The GLENELG
COUNTRY
SCHOOL

A
Margaret Wesley
BIRTHDAY
BOOK

· presented in honor of ·

Bailey A. Doloff
On his 17th Birthday

· given by ·

Mom, Dad & Dustin
September 29, 2015

SCHOOLING AND RIDING THE SPORT HORSE

PAUL D. CRONIN

SCHOOLING AND RIDING THE SPORT HORSE

A Modern American Hunter/Jumper System

UNIVERSITY OF VIRGINIA PRESS
Charlottesville and London

Publication of this volume was assisted by a grant from the Kookaburra Foundation.

University of Virginia Press
© 2004 by the Rector and Visitors of the University of Virginia
All rights reserved
Printed in the United States of America on acid-free paper
First published 2004

9 8 7 6 5 4 3 2

LIBRARY OF CONGRESS
CATALOGING-IN-PUBLICATION DATA

Cronin, Paul D.
  Schooling and riding the sport horse : a modern American
hunter/jumper system / Paul D. Cronin.
      p.   cm.
Includes bibliographical references and index.
  ISBN 0-8139-2287-9 (cloth : alk. paper)
  1. Jumping (Horsemanship) 2. Hunt riding—United States.
3. Horses—Training. I. Title.
      SF295.5.C76 2004
      798.2´5—dc22

2004007956

For

The horses and students who have taught me all I know,
especially those at Sweet Briar College

Captain Littauer, his support and guidance from age fifteen
well through my adult career as a teacher

Sara Lycett, who helped organize and edit my writing

Joe Fargis, teacher and horseman, who helped me finish

Pupils and colleagues who read and reacted to the manuscript

and for Ann

Contents

Foreword

In recent years, horses have come to be used mainly for sport rather than for farming and military purposes. If the horses we ride could talk, they would say, "Read this book; this is how to ride me." Paul Cronin's book on forward riding clearly explains the importance of a secure, noninterfering seat and soft controls as a basis for cooperative performance. Our horses are the most generous of creatures. Once the rider establishes trust with his horse, it will go anywhere he asks: over high and airy-colored obstacles, over solid unforgiving fences, and into water of unknown depth. Horses deserve the best treatment we can give them, and the forward riding system provides just that. By its logical step-by-step progression from stabilized gaits, poles, and small jumps, it builds confidence and makes the horse comfortable in any situation.

My roots are in forward riding, and it has always made sense to me. It provides the basic skills in the horse and rider from which to go forward into any discipline. The rider is secure, and the horse is confident on the flat and over fences. Once the horse is calm, straight, and forward, it can go on to field riding, show hunter courses, more advanced flat work, higher fences, and jumper courses. And if problems arise, the rider can always go back to the basics to reestablish confidence.

Paul Cronin and I share a common background in forward riding. I rode with Jane Dillon as a junior and participated in clinics with Capt. Vladimir Littauer, who reinforced our grounding in forward riding. Later I conducted riding clinics at Sweet Briar College where Paul Cronin was Director of Riding. Paul benefited from early exposure to Captain Littauer's clinics in Massachusetts and his lifetime association with Captain Littauer in New York and at Sweet Briar. Jane Dillon was also a clinician at Sweet Briar. In his book Paul clarifies and confirms my ideas about forward riding as a noninterfering, cooperative method of communicating with the horse. Our teaching and training methods are remarkably similar, though I have concentrated on show jumping and Paul on training hunters, field riding, and teaching.

Horses everywhere will appreciate this book. I believe Paul's book should also be of great help to riding teachers. The clear explanations it provides of position and controls will aid teachers in articulating the reasons a certain position works or why to use the aids in a particular way. For amateur riders of all ages seeking to improve their skills or school their own horses, it will give them the building blocks they need and provide a systematic methodology for progressing. The book is well organized and provides clear explanations of common terminology. I think the book fills a need in the current riding scene, providing us with a clear understanding of the forward riding system and its goal of creating a soft, secure rider on a calm, cooperative horse.

JOE FARGIS
MIDDLEBURG, VIRGINIA
October 1, 2003

Preface

Mary Aiken Littauer on the Author

Paul Cronin was a very gifted student of my husband, Capt. V. S. Littauer, and a riding teacher who carried on my husband's legacy, Forward Riding, with great success. Captain Littauer first noted Paul's equestrian abilities at a riding clinic my husband gave at the Groton Hunt in the late 1950s. That initial contact eventually bloomed into a friendship of mutual respect that endured until my husband's death. Over the years, Captain Littauer had a close affiliation with the riding program at Sweet Briar College: at first working with the Director of the Riding Program, Harriet Rodgers, and then with her successor, Paul Cronin. That riding program, directed by two such able teachers, was known to have had the highest standards of horsemanship in the United States.

As someone who has known Paul Cronin for more than forty years, I can recommend this book without qualification.

MARY AIKEN LITTAUER
SYOSSETT, NEW YORK
June 29, 2003

Acknowledgments

We are very grateful to many people who have made this book possible through their logistical support, technical expertise, and advice:

Editors, University of Virginia Press
The Kookaburra Foundation
National Sporting Library
Sweet Briar College
Pam Baker
Lisa Campbell
Coleen Catalon
Dr. Reynolds Cowles, DVM
Joe Fargis
Shelby French
Lendon Gray
Honora Haynes
Marion Lee
Keedie Grones Leonard
Mary Aiken Littauer
Sara Lycett
Sally Lynch
Jill Randles
Margaret Simpson, PhD
Molly Sorge
Stephanie B. Speakman
Cathy Staples
Mimi Wroten

ILLUSTRATOR

Elizabeth R. Manierre

PHOTOGRAPHERS

Janne Bugtrup
Liz Callar
Al Cook Photography and Video
Fallaw Photography
Flash Point Photography
Brant Gamma
Ira Haas
Keedie Grones Leonard
Mandy Lorraine
Pennington Galleries
Tish Quirk
Teresa Ramsay
Rick Photography
W. A. Robertson
Judith Buck Sisto Photography
Reinhold Tigges

We are grateful to those who participated in the photographs:

Winn R. Alden

Elizabeth Coughlin

David R. Cronin

Sari Deslaurieres

Pam C. Dudley

Mike Elmore

Joe Fargis

Lendon Gray

Frances C. Hooper

Anne Kursinski

Keedie Grones Leonard

Jamie P. Martin

Cindy R. Prewitt

Megan S. Proffitt

Ramiro Quintana

Jill Randles

Pam W. Renfrow

Mary S. Robertson, MFH

Christi Rose

Louise W. Serio

Lorraine H. Stanley

Anne V. Swan

Kenny Wheeler

James Young, MFH

Sally Young

The information in this book is true and complete to the best of our knowledge. All recommendations are made without guarantee on the part of the author or UVA Press. The author and publisher disclaim any liability in connection with the use of this information.

SCHOOLING AND RIDING THE SPORT HORSE

Forward riding. A modern American System for Schooling and Riding Hunters, Jumpers, and Field Horses. *(Louise W. Serio, rider; Mandy Lorraine, photographer)*

Introduction
Historical Perspectives, Concepts, and Definitions of the Modern American Forward Riding System

THE FORWARD RIDING SYSTEM AND THE GOAL OF THIS BOOK

This book presents a system of riding and a method of schooling for hunters, jumpers, cross-country, and pleasure horses based on concepts developed and practiced over the latter part of the twentieth century and the beginning of the twenty-first. It will be useful to the serious rider, to professional teachers, and to both amateur and professional trainers of horses in the twenty-first century.

The system of schooling and riding detailed here is called *forward riding*. It comprises three central interacting elements: position, controls, and schooling. The position used for forward riding is the American hunter seat. The controls are soft, precise aids that invoke close cooperation between horse and rider. Schooling in forward riding seeks to develop a natural equine athlete under the weight of the rider, and it produces a "connected" athlete that moves forward in long, low, ground-covering, efficient strides with a result known as *forward balance*.

These three elements—position, controls, and schooling—in the forward riding system can be fundamentally distinguished from those of the classical dressage school. While the central balance of advanced dressage is capable of producing brilliant gaits, the alert state of mind needed to perform such movements is fundamentally different from the goals of forward riding. Such a consistently high level of energy and mental alertness is not conducive to natural athletic jumping, good hunter movement, and the manners or calmness appropriate for most sport horses participating in hunter, equitation, and jumper divisions; hunter trials; field riding; and other group activities. It should be noted, however, that in the twenty-first century some riders and teachers of modern dressage, including some of my former students, have successfully adopted the principles of schooling on the flat presented in this text and use them as a foundation for advanced work.

USING THIS BOOK TO YOUR ADVANTAGE

Schooling and Riding the Sport Horse is designed in such a way that it can easily be adapted for the schooling period that best suits the particular horse in training. In part 1, the first and second chapters are a summary of the fundamentals of forward riding position and control theory and practicum.

Schooling the horse, the third element of the forward riding system (position, controls, schooling), is the main focus of the text. In part 2, the schooling component presents forward riding theory and principles as well as sections on handling the young horse, evaluating a prospect for schooling or purchase, and a review of conformation.

Part 3, which assumes at least a high-intermediate level of position and controls, is a progressive practical schooling guide in seven periods. The schooling exercises are organized in chronological order. While you will want to start at the beginning with a "green" or young horse, for a horse with a bit of education or one that is being retrained, you may find your starting point midway in the schooling system; i.e., chapter 9 or 11. However, in this case you will still want to return to the early "periods" so as to work in recommended exercises.

A HISTORICAL PERSPECTIVE OF THE
AMERICAN RIDING SYSTEM

In educated riding, there are two main systems of riding and schooling. Most methods, articles, and treatises on riding can be documented and placed under one umbrella or the other.

The first and older system is the classical dressage system or the classical high school system. The horse is schooled to be in central balance in order to perform the required objective of quality collected gaits in a flat arena. The dressage seat and traditional dressage controls fall correctly in line with this schooling objective.

The second, and younger by more than three hundred years, is the classical sport horse system or, as the United States Equestrian Federation (USEF) calls it, "the hunter equitation" (system) or, as it came to be called in the 1950s, the forward riding system. The horse is schooled under the weight of the rider to be in connected forward balance with ground-covering, efficient strides. The horse's natural athletic abilities are gradually developed to the point that the horse can shorten and lengthen his stride, turn, and jump with speed and agility, whether on the flat or over uneven terrain. The hunter/jumper seat or position and the emphasis on a *calm, alert, cooperative* horse under *soft, precise controls* fall correctly in line with the balance and agility objectives in schooling the hunter/jumper/field horse.

Neither system is superior to the other. Use of one or the other depends on the intended purpose, whether the goal is a hunter show horse, a field hunter, a pleasure horse, a jumper, a cross-country horse, or a high school dressage horse. The objectives in schooling the horse determine the system used.

Scholars believe that the written history of educated riding began with Federico Grisoné and his complete system (*Gli Ordini di Cavalcare*, Naples, 1550). Made more available by the invention of the printing press (Germany, 1450), it was the first complete description of a three-part system of position, controls, and schooling. It discusses the developing classical high school dressage system, the first and older system of educated riding. It was very well suited to the social and economic conditions of the Renaissance and Baroque periods. Masters such as Salomon de la Broue (*Le Cavalerice François*, Paris, France, editions 1593, 1646), Antoine de Pluvinel (*Manège Royale*, Paris, 1623), François Robichon de la Guérinière (*Ecole de Cavalerie*, 1729, 1733), William Cavendish, Duke of Newcastle (*A General System of Horsemanship*, London, editions 1667, 1743; first published 1658 in French), François A. Baucher (*Methode de'Equitation*, Paris, 1842), and James Fillis (*Principes de Dressage et d'Equitation*, Paris, 1890) developed the classical high school system. This was based on schooling for full collection, which was essential for the high school movements of the *manège*, on controls that provided dominance of the rider over the horse, and on a position based on the seat, not the stirrups, as most efficient for the desired and necessary change to central balance.

As a result of such events as the French Revolution and Napoleonic Wars, social and economic conditions moved the study and development of the classical high school dressage system from the patronage of the nobility and aristocracy to the military. In the mid-nineteenth century, men like Count d'Aure of the French Military Academy at Saumur, who were interested in training racehorses and field hunters, challenged the usefulness of the classical dressage method for the training of the sport horse. D'Aure's ideas were not accepted, however, by the academy, which clung to classical dressage training methods. In the late nineteenth century and early twentieth century, more leaders and writers on educated riding and practical military officers began to openly question the usefulness of the high school system for training recruits to ride efficiently and quickly cross-country and for training the horse to be controllable and fast cross-country with efficient, ground-covering strides.

In Italy, in particular at the turn of the nineteenth century, a completely new system evolved at the Italian Cavalry School under a Cavalry officer named Frederico Caprilli. The Caprilli system, which was adopted by the Cavalry School by 1907, set the foundation for the forward riding system, as riders were now being taught to follow the forward motion of the horse. While the European and American riding establishments of the early twentieth century in general did not understand or accept the differences in Caprilli's new natural system, especially the schooling and controls, they did recognize that the rider's position over jumps improved jumping performances.

After World War I, economic and social changes required the military cavalry institutions to change. The traditional formalized high school dressage system used for the training of the horse and rider was considered obsolete and was replaced by methods that mixed elements of the classical dressage system and the new natural riding system. Some of the leading authors on horsemanship from the 1930s to the 1950s wrote books presenting a mixed system, combining a certain degree of classical high school on the flat and some forward balance movements for the field and jumping. These books did not, however, provide the basis for a clear understanding of principles such as how a horse balances himself in motion and the mechanics of the jump. The mixed system was more politically acceptable to the old guard, if not as desirable for the progress of the new forward riding system in Europe. Military horsemen such as Col. M. F. McTaggart (1925), Gregor de Romaszkan (1940), and Lt. Col. A. L. d'Endrody (1959) wrote informative books but ones that often partially compromised, missed, or ignored some of the basically contradictory principles in the two systems of classical dressage and forward riding.

In America, however, where "traditional wisdom" in educated riding was not so deeply rooted, the new forward riding system developed rapidly. Riding to hounds, racing over timber, hunter trials, and hunter horse shows—the latter two judged on the quality of the rider's or horse's performance on the flat and over a course of jumps—provided a laboratory for the development of modern forward riding, sport riding, or hunter equitation in America. What has come to be currently known as the *hunter seat* is the result of the development of the *forward seat* as outlined by modern teachers such as Frederico Caprilli; Maj. Piero Santini of the Italian Cavalry (Caprilli's pupil), who taught and wrote in the 1930s; and Col. H. D. Chamberlin and Capt. Vladimir S. Littauer, both of whom had been strongly influenced by Caprilli and also by the Americans' practical and efficient approach to riding at speed and jumping in the open.

Col. H. D. Chamberlin studied at the French (Saumur) and Italian (tor di Quinto) cavalry academies in the 1920s. He brought modern Italian and French concepts home to the U.S. Army Cavalry School at Fort Riley, where he was to teach, write, and train the U.S. Army Equestrian Team in the 1930s and early 1940s. Chamberlin's method was generally based on the Italian school of Caprilli. His books, which included the Fort Riley cavalry manual, set forth these ideas very clearly. Fort Riley pupils (enlisted men and officers) had an enormous influence on American riding from at least the 1930s through the 1970s.

Another major influence on American riding, especially on the rapidly developing civilian side, was Capt. Vladimir S. Littauer of the Russian Cavalry. Captain Littauer came to the United States in the 1920s and, with two other émigrés, founded the "Boots and Saddles" riding school in New York. Deeply influenced by the French and Italians, Littauer wrote his first book on forward riding in the 1930s and continued to teach and write well into the 1970s. His interest was not the male military rider but in teaching the civilian amateur rider.

The Americans were able to adopt the forward riding system with great success. It is important to emphasize that Caprilli, known as the father of modern riding, had a complete system of riding and schooling. The forward seat is what most people saw in his method. Control and schooling techniques of the horse were components that required more intellectual comprehension, expertise, and study. Chamberlin and Littauer's work significantly advanced the schooling of the horse as the forward riding system developed.

Charles Chenevix-Trench, who made a serious contribution to accurately analyzing the development of educated riding (*A History of Horsemanship,* 1970), including American riding and specifically the works of Littauer and Chamberlin, wrote: "Chamberlin . . . rewrote the American Manual of Horsemanship and Horsemastership and had an influence on American riding second only to that of Vladimir Littauer. . . . The fruit of their teaching was the success of America in international competition between the wars" (257).

In the twenty-first century, there is a possibility that Americans will lose a connection with the roots of their dramatic success in schooling and riding show hunters, cross-country horses, and jumpers. No one organization supports the complete system known as Hunter/Jumper Equitation—or the American Forward Riding System, as the author has called it. Other than the USEF Jumper, Hunter, and Hunter Equitation Committees and smaller organizations such as the Affiliated National Riding Commission (ANRC), the United States Hunter/Jumper Association, the National Hunter/Jumper Council, the American Hunter/Jumper Foundation, some education-oriented secondary school and college riding programs, and possibly some commercial competition-oriented privately owned farms, few formal organizations exist to preserve and develop the complete system, Forward Riding.

As in all American sports at the start of the twenty-first century, specialization has led equestrian organizations to divide based primarily on the format, rules, and regulations of a particular equestrian competition, with training/schooling and teaching geared to competition rather than a system of riding and schooling the horse. Furthermore, coaching has often come to replace teaching. There is a growing interest in the classical dressage system (traditionally considered an art form) for competition in America, at least on the lower levels. Larger numbers of eventers are starting to learn to jump in horse trials (judged on the horse's faults at approximately two feet, six inches, to three feet) rather than in the hunter equitation, hunter horse shows, or hunter trials format (judged on quality of performance, which serves as an evaluation of horse and rider performance). Interest in Grand Prix jumpers is also growing. Upper-level jumpers require a degree of collection for the turns and distances on some advanced jumping courses. The classical dressage flat work for jumpers is still being promoted because of some lingering European military influence (the argument of the military nearly a hundred years ago that it is all the same system—classical dressage on the flat and something else over jumps, a "style"). With the closing of the American countryside and the growing commercialism and specialization of the hunter show horse, it is possible that future generations of Americans might not clearly understand the complete forward riding system.

Documentation for some of these comments may be found in the three scholarly historical texts by Felton, Littauer, and Trench discussed in appendix

The Two Central Educated-Riding and Schooling Systems

FORWARD RIDING SYSTEM
1920 to the Present

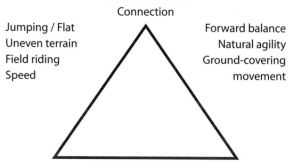

SCHOOLING GOALS
Connection

Jumping / Flat
Uneven terrain
Field riding
Speed

Forward balance
Natural agility
Ground-covering
movement

POSITION
Hunter / Forward seat
based on **the stirrup**
for flat riding and jumping

CONTROLS
Cooperation
Three levels of control

CLASSICAL DRESSAGE SYSTEM
1550 to the Present (Golden Era: the 18th century)

SCHOOLING GOALS
Collection

Manège
High school

Central balance

POSITION
Dressage seat
based on **the seat**
for advanced dressage

CONTROLS
Intensive influence
Obedience
Precision

2. It is this author's hope that more riders will be interested in gaining some understanding about the social and economic influences (for better or worse) that have historically influenced equitation and that they will be interested in sorting out what is often either oversimplified or erroneous about the history of educated riding and its two primary systems, classical dressage and forward riding. The aforementioned texts can help to develop that understanding.

CONCEPTS AND DEFINITIONS OF THE MODERN AMERICAN FORWARD RIDING SYSTEM

Concepts and terms of the riding and schooling system are set out in this section and further discussed in the rest of the text. Riders, trainers, and teachers interested in understanding more about position, controls, and schooling should have an understanding of modern riding and schooling concepts. It is important to be comfortable with these concepts before teaching position and controls and before moving on to the schooling part of the system.

Forward riding is a modern system of riding and schooling hunters, jumpers, and field horses in the most efficient and practical way. This system consists of three interacting parts: forward position, forward controls, and forward schooling. It is based on the natural dynamic balance of the horse with athletic agility under the weight of the rider and on the horse's mental stability and cooperation, which are established through progressive education in the forward riding system.

Balance of the horse in motion is described as *dynamic balance;* that is, the constant loss and recapturing of his equilibrium forward. The balance changes at each gait, turning, and transitions. All animals move in dynamic balance, a vital point missed in many riding theories, texts, and teachings. The use of a balancing gesture of the head and neck assists the horse in this process.

Static balance means that while motionless the horse has approximately 60 percent of his weight in front of the withers and 40 percent of his weight behind the withers.

Good movement in a hunter or sport horse is defined as connected, long, low, ground-covering, efficient strides. This means that the horse moves in one piece (is connected) and travels straight in front and behind. All animals, including horses, move with the constant loss and regaining of equilibrium forward (dynamic balance).

Horsemanship consists of obtaining the best possible performance from the horse using the least of his physical and nervous energies. This means the best possible performance should be obtained through the right combination of position, controls, and schooling.

Cooperation of the horse with the rider, one of the primary tenets of the forward riding system, results from the rider using a system of aids and techniques that the horse can learn to understand over time during the schooling process. Cooperation with the horse, rather than domination of the horse by the rider, is the goal.

Stabilization, a very important concept in forward riding, is often misunderstood. It is a very valuable foundation for horses on all levels. *Stabilization provides the horse the ability to maintain the gait and speed asked for whether on the flat, on uneven terrain, jumping, alone or in company, with the rider using elementary control techniques of weight, voice, hand (off contact), and leg.* In forward riding on the elementary level, the preferred technique is looped reins (see photographs). This is not a rein on the buckle. It is loose rein, short enough that the horse can be quickly corrected in case of disobedience but long enough that there is no contact with the mouth. He must learn to be stabilized on educated loose reins. It takes a high-intermediate or advanced rider to train a young horse so that he eventually has the foundation of stabilization. See illustrations throughout the text.

Connection is also an important concept in schooling. It is not to be confused with collection, as correctly used in the classical dressage school. *A connected horse is one that is moving in one piece—united—with the hind end connected to the front end.* Connection will vary with the level of reserve energy, alertness, type of horse, and task at hand. It is an essential ingredient of good hunter/sport horse movement and performance. See the earlier definition of good movement as well as illustrations throughout the text.

Collection is a classical dressage school concept. The horse is in central balance and is fully "on the bit." The head is raised and in a vertical position, the croup is lowered, and the horse moves with shortened, high, light, condensed steps.

Impulse is reserve energy. There are different types of reserve energy. A horse can be nervous, upset, or overfit and have considerable reserve energy. However, the term *impulse* as used in the training of horses in forward riding means an *educated impulse* or a reserve energy that is created by the leg. A horse is energetic and alert but remains calm and cooperative with the rider. Impulse can also be increased through speed.

Piaffe, a trot in place. This advanced dressage movement demonstrates full collection, central balance, and the vertical engagement of the hind leg. The quality riding and the quality performance of the horse are made possible by a special partnership between horse and rider over years of progressive and specialized training. *(Lendon Gray, rider; Reinhold Tigges, photographer)*

Contact is the feeling of the horse's energy or impulse forward created by the leg through a definite cooperation between the rider's legs and hands and the horse's movement. Contact connects the horse. The horse's head and neck should be extended and his mouth closed.

The concept of contact in forward riding is essential to understanding the system. There are progressive degrees of contact. They might vary with the mental stability and conformation of the horse, the education and skill level of the rider, the particular horse's needs, and/or specific movements. Contact can be passive and following. At a more educated level it is *a soft contact with varying degrees of reserve energy or impulse.* This level of contact is used in forward riding on the intermediate level and for most of the advanced level. The degree of impulse varies with the task, gait, and specific horse. Lastly if needed, more impulse than is normally necessary for hunters and jumpers may be used at certain gaits by some advanced competitive jumpers; i.e., an exercise at the short canter for short periods of time. See the illustrations in the text for passive contact and for soft contact with impulse.

Contact gives a feeling in the hand of reserve energy or impulse that is created by the rider's leg and is felt in the bit, reins, and hand. Educated contact is not a horse or rider that pulls. Contact is not feeling the energy of an aggressive, upset, or rank horse.

There are two reasons for training a horse to go on contact. One is that it will improve the quality of the horse's movement. The second is that it improves the quality of the controls. The transitions become softer and more precise. The horse is connected through contact.

A horse is ready to learn contact when he has achieved the foundation of stabilization.

Riders are ready to learn passive contact when their hands are independent of their body, and when they have enough education on the elementary level to do basic movements involving the coordination of legs and hands for

Posting trot on soft contact, head and neck extended, mouth closed. The rider's position is based on the stirrup, allowing unity of horse and rider on the flat, jumping, and over uneven terrain, as well as the efficient and effective use of aids. Ground-covering movement in forward balance with the horizontal engagement of the hind leg. *(Cindy R. Prewitt, rider; Brant Gamma, photographer)*

transitions and turning. Riders cannot be ready to learn schooling until their position and controls are on the high-intermediate level.

Engagement in forward riding is a horizontal engagement. It requires the swing of the hind leg well forward under the horse's belly, with the hoof coming in contact with the ground on or forward of the front hoof track. The disengagement follows.

Disengagement is important to keep in mind when discussing horizontal engagement in sport riding. The goal is to have the horse thrust forward with long, low, ground-covering, efficient strides. The disengagement should about equal the length of the engagement. This is important for connection, forward movement, and overall performance.

Longitudinal agility is the ability of the horse to shorten and lengthen his gait (stride). An example of a gradual longitudinal agility exercise is canter–trot–walk–halt–walk–trot–canter. A prompt longitudinal agility exercise is canter–halt–canter. In order to stay lightly on contact and not be mentally distressed by the abruptness of this exercise, the horse has to be trained on a fairly high level of forward schooling. One could, of course, force this exercise, but it would lead to an upset and stiff horse. The progressive steps to teach longitudinal agility from gradual transitions are important. Practicing the three speeds of the canter is a longitudinal agility exercise. Trotting and cantering over uneven terrain is another example of a longitudinal agility exercise.

Lateral agility is the ability of the horse to turn athletically and with agility. Younger horses and less-schooled horses need to learn to be connected and mentally calm on large circles and turns before moving to a good performance on smaller circles and sharp turns. Also, lateral movements need to be done well at the slower gaits first.

Following arms describes the ability of the rider to follow the natural balancing gestures of the head and neck whether on looped reins or on contact at the walk, the canter, and the jump. This allows the horse the athletic balancing gestures of the head and neck without interference from the rider. For example, the advanced rider uses the following arm to regulate the stride in rhythm with the gait, rate the stride to the jump, and have instant contact/control on landing from the jump, all without putting the horse off balance or mentally upsetting him.

Check-release is an elementary-control technique for slowing or stopping the horse while riding on a looped or loose rein. The rider gives a check-release. The release immediately returns to a loose rein. Several short checks may be necessary. This is always combined with the voice aid.

Give-and-take is a technique of the hand for riding on the intermediate through the advanced level. It is used riding on contact when shortening or stopping the horse and consists of taking and giving immediately back to soft contact in a short series of educated give-and-take actions. The give is back to the contact, not to looped reins. It grows out of check-release on the elementary level, when stabilizing a horse off contact. The relatively crude action of check-release (elementary level) becomes a nearly invisible technique of give-and-take (intermediate/advanced level). Give-and-take correctly used can progress to longitudinal flexions of the lower jaw as the rider becomes more skilled and/or if the horse needs to learn flexions (advanced level). Often the correct use of give-and-take leads to the use of flexions without a special effort.

Vibrations to soften the mouth can be used if give-and-take does not work consistently. This is accomplished by alternating closing the fingers on one side while lightening the pressure of the fingers on the other side. It is a very light repeated pattern side-to-side to help soften the horse's mouth. The head should not be moved from side to side, nor should this be used to punish.

For advanced control a *half-halt* is a cue used to decrease or rate speed, or to lighten the horse on the reins. The rider opens the hip angle while closing the fingers and lifting the reins for just a fraction of a moment, then returns to the direct line contact created by the leg. The energy felt in the contact should not be affected. A half-halt can be repeated two or three times if necessary. A half-halt is not a jerk in the mouth. A full halt stops forward motion and can be done through a gradual or a prompt transition. Give-and-take should first be mastered by the rider and then taught to the horse. Depending upon the characteristics and purpose of the horse, his responsiveness to give-and-take, and the level of his rider, a half-halt lesson may not be needed.

On the line means that, whether on a straight line or on a turn, the horse's hind foot steps up into the place of or forward of the front foot track. The head and neck are slightly bent in the direction of travel. The horse is straight and connected.

There are *three levels of controls* in forward riding schooling:

Elementary control aims for authority over the horse through definite and quick control. The central elementary control techniques utilize the four natural aids with emphasis on voice, loose rein, check-release, and tapping leg in the three leg-aid positions. An example of the aids for a transition on the elementary level from the trot to the walk would be: (1) weight (stop posting and sit), (2) voice ("walk"), (3) hand (check-release), (4) urging leg (alternating/tapping) to walk forward in one piece. This level of controls is especially useful while starting young horses. It often takes an advanced rider to achieve a good performance with a young horse on this level of schooling.

Intermediate control aims for soft and precise transitions—a soft but definite cooperation of the rider's hands and legs with the horse's efforts and reactions. Contact helps achieve better control (soft/precise) and better movement (efficient, long, low, ground-covering strides).

Advanced control aims for the highest quality of performance that an able horse can produce. This would require a mentally relaxed, physically alert and responsive, athletic, and educated horse.

There are *three corresponding levels of control in jumping:*

Elementary-level jumping:

Horse: Approaches on loose rein

Rider: In galloping position, grabs mane

Purpose: (1) Advanced rider schooling a horse, (2) beginning rider on a made horse learning to jump, (3) upper-level rider correcting a position fault

Intermediate-level jumping:

Horse: Approaches on contact that is gradually and rhythmically lightened to loose rein (with the urging leg at the girth) so that the jump itself is on a looped rein

Rider: In galloping position, rests hands on neck with a looped rein while going over the top of the fence (crest release)

Purpose: Allows softness, precision, subtle rating of stride between jumps on contact, and full use of the horse's balancing gestures over the jumps; and the rider's hands rest on the crest of the neck to ensure security and the non-abuse of the horse

Advanced-level jumping:

Horse: Contact is maintained throughout turns, approaches, and the jump itself (although there may be some rhythmic lessening of tension between bit and hands combined with an increased urging rhythmic lower leg while on the approach)

Rider: Following arms; may use galloping position or deep two-point to fit the needs of the course

Purpose: Quality performance of horse and rider

Qualities of a good jump are a calm, connected approach; a jump out of stride at the takeoff; a straight, even arc with good head and neck gestures; even folding of the legs in front and behind (above horizontal); and an even pace similar to the approach when departing the jump.

Mechanics of the gaits: See the illustration on the next page as well as photographs throughout this book.

Stages of the jump include approach, takeoff, flight, and landing. See the discussion of the jump and the photographs in chapter 2, and the photographs throughout the book. The approach can be at the walk, trot, or canter. The takeoff starts with the "fork" and finishes after the "double engagement."

Four fundamentals of a good position are (1) unity of horse and rider, (2) security of the rider, (3) nonabuse of the horse, and (4) efficient and effective use of the aids.

Four natural aids are (1) leg, (2) hand, (3) weight, and (4) voice. These natural aids are used in a specific order depending upon whether the transition is forward or downward and with specific techniques depending upon the level of control.

Educated hands are responsive hands. Together with the leg aids, they create actions of fingers, hands, and arms that in the shortest time obtain the best results with the least expenditure of the horse's mental and physical energies. Degrees of contact are passive contact, soft contact with reserve energy, and soft contact with more reserve energy.

Passive hands have a light feel of the reserve energy. Riders should have a position independent of their hands. Educated hands should be able to be passive much of the time. Passive hands can therefore belong to a talented but uneducated rider and can also belong to an educated rider who is intentionally and correctly riding a young horse with passive contact. In forward riding it is not a matter of constant drive, hold, drive, hold. In forward riding, on passive contact or on soft contact with more reserve energy, the gait, the pace, and the degree of reserve energy are established; and the hand is passive except when needed to shorten, stop, or turn. If it is the walk, canter, or jump, the hands follow the balancing gestures.

Heavy hands insensitively hang, pull, or are fixed against the horse's mouth. They are hands that disturb the horse and may be called abusive. They often go with a rider who has a position that does not have the four fundamentals or any of the seven physical characteristics of a good position discussed in chapter 1 of the text; the hands are not independent of the body. Sometimes they belong to a tense or nervous rider. Heavy hands most often

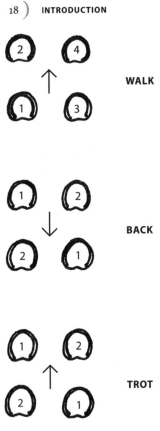

WALK

BACK

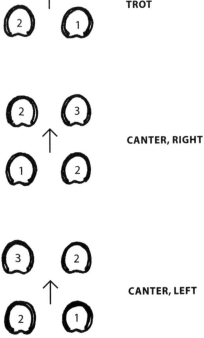

TROT

CANTER, RIGHT

CANTER, LEFT

MECHANICS OF THE GAITS

The horse moves in dynamic balance. There is a constant loss and regaining of equilibrium forward. The walk has four beats. The canter has three beats. Both gaits have a balancing gesture of the head and neck similar to the balancing gesture of the head and neck over a jump. The trot and back each have two beats in diagonal pairs. Not shown, the fast gallop has four beats. The diagonal pair touch ground separately, then the leading foreleg (fourth beat), and the first beat (hind leg) starts again. Both the canter and the gallop have a period of suspension after the leading foreleg.

result in a mentally unstable horse and/or a horse with a hard mouth. The more sensitive the horse, the more damage heavy hands can do. They create stiff movement and inhibit the athletic movement and development of the horse. These hands can also belong to an experienced rider who has ridden only horses that pull. This rider becomes unaware and insensitive to a young or an educated horse because of poor habits learned.

Abuse is the unintentional mistreatment of the horse as a result of uneducated riding and schooling. An example is posting with moving hands, which causes the horse's mouth to be abused, or through ignorance using improperly adjusted gadgets. The rider is not intentionally hurting the horse.

Cruelty is the intentional mistreatment of the horse. The rider deliberately and consciously acts in a way that mistreats the horse. Examples include angry whipping, overworking, or overfacing the horse.

Discipline is the intentional treatment of the horse to correct or discourage inappropriate behaviors. An example is using a crop at the girth or a sharp voice to reinforce the leg aid or to discourage undesirable habits a horse has learned through poor riding or training.

Cavalletti in forward schooling are a series of poles at specific distances that relate to the stride or gait and the schooling needs of a specific horse. When jumping is first being taught, a horse is stabilized over single poles and then a series of poles. Eventually cavalletti poles are used to stabilize the approach to an X, which leads up to stabilizing the approach to the jump. Types of cavalletti can be used throughout schooling to maintain stability, to integrate jumping with flat work, and for some corrective jumping. Cavalletti and combinations were used in teaching and schooling hunters to a fairly sophisticated degree by the 1950s in the United States. They were later used by a cross-section of Americans focusing on jumpers. (See appendix 1 for distances.)

Combinations or jump gymnastics are used after the horse has been stabilized on the approach and departure of the jump. They help to teach the horse how to determine correct takeoff. As horses become more skilled in figuring correct takeoff, combinations help teach them to improve form and to develop experience seeing a distance and jumping to the best of their natural ability. Combinations move from the simple to the complex. Riders must be careful not to mentally stress the horse by pushing him beyond the height and the distances that he can physically and mentally handle. Combinations of varying distances can also be a longitudinal agility exercise.

Hunter exercises are for teaching calmness in company (note the illustration in chapter 9). They are done in groups of two to ten horses. They are useful for the show hunter that must work in an under-saddle class in company, for the field horse that must go out in a group, and for the young horse that is going to compete individually but must warm-up in company. They are a series of exercises that teach a horse to calmly cooperate with a rider while being passed, to have a horse come toward him, to lead the way, or to go behind other horses.

I POSITION AND CONTROLS

1 Overview of Position and Its Theory

Position is one of the three foundation parts of the forward riding system. The type of position used in a system to school and ride a horse affects the balance of the horse, and the balance of the horse relates to the objectives of the sport. An educated, modern position is essential to the efficient use of soft, precise aids or controls. Further, well-rounded schooling (training the horse on the flat, on uneven terrain, and for jumping) requires a good working position. In this and in other sections of this text, there are examples of how the position, the controls, and the schooling interact on different levels to produce quality riding for the field horse, hunter, and jumper.

This position, on the flat as well as over jumps, is essentially based on the stirrup rather than the seat, because that is the most efficient position for riding a well-balanced, ground-covering mover. The stirrup is especially necessary at the posting trot, when riding over uneven terrain, at the gallop, and during the jump.

A good position on the flat helps produce a quality position over jumps. Modern American riding uses the same position on the flat, on the jump, and in the field. This point is often the most misunderstood when learning this forward riding system. For example, many today now see the value of the hunter/jumper position for jumping and at least some modern schooling methods for teaching the rider and horse to jump but have barely a notion as to the importance of forward riding flat work. Further, some talented competitors with able horses have studied winning performances in competitions and have been able to copy parts of the hunter system. However, they cannot verbalize the modern principles and do not understand it as a complete system. Another confusing situation occurs when classical dressage terms are used incorrectly in clinics and magazine articles. This common problem is rightfully very annoying to classical dressage teachers trying to accurately explain terms and concepts that historically belong to the high school system, such as *collection*. In the introduction, see the illustration of a horse schooled in collection and central balance with the rider's position correctly based on the seat rather than the stirrup. Compare this with the other photographs in this text.

This text provides theory, concepts, and terms that are consistent with what is taught and actually achieved in an American hunter/jumper system.

The position part of the forward riding system is based on the principle of a hunter/sport horse's forward balance and ground-covering, efficient movement. Regardless of the gait, all animals, including horses, move in dynamic balance—the constant loss and regaining of equilibrium forward. Further, in a hunter, jumper, and/or cross-country horse, *a good mover is defined as one that moves with long, low, ground-covering, efficient strides.* Efficient means that the horse is square in front and behind (moves straight without interference) and moves in one piece; that is, the hind end is united to the front end. He is "connected."

FUNDAMENTALS IN A GOOD WORKING POSITION

There are four fundamentals in a good working position that should be understood and achieved for successful riding in this system. This position was developed because it allowed the rider to (1) be secure on the horse, (2) be nonabusive to the horse, (3) be united with the movement of the horse, and (4) have strategic placement of hands and legs for efficient and effective use. It is a position that enables the rider to allow the horse to move with a connected, ground-covering, athletic stride.

In analyzing a correct American hunter position, we have, through the written work of the twentieth-century riding masters (Caprilli, Chamberlin, and Littauer), been given an outline of principles. In position theory this includes the above four fundamentals of a good working position and the following seven physical qualities of a good position.

SEVEN PHYSICAL QUALITIES OF A GOOD POSITION IN THIS SYSTEM

1. Correct design of position
2. Correct distribution of weight

3. Balance in motion
4. Spring
5. Rhythm
6. Grip
7. Physical and mental relaxation

This system utilizes a position that allows the rider to be united with the ground-covering stride of the ideal hunter, jumper, or sport horse. The position must be nonabusive to the horse on the flat, during transitions, on uneven terrain, and especially when in motion at the trot, gallop, and jump. A poor position is abusive in that the unstable hands can jerk the mouth, and a swinging leg can irritate the horse and cause the rider's weight to pound the back. This unintentional abuse, related to faults in the design of position, is abuse nonetheless.

The length of the stirrup is essential to creating angles and weight distribution. In general, when working on position, the rider should remove the leg from the stirrup and relax it down. The stirrup should fall at or a little below the middle of the ankle. In this way there is a hypothetical floor for the angles and weight to create the spring effect. Starting at the bottom and working up, the ankle is a hinge or spring to absorb the force of weight transferred down the leg. This combination of effort and gravity provides a bedrock for a secure position based on the stirrup. Two other angles, the knee and hip joints, act in concert as accessory shock absorbers that adjust and respond to the actions of the horse and rider. The weight must be correctly distributed through the correct design of the rider's position in order for it all to work. If the stirrup is too long, the floor necessary for the weighting of the springs is gone. It will not be possible to use the weight and the three angles to produce the spring, especially for the posting trot, the gallop, and the jump. For ordinary riding and for learning to ride, both on the flat and over jumps, the pupil should keep one stirrup length (at or just below the middle of the ankle) instead of regularly adjusting length for different tasks. It is more efficient and actually easier for the pupil to develop a better position this way.

Stirrup length depends also on the conformation of the rider and the conformation of the horse. For example, if the horse is wide, the rider may have to make the stirrups longer. If the horse is narrow, the rider may have to shorten the stirrups.

Later when the pupil has mastered the four fundamentals and seven physi-

Loose rein, ground-covering walk. The rider demonstrates a correct position with an alternately urging leg used at the girth and elementary control at the walk. *(Louise W. Serio, rider; Mandy Lorraine, photographer)*

cal qualities of a good position and has had riding experience, adjustments (one or two holes) to the stirrup can be made based on the riding task at hand. Generally, the experienced rider has three lengths of the stirrup. The middle length at the ankle is for ordinary riding and jumping to four feet, six inches. The second length is one or two holes below for riding and schooling with a longer, stronger leg on the flat, and the third is one or two holes higher than the ordinary for jumps over four feet, six inches. The shorter stirrup raises the floor so that the correct design of position gets the weight distributed to the heel, and more spring is created in the three hinges—ankle, knee, and hip—but it sacrifices some security. The longer stirrup allows a stronger leg but sacrifices spring.

The four fundamentals of a good working position interact with the seven physical qualities. The *correct design of position* (1) is essential for *correct weight distribution* (2) and for *balance in motion* (3). These three physical qualities are vital for the third fundamental, *unity of horse and rider*. Correct design of position with the correct weight distribution, *spring* (4), and *rhythm*

(5) are essential for the second fundamental, *the nonabuse of the horse by the rider.*

Correct design of position puts the leg where it can be efficiently used. The two central areas where the rider uses the inside lower calf are just at the girth (holding leg, urging leg) and four to six inches behind it (displacing leg). With correct design of position and correct weight distribution, *efficient and effective use of the aids*, the fourth fundamental, is possible.

The correct design of position and *grip* (6) are essential for the first fundamental, *the security of the rider.* Correct design of position is necessary for the weight to get all the way to the ankle. This allows an even grip with the inside lower thigh, inside knee, and inside upper calf, making the rider more secure.

Galloping in a field. Head and neck extended, mouth closed. The rider is in two-point with a following arm on contact. The horse is just leaving the support of the right lead, and the off hind will soon support the horse. The balancing gestures of the head and neck change forward and back in coordination with the beats of the gait. A fast gallop has four beats. The diagonal pair become two beats instead of one. Both the canter and gallop have a period of suspension. *(Anne V. Swan, rider; Reinhold Tigges, photographer)*

The weight needs to be distributed through the correct design of position. The correct weight distribution will be weakened or stopped if the rider grips more with the thigh, knee, or calf. Uneven grip makes it impossible to get the full depth all the way down to the ankle.

There are two types of grip used in teaching a correct "hunt seat" position: frictional and muscular. Frictional grip is when the correct design of position has the leg (inside lower thigh, inside knee, and inside upper calf) in place and in even contact with the saddle and the horse. Correct distribution of weight then provides frictional grip and rider stability. If a rider grips more with the knee, it takes the lower leg away from the horse and makes frictional grip with the upper inside calf impossible. Muscular grip is used when activity takes place—when the rider evenly grips the saddle or horse to gallop or jump

The horse is folding well during the flight phase of the jump, with his forearm above the horizontal. The rider has a secure lower leg position and following arms, allowing the horse's head and neck gestures, and the rider's following arms allow consistent contact into the landing and departure from the jump (advanced controls) *(Pam C. Dudley, rider; Fallaw Photography)*

Sitting a short trot on soft contact, the rider demonstrates the correct design of position and unity of the horse and the rider. *(Liz Callar, photographer)*

or if the horse is bucking. If the correct design of position is already there, the leg muscles simply close in and tighten, and the frictional grip becomes muscular grip. The leg position does not have to be moved—the muscular grip is instantaneous.

EXERCISES TO DEVELOP THE FUNDAMENTALS AND QUALITIES OF A GOOD POSITION

Correct design of position (1) is taught through "jump position" or "two-point," first at the walk, opening and closing angles. *Correct weight distribution* (2) is taught along with the correct design of position at the walk, posting trot, and canter; on uneven terrain; with cavalletti; and especially by jumping combinations.

One of the important exercises introduced to us in various forms by Caprilli and Chamberlin, and established as a teaching technique by Littauer, is the galloping or jumping position, thirty years later described as the two-point position now commonly used in the United States. This position is taken by standing and weighting the stirrups as though the rider were jumping or galloping. Correct design of position with the correct weight distribution is essential. The three angles and the three areas of even *grip* (6) are also essential. The rider can practice this exercise at the halt, the walk, the trot, the canter, approaching the jump, over uneven terrain, and through cavalletti and combinations. The rider can grab the mane in the two-point position or can rest the hands on the horse's neck for support. This helps develop a strong position based on the stirrup. Two-point should be integrated with the slow trot sitting so that the upper body has the habit of being adjustable. Also, the rider should practice sitting into transitions to the walk from the canter and from the trot. Some riders should work without stirrups for short periods to improve security and balance. However, consideration for the horse's back and mouth should be a priority.

Exercises to develop *balance in motion* (3) include the slow sitting trot on a smooth horse, the canter, the jump position or the two-point position

Two-point position, originally described as "jumping position" or "galloping position," at all three gaits is an exercise to develop qualities of a good position, including a correct design of position, correct distribution of weight, and spring. It is used in teaching jumping to horses and riders. The horse in the photograph is trotting on elementary controls (stabilized) in a field. *(Ramiro Quintana, rider; Liz Callar, photographer)*

at all gaits and transitions; i.e., walk–trot–walk. Low jumping (the horse will not receive much pounding at two feet or lower), riding over uneven terrain, working without stirrups maintaining the correct design of position, and riding different horses will help the intermediate or advanced rider.

The posting trot with a correctly adjusted stirrup, correct design of position, and correct weight distribution will strengthen the quality of *spring* (4). Spring can also be developed with the galloping or jumping position at the trot, canter, and gallop. Spring can be practiced with combinations and single low jumps. None of these exercises will work unless there is correct design of position (including correct stirrup length) and correct weight distribution all the way to the ankle.

Rhythm (5) can be developed through most of the exercises already mentioned. Other exercises include practicing transitions and changes of speed through the trot. For example, the rider can try ordinary trot posting, shorten to the sitting slow trot, and then move forward to the ordinary posting trot. Variations on this transition exercise can be practiced at the canter.

The last of the seven physical qualities of a good position is *physical and mental relaxation* (7). It is important that the other qualities of position and the four fundamentals of a good working position be well established. Then it will be possible for relaxation to come. Hacking out on trails on a quiet horse in the woods or in the field will help develop mental and physical relaxation, as will performing simple exercises successfully at the slower gaits.

On-the-ground stretching exercises are commonly used in other sports and are helpful before mounting. Exercises in the saddle, such as rotating the arms and ankles, will help stretch the muscles and relax the rider physically; exercises such as regulated breathing will relax the rider mentally.

To improve the rider's position at the sitting gaits (the ordinary and short canter, the sitting slow trot) practice the slow trot sitting, keeping the correct design of position with the stirrup. Avoid abusing the mouth. If necessary, use the pommel by pulling it up with one hand and hold both reins with the other hand. Master the slow trot sitting, keeping the correct design of position with the heel under the seat bone and the three angles of the ankle, knee, and hip in line. In this case, the rider will have less weight in the stirrup because some weight is in the seat.

The rider's position should adjust to the dynamic balance of the horse. With an increase in speed, the rider will increase the amount of weight in the stirrups, and the hip angle will close in order to unite the rider with the motion of the horse's faster gait. In decreasing the speed, the reverse will be true. The rider will gradually open the hip, being careful not to get behind the vertical, where the rider would be out of balance and behind the horse.

Further exercises to develop a correct design and correct weight distribution include having a teacher lunge the rider on a horse that is safe and quiet. Work without stirrups is recommended, provided the rider does not overgrip with one of the three parts of the inside leg—inside lower thigh, inside knee, or inside upper calf. Keep the three areas of grip even, and hold the design of position. When working without stirrups, hold the lower leg in the same position as with a stirrup. Otherwise, the lower leg can slip forward, the knee can be pinched up, or the lower leg can slide back. A frozen grip of the thigh and knee inhibits fluid riding based on the stirrup. All of these exercises are useful only if they are done correctly. Teachers should avoid making work without stirrups the major part of a lesson but should integrate it with work with the stirrups. This will take more preparation and effort, but the pupil will advance faster with fewer or no position faults to correct later.

In the forward riding system, the position of the body and legs in the saddle on the flat directly relates to the jumping position. If the rider has the correct design of position and the correct weight distribution on the flat—for example, at the posting trot—the rider will be much more prepared to correctly apply it at the jump, which lasts only about a second or even less, depending upon the jump. Most riders have only one or two horses on which to practice jumping. Therefore, if a correct hunter/forward seat position on the flat can be developed, there will be a better chance of having cooperative and successful horses over fences and rewarding riding experiences.

A VERSATILE POSITION UNITED WITH
THE HORSE'S DYNAMIC BALANCE

A good modern position is versatile. It allows for riding a horse on the flat or over jumps, riding over uneven terrain, and hacking out in company, all with the same basic position based on the stirrup. Study the rider's leg position in the photographs in this book, which include a variety of settings and activities. Starting at the bottom of the leg, the three angles are the ankle, the knee, and the hip. The faster the pace, the more weight will be put in the stirrup and the more the seat comes out of the saddle. The slower the pace, the more weight gets shifted to the seat; the hip opens and the rider sits softly (not heavily on the seat bones) in the saddle. In most situations the rider's center of gravity should be accommodated to the horse's center of gravity. If the position is mechanically correct, most riders will be able to keep this unity naturally and automatically.

There are times that a rider may want to intentionally sit slightly behind the center of gravity. For example, I teach transitions down from the trot to the walk as follows: stop posting; sit (weight aid); and, if on the elementary level, use the voice, check-release, or, for contact, give-and-take rein technique; and then use the lower leg to encourage the horse to walk forward into the transition. In this instance the weight aid is slightly behind the center of gravity, and the rider is signaling the horse before using the hand to walk or shorten the stride. The upper body is more upright at the slower gaits and the shorter-strided gaits.

In educated riding, it is not accurate to refer to the short gaits with hunters as classical collected gaits. That is a concept that has a special meaning in educated classical dressage riding. The hunters are not collected and on the bit but are connected and on soft contact. Some competetive jumpers at an advanced level of controls in the forward riding system do have a degree of collection for short periods (i.e. the short canter). To the uneducated eye, ordinary contact with the horse connected in forward balance might look collected, but in high school the word *collection* is a special term that is defined in the introduction. It has been a classical dressage concept for more than three hundred years. Unfortunately, some hunter teachers misuse the term, which is confusing to the pupils and muddles theory and direction.

In general, the hip angle should be at or ahead of the vertical depending upon the gait, the speed, and the movement. This relates to the horse's movement in forward riding: a long, low, ground-covering, efficient stride; connected, or moving in one piece. The rider is to be correspondingly in forward position, united with the horse's center of gravity and its dynamic balance. When the horse shifts to his connected shorter stride, such as when moving at the advanced-level short canter, the rider's center of gravity must concur with that of the horse. The rider therefore sits erect but not behind the vertical. The rider who is too forward or ahead of the motion at the short canter will be just as off balance as the rider who sits behind and erect on a horse in forward balance moving at faster gaits. The ability of the rider to feel movement and stay united with the horse's shifting balance is part of advanced modern sport riding.

In the section on controls (chapter 2), the mechanics of the gaits, the mechanics of the jump, and the three levels of control used when jumping in this system are discussed. There is further discussion on position when these areas are covered.

FINAL COMMENTS ON POSITION FOR RIDERS AND TEACHERS

The important details of the best ways to select tack, groom and tack the horse, mount, hold the reins, and start riding are presented in a large number of American hunter-oriented books and are not repeated in this text. However, a few position-related details are presented here for consideration for teachers to emphasize to their riders.

MOUNTING FOR ALL LEVELS

Before mounting, properly adjust the tack. Ensure that the girth is correctly fitted. Tighten the girth slowly and carefully to avoid pinching the horse or eventually giving him a sore back. At first, put the girth on loosely and then gradually tighten it after walking toward the mounting block. Mounting should always be taken seriously. Everyone should know how to safely mount from the ground. For the rider's safety, ensure that the reins are gathered short enough to cue the horse promptly if it starts to move away and that the mounting area has a barrier on at least one or two sides. Especially for beginners and aged riders, using a mounting block is often easier on the horse's back. Whether a mounting block is used or not, be certain not to slam down in the saddle. It will cause the horse to scoot off rather than stand, it will give many horses sore backs, and, over a period of time, it might interfere with their performance. Imagine having 75 to 150 pounds slammed down on a spinal column not built to carry weight. Mounting from the left side, swing the right leg over, meet the horse's side gently with the right knee, and take the right stirrup without sitting down. Especially with horses having sensitive backs, avoid sitting down until the horse has gotten used to the weight. Ask him to walk away while still in the two-point and then sit softly with weight in the ankle.

THE HORSE AS VICTIM

Abusive riding, lack of unity, and inefficient use of the aids all interfere with the horse's performance and his physical and mental well-being. Security is the one fundamental of a good working position that many riders have, but it can be at the expense of the horse. It is possible for someone to hang on the mouth and avoid falling. One can also bang the horse's back when getting "left." The result is that, in time, horses become unsound mentally, if not physically, and will not or cannot do their job. Poor position will also be at the expense of an efficient, fluid, and quality performance of the horse. An athletic horse with an excellent temperament will often put up with a great deal of abusive riding and be able to do the job in spite of the antiquated flat riding and disunited position over jumps. Further consider that if a pupil is riding only one or two hours a day five days per week, learning two positions (one for the flat and one for jumping) will be more difficult to do well.

RATIONALE FOR SITTING WELL ON THE HORSE

Security and proficiency are two reasons for wanting to sit well on the horse. A good working position will be safer and more secure. Another reason that a correct design of position and correct weight distribution are useful to develop is that hand, leg, and weight aids can be more efficiently used, making a more proficient rider who will have better success reaching the desired objectives. The rider will have a more cooperative and therefore better-performing horse. A technically correct modern position eliminates abuse of the horse in transitions and reduces the chance of being left behind over jumps and banging the horse's back on the landing. A horse ridden by a rider with a nonabusive position is able to do his job better. This horse will last longer mentally and physically. For the commercially minded, this horse will be a better investment. A correct position also allows the rider to be united with the horse's movement and, therefore, makes riding more comfortable for the rider as well as the horse. Unity of the rider with the movement of the horse leads to a better performance of the horse.

RIDERS WHO NEED A GOOD POSITION

The advantages of having a good working position are important not only for the beginner, the intermediate-level rider, and the general recreational rider, but also for the more experienced amateur rider and the professional.

A less-experienced rider with a good working position will have more productive experiences and progress faster with confidence. Intermediate- or advanced-level competitors with a good working position will be able to use their natural ability and skills most efficiently on a wider variety of horses. Very experienced athletes with good reflexes will, as they age past thirty years, be able to keep consistency in their performance by regularly working on the fundamentals of a good working position and its related seven qualities. Otherwise, the natural athlete with his own style deteriorates rapidly at a relatively early age.

Regardless of one's level of dexterity and age, a rider with a mechanically correct position relies less on athletic reflexes for balance in normal situations and generally rides more effectively.

Occasionally one sees examples of athletic riders with unorthodox positions who are able to recover with above-average timing and reflexes. An uneducated position requires more ability and strength on the part of the rider during certain segments of the jump in order to avoid banging the horse on the back or jerking his mouth. It also requires more dexterity and quickness on the part of the rider to avoid abuse of the horse and lack of unity in transitions. The body and legs of the rider need to be in an efficient position to be quickly used. They have to be moved into place if a stable lower leg is not already at the girth.

There are many professional and amateur riders who once had a decent position but through habit have become comfortable with a changing design of position and weight distribution. They are not only at times unattractive to watch, but they are less balanced, less secure, less agile, and less united with the movement of the horse. They also are less efficient in the use of the controls (weight, hands, and legs).

A successful rider of any skill level will be a more consistent rider and performer with a good working position in the modern forward riding system. All riders need to do position work to keep the correct design and weight distribution, which will allow the four fundamentals and all of the seven physical qualities to function well and thereby lead to a better performance of the horse.

AVOIDING FADS AND APPLYING THE SYSTEM
FOR PROBLEM-SOLVING

Over the past fifty years, there have been many position fads. All of us have been known to take on a few either intentionally, in the short term, or mistakenly. Try to look behind some of the fads that artificially change position. Determine how they affect other fundamentals and qualities of the position and the horse's performance. A thorough understanding of the four fundamentals of a working position and the seven physical characteristics will help riders to both work through their own problems and analyze other people's riding.

Horse-show judges during some periods have actually pinned riders who sit behind the motion or whose toes point toward the horse's elbow, equitation riders who lie down on the neck at the flight phase of the jump, or riders who do a posting exercise at the canter. Often competitors try to please the judge and make changes to their position. These riders should be careful not to let this temporary effort for a prize become a permanent part of their position.

In educated riding the conformation of the rider adjusts to the conformation of the horse. A long-legged person on a thin horse is going to have to turn his toe out to get his lower leg in contact with the horse. The horse and rider are not a good fit, and it is not a "pretty picture" for a hunter equitation class, but the lower leg is effective and the position works on this horse. If this long-legged rider points the toe inward and thereby takes the lower leg away from the smaller horse, it will not be an effective position or a decent ride.

A trend has been to integrate some currently popular and useful German dressage methods originally designed for classical dressage and for their breeds of horses into the schooling of the American hunters and especially the jumpers. This has led to a change in position that is based more on the seat than on the stirrup. Teachers and riders doing this are now wondering what happened to the quality of the American forward seat/hunter seat riding of the 1950s through the 1970s. They have confused two systems with different objectives. In the military in the 1930s some able riders could do both satisfactorily because they used different or exceptional horses and rode a full day for the army. Following this old approach today can be inefficient and unwise for the American amateur and professional. Most have only limited riding time and horse resources. The principles involved have been thoroughly discussed and resolved years ago, but some riders seem to need to revisit this approach as though it were original.

IN SUMMARY, POINTS CONCERNING POSITION

Nonabuse of the horse, unity of the rider with the horse in motion, the security of the rider, and efficient and effective use of the aids are the four fundamentals of a good working position.

The rider should know well the seven physical qualities of a fluid position and exercises that help develop each of them.

The three hinges, angles, or springs in the leg position are the ankle, knee, and hip.

The three areas of grip are the inside lower thigh, inside knee, and inside upper calf.

All horses move in dynamic balance, and the rider's position must be efficient and flexible to be in balance with the horse at different speeds, on uneven terrain, and during the jump. The modern forward riding position, or "hunter seat," is based on the stirrup for this reason.

In educated riding over the past three hundred years, two main systems of riding have emerged. One is the classical dressage system based on principles of *manège* riding from 1550 to its golden era in the eighteenth century. The second system is the forward riding system/American hunter system based on field and sport riding with jumping. It is a complete system that has evolved from the 1920s through the work of Caprilli, Chamberlin, and Littauer. Please review the introduction (especially the section entitled "Concepts and Definitions of the Modern American Forward Riding System"), see the references in appendix 2, and study the rider's position in photographs throughout this text.

2 Levels and Characteristics of Controls in the American Forward Riding System

OVERVIEW OF CONTROLS AND ITS THEORY

The forward riding system is a modern system of riding for hunters, jumpers, hacks, and cross-country horses and consists of three major components: position, controls, and schooling. In this section, we discuss controls. There is no question that the average American rider and many Europeans know more about position from observation and reading now than at any other time. Although unfortunately emphasizing the seat (position) even in the title, the USEF hunter seat equitation division has done a great deal to help educate the general public. However, the area of controls and understanding them has not come through as strongly as the position part of the system. It is very important to understand that modern American riding has a complete system of controls, one level relating to the next. This system emphasizes cooperation with the horse using soft, precise controls. The method and techniques of controls relate directly to the schooling of the horse and, together with the position of the rider, form a complete interacting system.

This chapter on controls emphasizes the three fundamental leg aids and the six rein aids as they relate to the appropriate schooling level—elementary, intermediate, and advanced. These aids are used in coordination with the horse's efforts and reflect the rider's understanding of the horse's physical and mental characteristics.

The three levels of controls each have different aims. In the discussion of the schooling component and the progressive periods of schooling (part 3), there is more information on the importance of controls to the performance of the horse. At this point we are putting forth the aims and levels of the controls for the rider. It is important for the rider/teacher to be at least mechanically correct and clear in applying the aids.

ELEMENTARY CONTROLS

The basic level of controls aims for authority over the horse through definite and quick controls. It utilizes the four natural aids (weight, voice, hand, and leg) and emphasizes such techniques as loose rein, check-release, tone of voice with consistent vocabulary, and tapping leg.

The aids for a transition down on the elementary level from the trot to the walk are: (1) weight: stop posting and sit, (2) voice: "w-a-l-k" spoken in a drawn-out manner, (3) hand: check-release to loose rein, and (4) leg: alternating tapping/urging to walk forward united, following on a looped rein the gestures of the head and neck. The elementary level of controls is especially useful when starting young horses. It often takes an advanced rider to achieve a good performance on this level with a young horse. For more detailed instruction and discussion of schooling on this level, see chapters 7, 8, and 9.

INTERMEDIATE CONTROLS

The intermediate level aims at harmony with the horse using soft and precise controls that require the rider's hands and legs to coordinate with the horse's efforts. Contact helps achieve softer, more precise control; more connected movement; and efficient, long, low, ground-covering strides. This level is often considered advanced in most modern sport riding today. The aids for a transition down on the intermediate level from the trot to the walk are: (1) weight: stop posting and sit, (2) hands: give-and-take, and (3) leg: squeeze-release action, alternating, urging the walk forward. Hands follow the balancing gestures on contact.

ADVANCED CONTROLS

This level of controls in schooling aims for a specific function such as riding to hounds, jumper competition, or competing as a show hunter and is designed to elicit the highest-quality performance that an individual horse is capable of producing in his specialty. The level requires a mentally relaxed, physically alert, responsive, educated, above-average, athletic horse. The same position, aids, and techniques are used in all settings and transfer from flat work to the American hunter or jumper course.

A key objective in successful modern schooling of the horse is to develop controls that are soft and precise. They produce the best-quality performance from the horse using the least amount of the horse's physical and nervous energy. This is the reason that this system is more efficient and effective for schooling hunters and jumpers on the flat.

TWO FOUNDATION CONCEPTS OF FORWARD RIDING CONTROLS

For the rider to better understand controls, it is appropriate at this time to mention two important concepts frequently misunderstood in the schooling component of the modern forward riding system: (1) stabilization as the essential foundation in the first stages of schooling and (2) forward balance, which is different from the classical dressage school's central balance. For the sport horse the goal is to cultivate his natural agility and balance under the weight of the rider, producing connected, ground-covering, efficient movement and mental alertness while keeping him calm. See the illustrations in the introduction to compare forward balance trot and central balance trot. Also see other illustrations in the text.

After training on the foundation level, stabilization (elementary control) is achieved. The horse is mentally and physically stable, maintaining the gait and speed asked for on looped rein, over uneven terrain, on the flat, alone or in company, and over jumps. This is an essential step before proceeding to work on contact and developing the prospect; i.e., teaching the horse to jump courses.

POINTS AND DISTINCTIONS OF CONTACT IN THE
AMERICAN HUNTER SYSTEM

Contact is used for the intermediate and advanced controls levels. In forward riding the dividing line between a quality elementary control performance and the intermediate and advanced levels is riding on contact. There are different levels of contact in this system. One level of contact is passive contact, and another is soft contact with consistent reserve energy. Horses may be schooled to varying degrees of this consistent reserve energy, some more and some less. These two levels of contact will ensure attainable objectives and goals for most horses, riders, and combinations of horses and riders. Some horses have more natural reserve energy than others. Many hunters/jumpers perform well on soft contact. Some may move better at one gait than another, requiring less schooling to improve movement at the better gait. A third level is a contact with more impulse and connection, applied for short periods with specific objectives (i.e., at the short canter for certain competitive jumpers).

There are two reasons to ride on contact. The first is to improve the quality of the horse's movement. The second is to improve the controls, which, when used correctly (soft/precise), improve the quality of the horse's overall performance.

ACHIEVING CONTACT

Riders are ready to ride on contact when their hands are independent of their bodies.

When is the horse ready for it? How is contact established? How is contact introduced to the horse and the rider learning contact? What influence does it have on the quality of the horse's performance?

The horse is ready to ride on contact when he is stabilized. This means he can maintain the gait and speed when asked off contact, but with a degree of connection under the weight of the rider, and he is responsive to the lower leg. If the rider loops the reins and the horse increases speed, he is not stable and not ready for further training. The rider should stay with the elementary foundation of schooling before going on with the contact.

Contact is both a fairly sophisticated and a simple concept. It is a feel of the horse's impulse or reserve energy created by the rider's leg. It is important to emphasize that an educated rider establishes contact from the leg to the hand. The rider's hands feel the reserve energy through the reins. It might be like dew on grass, a very soft feel of reserve energy that is created by the leg.

Speed also produces reserve energy and in an educated, calm horse can be used to the rider's advantage when schooling on contact; i.e., canter or gallop and then go to a trot on contact.

However, a horse that has been upset by previous riding will also give the rider a feel of energy through the reins. He pulls or tries to bolt. He might be a horse that is afraid of the rider's spur or a horse that is unbalanced and nervous from being on the lunge line with improperly adjusted gadgets. Horses in these situations can be full of nervous energy and be thought of by some riders as being on the bit, but these examples do not show educated contact and riding. They simply reflect upset energy from a nervous, partially ruined, or frightened horse.

The trot is a good gait to start riding on contact because it has no balancing gesture for the hands to follow, and the two-beat gait gives steady energy.

The rider establishes a direct line from bit to elbow (the arm can be seen as an extension of the rein) and feels the reserve energy created by his own leg. The rider should keep in mind that: (1) the faster the gait, the more reserve energy or natural impulse (impulse at the walk can be difficult to feel on some horses), (2) the balancing gestures need to be followed at the walk and canter, and (3) it is difficult to maintain contact during transitions, even for some talented amateur riders and some professional riders. (This affects the performance of the horse.)

At the trot as the rider posts down, the insides of both lower legs close, producing a little squeeze-release that increases the engagement of the hind leg under the horse's belly and produces the thrust forward (disengagement). Put as much emphasis on the disengagement as the engagement, because it is the push-off that produces the power and energy. Engagement in the classical school often means a vertical engagement and a vertical disengagement. In the sport horse, the goal is a good horizontal engagement/disengagement.

Sometimes the conformation of some horses makes engagement difficult, and it is therefore hard to put the horse on contact. An experienced eye can evaluate the conformation and predict schooling problems or advantages.

After stabilization, teach the horse passive contact before proceeding to the next stage of contact.

Soft contact—the horse's ability to extend the neck and head and accept the hand—is a soft feel of the horse's reserve energy created by the rider's leg. There are degrees of reserve energy, and they produce a connected horse. The neck and head are extended with the nose in front of the vertical at ordinary gaits and transitions. An older horse warming up or a young horse being trained should not develop the habit of being behind the vertical or above the bit, nor of leaning down on the bit unbalanced (heavy-headed). The horse has balancing gestures at the walk, canter, gallop, and jump. It is a fundamental principle that the rider should be able to follow the natural balancing gestures. A hand set against the natural balancing gestures will restrict movement, teach pulling or hanging, cause pain, and may mentally disturb the horse. Horses often escape this hand by poking their nose up or overflexing, or they may develop an abused, numb mouth.

Riding "on the bit" can have more reserve energy than is necessary for most horses and most movements. For some jumpers, it can be a form of semi-collection used at the short gaits as an exercise. The horse has more reserve energy and also has a higher head and neck carriage.

The short canter can be used to help the horse prepare on the flat to canter to a combination that requires a short, energetic stride for a short arc on the first element, but it needs to be integrated with normal gaits and lengthening. *Horses with a good temperament, natural impulse, and above-average agility will not need to be "on the bit" in order to do the short canter or abrupt transitions and turns.* Too much work on the shorter gaits with a high reserve energy can negatively affect movement and temperament. For example, the ground-covering stride may be restricted, the temperament may become aggressive, and/or the horse may become too energetic for the schooling objectives and too sensitive for his rider.

In schooling the hunter and jumper, the short-gaited work needs to be tempered by lengthening work in order not to distort the quality of the horse's ground-covering movement. Normally a naturally good mover may need less lengthening work, and a less-than-average mover will need considerably more lengthening work.

To summarize, contact is initiated by the leg aids and results in the reserve energy the rider feels in his hands. The reserve energy is created by the horizontal engagement and disengagement of the hind leg, which connects the hind end to the front end. The goal in forward riding is to produce connected, ground-covering, efficient strides for an athletic sport horse, enabling him to gallop, shorten, turn, stay connected, and jump efficiently and with agility. He must remain calm but alert. This can be successfully achieved with a horse in forward balance that is connected on soft contact with reserve energy.

The goal does not include schooling in full collection and central balance. As a child I remember my instructor telling me to shorten the reins and collect the horse, which was a common misuse of the term. Collection is a very important concept in the classical dressage school, but in teaching contact for modern hunter, jumper, and/or cross-country riders and horses, it is best to avoid this term and emphasize instead the concept of connection.

To be certain, quality, classical high school dressage is an important educated type of riding; but it should not be confused with the flat work, the position, or the level of controls that are the aim in modern hunter/jumper riding. Riders should not look to influence each step, nor perfect a movement that is a schooling exercise, or look for a high degree of short elevated gaits and central balance. Riders should work at the shortened gaits to teach certain horses (i.e., upper-level competitive jumpers) to be agile making a turn, or approaching a specific jump or combination. The schooling should emphasize natural connected movement (long, low, ground-covering, efficient strides) in a forward balance suited for uneven terrain, the flat, and jumping.

THE HORSE'S INDIVIDUAL CHARACTERISTICS AND MOVEMENT AND THEIR EFFECTS ON CONTROLS

Movement, temperament, and athletic ability will predetermine the success of the horse and rider in each of the levels of controls.

First consider the horse's character and physique. What is the horse's mental attitude and level of cooperation toward accepting the aids? What is the horse's conformation? Is he an athletic, connected horse that will take the weight of the rider and a higher level of schooling in a manner that is physically easy for him? Is he a horse of fairly insensitive nature, not a naturally connected horse, perhaps long in the back, camped out behind, even ewe-necked? Even with an excellent temperament, this type of horse will have a great deal of trouble accepting contact on the intermediate and advanced levels of forward riding.

The horse may be high-headed or crooked-legged behind, which could cause him to disengage longer than he can engage. It may be physically difficult for him to engage, making connection and contact difficult, and it will be hard for him to travel in one piece under the weight of the rider. The conformation nature gave the horse will often determine its potential level of schooling. Trying to force the flat work on horses whose conformation restricts good natural movement may cause mental and eventually physical unsoundness.

If the horse is in any kind of physical discomfort or if the horse is extra-sensitive, perhaps from previous bad riding, its potential is limited. If the horse pins its ears, resists with the head and neck, "cranks" his tail, and/or shows other signs of unhappiness, these are signals that the horse is sour. Although limited, these horses can possibly be reclaimed to be useful. The rider's ability to feel the horse's physical efforts and to be aware of his mental attitude is *essential* to applying the appropriate level of controls.

Good conformation and temperament as well as inherited athletic ability are important in schooling. A horse traveling "straight" is in the best position to maintain his balance. The hind end needs to be connected to the front end. Good engagement of the hind leg (swing of the hind leg under the belly) and the proportionate disengagement (push-off/thrust forward), coupled with the free swing of the shoulder, are essential to good movement.

It is not possible to "make" an advanced horse in this system from a horse that has limited athletic ability and/or movement. For example, a horse that tends to be naturally low-headed (in the old days this was called heavy on the forehand) with the hind end disconnected from the front end or a horse that is built much higher behind than in front will always be difficult to connect even with good schooling. Horses with this kind of conformation can often lack natural coordination and agility, making it impossible for them to achieve higher levels no matter how well the controls are administered and how carefully the stages of training have progressed.

It is important to note that if such a horse is sound and nicely tempered he might make an excellent elementary-level horse. There is a use for the horse that can walk, trot, and canter—off contact or on a light, passive contact—and be ridden by someone learning to ride or by someone who does not wish to do more than hack or hilltop. Not all horses and riders will be able to achieve the advanced level of control nor do they need to in order to experience safe, enjoyable riding.

At the same time, if a horse is beautifully conformed and moves efficiently with a natural connection, has a nice topline (the head, neck, withers, back, loin, and croup proportionate to each other and in balance with the parts below), and looks to be athletic, then it may be realistic to plan advanced-level schooling objectives.

One would, of course, need a rider educated through the three levels of control and stages of schooling as well as a rider with the mental and physical ability to train a horse to an advanced level.

The horse's mental as well as physical qualities for each of the levels of controls are necessary for success. The elementary level is better suited to a fairly docile horse or what is called a half-bred. However, this type is often not a quality mover and does not have a natural reserve energy desirable for a higher level of schooling. A three-quarter-bred temperament is often ideal for intermediate riding and schooling. The advanced-level horse must have an athletic build and natural quality movement with reserve energy, in addition to sensitivity and a cooperative attitude.

There is no clear way to predict a horse's jumping ability through conformation. Unfortunately, a schooling prospect can have quality temperament, reserve energy, conformation, and movement but not sufficient jumping ability to reach the higher levels of education in this system of riding. A "green" horse or an able but poorly trained horse can jump awkwardly until (re)trained. However, a horse must show consistent jumping form (i.e., fold) from the start, or the odds are against success at a higher level. The prospect will develop under the weight of the rider in a progressive schooling plan into a skilled jumper only if he has some natural jumping talent.

In conclusion, conformation is important, but cooperative temperament and talent for jumping are also important. Conformation is discussed in more detail in the section on schooling (part 2, chapter 4).

APPLYING CONTROLS: FOUR NATURAL AIDS

The four natural aids (weight, hand, leg, and voice) are used in a very specific sequence. For example, in going from the canter to the walk, the rider should have depth in the ankle with the three position angles or springs (ankle, knee, and hip). At the intermediate or advanced level, the rider should sit through the crotch of the britches by opening the hip, bringing the upper body back but not behind the vertical, and then, in rhythm with the balancing gestures, use give-and-take. For a gradual transition from the canter through the trot to the walk, the rider should sit the trot gait, thereby alerting the horse to come back to the weight of the rider, and then use the leg aid just as the horse is about to walk. At the intermediate and advanced levels, the voice is not used unless the horse ignores or resists the aids. A "sharp" voice and/or a stick should be used at the girth to correct any disobedience to the leg aid when it is time to walk frankly forward. The rider needs to practice using the four natural aids and the coordination of the specific rein and leg aids. The specific techniques for each level are an important part of this system. Exercises are included below to help the rider become skilled on each level of controls.

Student riders and teachers should memorize the combination of six rein and three leg aids. Some of the more talented and experienced riders who ride many horses a day instinctively work out these aids without labels. However, when teaching or when riding just one or two horses a day, or if pupils are less experienced, it is advantageous to practice the aids after understanding how and why they are used.

Some would argue that teaching a rider to use these aids mechanically might inhibit their natural talent, and perhaps this would be true with a rider in the middle of a competitive season. If a rider knows the mechanics of the six rein aids and three leg aids and has developed the ability to feel movement and coordinate these rein and leg aids with the movement of the horse, then the rider is riding on a high-intermediate or an advanced level. A serious rider

TABLE 1

THE FOUR NATURAL AIDS PROGRESSIVELY TAUGHT THROUGH LEVELS OF CONTROL

Natural Aids	Elementary Control Level	Intermediate Control Level	Advanced Control Level
Weight	Precedes voice in all transitions down except when teaching beginners position	Used in all transitions Precedes hand and leg in all transitions down Used at short gaits	Same as intermediate level
Voice	Actual word and tone. "Walk,""trot,""canter," "whoa,""slow,""no,""good" Used in all transitions Precedes weight and leg in transitions Key aid in teaching stabilization and controls	Used to warm up off contact Used on contact only to reinforce weight, hand, leg	Same as intermediate level
Legs	Tapping technique—3 leg aids Used in rhythm with mechanics of the gaits	Squeeze/release technique—3 leg aids Objective with other aids is to "connect" the horse to improve movement and controls (soft, precise transitions) Used in rhythm with the gaits and transitions	Same as intermediate level Create more impulse as needed for connection, quality movement, and soft, precise controls Objective: Produce best performance a particular horse is capable of on this level
Hands	Looped rein Check-release technique Opening rein for turning young horses 1st combination rein used is inside direct/outside opening Avoid corrective reins 5/6	Contact: (1) Passive contact, (2) Soft contact with degrees of reserve energy/impulse Give-and-take technique Head and neck extended—mouth closed Following arms All 6 rein aids used in coordination with 3 leg aids	Contact: Soft contact with more reserve energy, if needed Flexions and half-halt technique, if needed Increased reserve energy risks mental stability Excessive work at short gaits risks quality hunter movement Same as intermediate level

should know these aids well enough to teach them to another rider and to communicate them to a variety of horses.

Littauer was among the first to present the aids in an organized way. See the illustrations on rein aids and leg aids, which are altered but based on his work. In the past twenty years, we have integrated the "neck rein" and increased the use of it in forward riding.

THE WEIGHT AID

At the elementary level in the forward riding system the weight aid is used to help the horse anticipate shifts and transitions. For example, if he is going to go from the walk to the trot, the beginning rider should prepare the horse by stepping down deep in the heel, closing the hip, saying "trot" with a sharp voice, and using a tapping lower leg. When a trained school horse moves forward, the starting rider can be "a nickel's worth" ahead of the motion for the first moment. In that way the beginning rider gets to feel the unity much faster. He can easily later correct the disadvantages of riding a little ahead at the start of the transition. This same weight aid technique can help a green horse understand what is being asked of him. At the intermediate and advanced levels, the weight can be used to produce invisible, soft, and precise transitions down.

Exaggerate it to own it. Start with the simple elemental exercise of walk–trot–walk off contact. It can be useful for all students from the beginner to the advanced/intermediate needing a tune-up. It is also good for young horses learning to take it as a signal to shorten. When trotting, sit, try not to touch the mouth (most riders go for it), and use the voice and if necessary the hand (check-release) to get the walk. Soon the horse will walk without the hand. The rider closes the leg to walk forward into the first steps of the walk. In very gradual transitions use each of the four aids separately to learn the order in which they are applied. Repeat over and over. Never confuse the weight aid with a "driving seat" or sitting heavily on the seat bone.

The rider should learn the movement of the horse through the transition. For downward transitions use (1) the weight aid (sit through the crotch with weight in the ankle), (2) on contact, give-and-take of the hand (several if necessary) for just fractions of a second, and then (3) closing the leg so that the horse walks forward with a good swing of the hind leg under the belly (engagement), followed by a thrust of the hind leg (disengagement). In this way the horse will learn to respond to the weight signal before the hand and will be connected in transitions down. The rider can learn to better feel the movement of the horse through the transition. If the rider is soft and accurate and the horse comfortable, the result should be a better-quality transition.

THE VOICE AID

This aid is used in coordination with the other three natural aids. The voice can be a useful aid on the elementary level, both for teaching riders and for schooling young horses or reclaiming horses. The voice can be useful on the higher levels as a reinforcement.

At the elementary level, the voice is used for all transitions. For example, when walking, to let the horse know he should trot forward, use a tapping leg and the voice ("trot") at the same time. The weight aid forward comes into play, especially for beginners. The teacher must make certain that the beginner is stepping down in the heel and has an angle at the hip. The hand is used only if the horse trots at a faster gait than is necessary. The trained "school horse" trots at an even pace. The check-release hand technique of the elementary level may not even be necessary. On transitions down at the elementary level, from the trot to the walk, the beginning rider should (1) use the voice ("walk") in a drawn-out, low tone and (2) if it can be done by a beginner without being abusive, stop posting (weight), sit down, and then use (3) check-release hand technique and (4) a tapping, alternating leg aid to ensure the horse walks forward. When the beginner's position becomes united with the movement and is nonabusive, the weight aid precedes the voice on the elementary level.

The aids for a transition forward at the intermediate and advanced levels are the (squeeze-release) leg and dropping the voice except to cue a correction to the leg or hand. The contact should be consistently maintained throughout the transition forward.

Because using the voice is often penalized in equitation competitions where the rider is to demonstrate effective hand and leg aids on a horse schooled to the intermediate or advanced level, many "coaches" of the junior competitors have forbidden it in practice to avoid a mishap (habit) in competition. This might be the reason that in training horses the voice is currently often used in a fairly primitive and hidden manner, such as "whoa" for all transitions down and "cluck" for all forward. All horses should be able to learn to respond to these words used with a different tone or inflection: "walk," "trot," "slow trot," "canter," "slow," "whoa," and "good."

THE THREE LEG AIDS: USES AND TECHNIQUES

In the early stages of learning to ride, the technique to use is a tapping leg, which later for intermediate and advanced riders develops into a squeeze-release technique. The latter becomes an almost invisible technique. Avoid a leg, leg, leg–hold, hold, hold attack, as seen in some approaches to riding on the flat. Also avoid a vising, clutching leg, where the rider closes the inside lower leg and does not let go until the horse responds. This will make many horses numb-sided and others unhappy with leg aids. These aids are to be applied with a soft, rhythmic technique coordinated with the horse's movement.

When teaching the young horse to respond to leg aids, a tapping action is first used; and later, when he understands the signal, it becomes a soft, invisible squeeze-release technique. A less attentive young or green horse does not usually understand the squeeze-release leg at first. He will need a little tap and a sharp voice and/or crop at the rider's calf (girth) to reinforce the voice and leg aids.

At the elementary level if the horse is walking and the rider wants it to trot, the rider should use a sharp voice ("trot") and the lower leg (tap, tap). If the horse has been taught the word "trot" on the lunge line, it will be easy for the young horse to make the association. It is useful in teaching beginners trying to stay in balance to say "trot" along with using the tapping leg. The beginner on a horse trained to the voice will be rewarded with a response. The experienced horse used for teaching will need to be periodically "tuned" to the elementary controls by the instructor.

If there is a disobedience to the elementary or intermediate/advanced leg techniques, correct it with a voice and/or a stick exactly where the leg is used. The horse will have no problem making an association. The leg technique is first the soft tap; if no response, then a sharp voice; and next, if needed, a leg, voice, and crop at the girth. The spur is also used to correct disobedience to the leg. High-intermediate and advanced riders can use dull short spurs (pointed down) on some horses. It is foolish and unkind to the horse to put spurs on beginners. Horses will lose their value as they become sour, and pupils might sometimes get involved in a bolt or a buck when they misplace the spur. Misused aids including spurs will often sour horses. Horses that have the spur constantly used or a constant vising leg may begin to swish their tails, pin their ears, and become very uncooperative to the rider's leg requests; and it is difficult behavior to reverse once it has been learned. That is one reason for using the voice with the elementary-level rider and with the young horse. If the leg aid is not being correctly applied, the voice can help the horse understand. If it is a green, sensitive horse, he can make the association with voice reinforcement much faster without being frazzled and distracted by a stick or spur. Please note the illustrations on leg and hand aids.

THE URGING LEG (1)   The urging leg is used at the girth to ask the horse to go forward—i.e., walk to trot—with two legs used simultaneously at the girth. To lengthen the walk, use alternating legs at the girth. To lengthen the canter, use one urging leg on the side of the lead.

THE HOLDING LEG (2)   In modern sport riding, the leg at the girth is a holding leg. It prevents the horse from falling in and can move him over laterally. The holding leg is normally used on the inside for turns. In the past the holding leg used at the girth was called the bending leg. The skeleton was somehow supposed to bend around the inside leg. The bending leg term is a holdover from the sixteenth-, seventeenth-, and eighteenth-century classical dressage school. Unfortunately for the horse, some strong, forceful riders still try to bend the horse's skeleton around the leg, resulting in soured horses.

THE DISPLACING LEG (3)   The displacing leg refers to displacing the haunch; i.e., to turn on the forehand the haunch is moved around the front end (see the illustration) or when cantering a turn the outside displacing leg holds the haunch on the line or prevents the haunch from falling out.

The urging and the holding leg aids are applied at the girth. The displacing leg may be used three to six inches farther back. If the rider's leg size fits the horse, he should ride off the inside lower part of the leg rather than the back of the calf, although the latter will occasionally be necessary for a stronger leg.

There are other leg aids that have been used and suggested in modern times, but they do not relate to this system. For example, one that is three hundred years old is the tapping of the leg on the shoulder, an aid believed to have been used by riders in armor. In modern American riding, the legs are used in coordination with the rider's hands while feeling the horse's movements but not usually at the same time. It is not a drive-hold approach. The rider asks for the gait and speed, and the horse responds, maintaining a certain level of impulse and connection. The rider's design of position and schooling objectives in forward riding are directly related to the controls.

THREE LEG AIDS

The urging and holding legs *(left)* are used at the girth. The technique of the urging leg at the walk is alternating; at the trot, both legs act simultaneously in rhythm with the two-beat trot as the rider posts down; and at the canter the urging leg is used on the side of the lead. The holding leg helps keep the horse on the line, often on the inside. In previous centuries this leg was called by many a bending leg. This implied the impossible, that the rib cage at the girth bent around the rider's leg.

The displacing leg *(right)*, placed approximately four to six inches behind the girth. It affects the haunch and is used on turns or lateral movements. The technique at the elementary level is a tapping lower leg and at the intermediate and advanced levels is a squeeze-release lower leg. (See also tables 1 and 2.)

The approach of seeking cooperation and soft, precise transitions is a major part of this system. The conformation of the horse and the mental attitude of the horse, which also tie in to the breeding, will influence the success of this schooling objective. Forward riding is most successful with a physically athletic and mentally kind type of horse.

HANDS AS AIDS: THE TECHNIQUES AND THE SIX REIN AIDS

The elementary level has been developed for the advanced rider to start the green horse and for the beginning or limited rider to efficiently and safely enjoy riding on a made horse trained in elementary controls. Please note the leg and hand aid illustrations.

Beginning riders should be riding without contact on stabilized horses until their position allows their hands to be independent of their bodies. The reins are loose, and the horse is stabilized. The beginning rider should not try to have a feel of the mouth, because doing so will be abusive to the horse. If the rider loses his balance in a transition, he is going to grab the reins for balance and jerk the horse's mouth. Certainly a horse experiencing this will not perform better and may go sour. With an insensitive horse, a few teachers have allowed the rider to hang on to the mouth for balance. I have observed that this creates all sorts of rider and horse problems. With this hanging-on

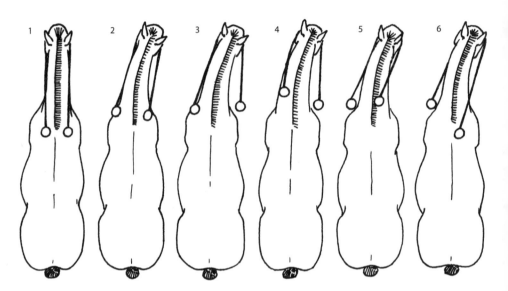

SIX REIN AIDS

All six are used in combination with the appropriate leg aids for the movement. (1) Two direct reins of opposition used to slow or stop the horse. The techniques are check-release on loose rein at the elementary level and give-and-take on contact for the intermediate and advanced levels. (2) One right direct rein of opposition for turning on contact. (3) One right opening rein for turning at the elementary level (loose rein for young horses, beginning riders, and all levels warming up). Used at the advanced level to avoid shortening the stride when turning at speed. (4) One left bearing or neck rein combined with a direct or slightly opening right rein. The left neck rein should not cross the neck but should bear or press on the neck. Next are corrective reins five and six. (5) Inside indirect rein of opposition in front of the withers shifts the weight to the opposite shoulder. This rein is often incorrectly used in lateral movements in place of an effective holding leg. If consistently used incorrectly it cocks the horse's nose to the inside and makes educated lateral work on contact difficult. (6) An indirect rein of opposition behind the withers shifts the weight to the opposite haunch; i.e., in backing, it can be used to help straighten a crooked step back. It is a severe corrective rein aid and should not be overused. (See also tables 1 and 2.)

approach, riders learn the habit of heavy hands that will be a handicap when they try to step themselves up into the intermediate and advanced levels.

If a rider is off contact (elementary level) and wants to use two direct reins of opposition to go from the trot to the walk, the order of the use of the aids is weight, voice, and check-release technique. Repeat voice and hand until the desired pace or gait is achieved. The tapping leg (alternating) is used to get the horse to walk forward into the transition. Check-release gives the horse nothing to lean or hang on if he is green, and it does not allow the beginning or awkward rider on a stabilized horse to hold on to the head for balance during the transition. A rider is ready to ride on contact when his position has allowed his hands to be completely independent of the rest of the body, including during transitions.

The horse is ready to be on contact when he is stabilized (the foundation). If the rider has a looped rein and the horse becomes uneven in his gaits or goes faster or slower, he is not stable. The net result is a horse that is pulling or a rider who is constantly regulating pace with a leg or a hand. It is not educated contact—that is, reserve energy created by the leg and felt by the hand.

Teaching riders the foundation of forward riding elementary controls provides them with a method to reclaim a racehorse or a horse that pulls or to improve a rider's heavy hands. Training the horse to be stabilized may take four to eight weeks, but progress toward the intermediate and advanced levels goes faster once stabilization is established. Both the horse and the rider will have a better chance of achieving a higher level of performance once they have the foundation of stabilization.

GIVE-AND-TAKE TECHNIQUE   Give-and-take is a technique used when riding on contact at the intermediate and advanced levels of controls that builds out of the check-release technique (elementary controls level). It enables the rider to maintain rhythm with the horse's movement, including the balancing gestures. It is done in coordination with the weight, leg, and, if necessary, voice aids. It is a soft taking of pressure and then giving back to soft contact. The higher the level, the more invisible it is. When a downward transition starts, the rider gives back to soft contact and follows through with the leg as needed. Educated hands are the actions of the fingers, the hands, and the arms, which in cooperation with the leg and weight aids attain the best results in the shortest time and require the least expenditure of the horse's mental and physical energies.

TWO DIRECT REINS OF OPPOSITION (1)   Two direct reins are used for slowing or shortening the gait, for halting, and for backing. They are used in rhythm with the balancing gestures with appropriate technique for the level. This technique to shorten or halt the horse using two direct reins of opposition can be used on a looped rein or when riding on contact. The horse should not lean or develop the habit of leaning. At the advanced level, flexions can come into play, where the rider feels the horse soften in the jaw and the rider's hand then instantly softens. For more information on flexions see chapter 9.

ONE DIRECT REIN OF OPPOSITION (2)   One direct rein is used for turning on contact and for intermediate and advanced levels of controls. It tends to slow the speed of the gait. The horse's head and neck should be positioned in the direction of the turn.

LEADING OR OPENING REIN (3)   For turning, a leading or opening rein is used by elementary riders and by experienced riders on green horses. Elementary riders can use this rein for turning without being on contact if they have an insecure position or do not have hands independent of the body. Young horses can easily understand this guiding rein.

The leading rein is occasionally used at the intermediate and advanced levels for turning at speed or when the rider does not want the horse to shorten stride. With a little opening inside rein, the horse will turn, keeping a longer stride; turning on a direct rein will shorten the stride. The direct rein turn might help get the horse connected and in a shorter stride for the next problem off the turn. However, if the problem off the turn requires a galloping stride, an opening rein can be used for the turn.

NECK REIN OR BEARING REIN (4)   One rein (inside or outside) presses against the lower half of the neck in combination with the leg to move the horse laterally. The hand should not cross over the mane. This rein aid works best with a connected horse.

Current variations on this rein aid and the techniques include the western riding neck rein now used by some on hunters and jumpers for turns on courses. The neck rein is used by simply pushing the rein against the neck on the inside or outside. It is not to be confused with an inside indirect rein of opposition (corrective rein). The inside neck rein should go back to being an inside direct rein on contact when the pressing-out has been accomplished.

For example, when jumping off a turn, the horse might need a little pressing out. The inside direct rein becomes a neck rein with the rein pressed on the neck. Both will be combined with a slightly opening outside rein and the inside leg at the girth. Western American riding has been using it for generations, and it has been incorporated into American hunter riding by some riders and teachers.

CORRECTIVE REIN AIDS (5/6)

Inside Indirect Rein of Opposition in Front of the Withers (5). The inside indirect rein of opposition in front of the withers is used with an inside lower leg (holding) and an outside opening or direct rein. It is a corrective rein. For example, the left indirect rein of opposition in front of the withers will shift the horse to the right or opposite shoulder. It is used to correct a "popped" shoulder, a term that means the horse is falling in at the shoulder, usually on a turn. The inside indirect rein of opposition "unpops" the shoulder and is used at the same time with an active leg that moves the horse over and also urges him forward, which will help to correct the falling-in as well.

The rider must be careful not to use the inside indirect rein of opposition for all turns. This rein is frequently incorrectly used. Riders should turn most often on a direct rein and an inside holding leg, keeping the horse connected and going forward. A consistently used inside indirect rein of opposition in front of the withers will cock the horse's nose to the inside and prevent the horse from taking educated contact. At the advanced level it is very hard to teach lateral flexions if the horse has learned the habit of cocking the head to the inside as a result of the constant use of the inside indirect rein of opposition for all turns. The rider and horse must learn to use and respond to the holding leg. When the holding leg is weakly used or not used in turning, the rider often "fills in" with the corrective indirect rein of opposition in front of the withers for all turns.

Inside Indirect Rein of Opposition Behind the Withers (6). The rein of indirect opposition behind the withers is also a corrective rein; i.e., if, when backing the horse, the haunch swings toward the right, then the right indirect rein of opposition behind the withers is used to shift the haunch to the left. It can be a severe corrective rein and should be used softly and only when necessary. The indirect rein of opposition behind the withers is used with an outside slightly opening or direct rein and a holding and/or displacing leg as needed.

RIDING THE HORSE ON THE LINE   Normally when turning on a large circle, an intermediate- or advanced-level horse in forward riding is connected (moving in one piece), the hind leg having a long swing under the belly (engagement), with the corresponding strong disengagement. There is a good swing from the shoulder. The head and neck are extended, the poll is slightly flexed, and the nose is in front of the vertical. On the turn, it is an inside direct rein, not an indirect rein. The outside direct rein gives or softens, allowing the horse's eye to look where he is going and the neck to slightly bend (laterally) in the direction he is going. The rider keeps consistent soft contact throughout, always riding forward from the leg.

Riders should avoid teaching the horse to hang in or fall in from an outside opening rein. A common error when the horse is falling in is to hold the nose out when turning. When the nose is held out, the inside haunch will fall in, and the horse will be crooked. The rider should keep an active inside leg and keep the horse looking where he is going, using a combination of inside direct rein and an outside direct that can be a slightly opening rein. The outside opening rein will not be a "holding out" rein if it is used with the inside leg and hand. For all levels, the inside leg should be the stronger aid.

FEELING THE HORSE'S MOVEMENT: MECHANICS OF THE GAITS, THE FOUR NATURAL AIDS, AND LEVELS OF CONTROLS

Please note in the introduction the illustration showing the mechanics of the walk, trot, canter, and back. Also note both the mechanics of the gaits and the mechanics of the jump in the photographs in this book. All riders at all levels should know the mechanics of the gaits and the jump. I have met talented riders who could feel the gait but could not explain the beats and mechanics. Perhaps these people will never need to know these mechanics, but the average rider at the advanced or high-intermediate level and teaching professionals should know them well. A place to start is to memorize them. For example, the canter has three beats. On the right lead the sequence is the left hind leg, the diagonal pair, and then the right leading leg. Also watch horses move and see the beats from the ground. Study a video. Then ride different horses and feel the beats. When riders try this for six to ten days, they feel movement better.

As recently as forty years ago people talked about the horse being balanced equally on all four legs. However, even the fully collected horse in quality clas-

TABLE 2
LEG AND REIN AIDS

	Aid	Action	Effect
3 Leg Aids	(1) Urging leg	Acts at or just behind the girth	Moves horse forward, to increase speed and reserve energy
	(2) Holding	Acts at or just behind the girth	Holds horse's body on the line especially when turning
	(3) Displacing	Acts behind the girth, 4 inches to 6 inches, depending upon the goal	Displaces the haunches, holds the haunches in place, or moves the body laterally
6 Rein Aids	(1) Two reins of direct opposition	2 hands/reins straight back; direct line from bit to elbow	Slows down, stops, or backs the horse
	(2) One rein of direct opposition	1 hand straight back	Turns horse, positions horse's head slightly to the turn, tends to slow horse on turns
	(3) Leading or opening rein	1 hand inside opens or leads to the inside	Makes gradual turns on young horse or turns at speed (older horse)
	(4) Neck rein	1 rein pressed against the neck	Moves laterally
	(5) Corrective rein: rein of indirect opposition in front of the withers	1 hand/rein acts toward the opposite shoulder	Shifts weight to the opposite shoulder
	(6) Corrective rein: rein of indirect opposition behind the withers	1 hand/rein acts toward the opposite haunch	Shifts weight to the opposite haunch

sical collection (central balance) has a shifting balance based on the beats of
the gait. Long after the invention of the camera, which exposed serious flaws
in some traditional riding theory, there are still books on riding that at least
imply that the author does not understand the balance of the horse in motion and the related mechanics of the gaits, including the balancing gestures
of the head and neck at the walk, canter, and jump. It is important for the
rider to have an intellectual understanding of the mechanics and learn to feel
movement.

Try walking off contact; apply the urging leg aid to increase the walk by
using alternating leg pressure. Be sure your hands follow the head and neck
gestures in rhythm with the four beats of the walk.

On the intermediate level (on contact), the technique is squeeze-release
on the right, squeeze-release on the left, and so forth. If this does not come
naturally, the rider should stop and work on it. For the horse's sake, the rider
should do it off contact at first and on a trail or somewhere that the horse is
walking forward energetically and pleasantly. Once again, any disobedience to
the leg should be corrected by a sharp word ("walk"). If this does not get the
correct response, use a stick in the same place the leg aid is being used—or a
tap of the spur if appropriate—and at the same time repeat the voice aid. Be
sure to reward a positive response with a stroke or a voice aid ("good").

On the intermediate/advanced level, the pace of the walk increases as
the rider uses alternating leg pressure. The horse will begin to respond by
lengthening the swing of both the hind leg (engagement/disengagement) and
the shoulder. As the walk lengthens, the balancing gestures of the head and
neck become more noticeable. The rider needs to follow these gestures with
the arm, hand, and reins. When humans run with their hands in their pockets
they feel much more awkward than when they are swinging their arms and
running. It is the same idea with the horse. The horse can walk with a frozen
head and neck, but he will have a longer, more fluid stride if he is allowed to
use his natural balancing gestures.

Green horses learning to carry the weight of the rider will normally have
a longer, lower neck carriage and a less-natural connection under the weight
they are learning to carry. An older and correctly trained horse has learned to
carry the weight of the rider and is able to stay connected through transitions.
He has been schooled to carry his whole body in one piece and will carry his
head and neck somewhat higher. There continues to be a balancing gesture
of the head and neck at the walk, canter, and jump.

Consistent following contact will help the rider to apply soft, precise controls in rhythm with the horse's movement at all gaits. If the rider can master following the balancing gestures at the walk, the carryover to the canter and jump will be easier. The rider should practice with a passive contact and not try to feel significant reserve energy/strong contact at the walk.

In the 1960s, 1970s, and 1980s in the hunter and jumper rings, it was rare to find anyone who taught this, but many rode following the balancing gestures. In the early twenty-first century, there are some riders who follow the balancing gestures with educated hands. However it still is not often taught, so perhaps it came naturally to them.

The *trot* is a *two-beat gait, with the legs moving in diagonal pairs.* The horse maintains a fairly stable head carriage. The short trot (the slow sitting trot) is an important exercise in forward riding and schooling. At the slow trot a student can learn to sit softly. At the slow trot the young horse learns to shorten the stride and maintain the speed asked for at the shorter gait under the weight of the rider. If it is a green or young horse, it is best to sit only for short periods of time. Later the slow sitting trot helps the horse accept the weight in both the downward transitions and at the ordinary and short canter.

The rider in the posting trot should be united with the movement. The hands should be independent of the body lest the rider give signals unintentionally that will result in abusive riding and a poor performance of the horse.

To lengthen the trot, post and use two urging legs at the girth in rhythm with the diagonal pairs. When posting down, the squeeze-release of the lower legs is applied at the girth.

The *canter* is a *three-beat gait* with balancing gestures. As in all gaits, a horse moves with the constant loss and regaining of equilibrium forward. This is obvious at the strong canter and less so at the short canter.

There are three speeds of the canter, and also the fast gallop, which produce a period of suspension and four beats, with the diagonal pair of legs developing separate beats or footfalls.

The urging leg used at the girth is closed on the side of the leading leg in rhythm with the three-beat canter. It is important to remember that the balancing gesture of the head and neck is an important part of the gait. The short canter has the least gesture; the fast canter/gallop the most. In racing, modern jockeys follow the balancing gestures of the head and neck, especially at the finish, allowing the full swing of the head and neck to encourage the full length of stride.

Whether at the walk or the canter, the degree of swing of the head and neck influences the stride. In general, the shorter and higher the neck, the shorter the balancing gestures and the shorter and higher the stride. The longer the neck, the longer the balancing gestures and the stride.

If a rider can follow the balancing gestures of the head and neck through the three speeds of the canter and has learned to feel the movement, the rider has probably progressed beyond being a mechanically correct rider. To move from the ordinary canter to the slow canter, the rider should open the hip angle, thereby using the weight aid first, and while on contact use give-and-take in rhythm with the balancing gestures of the head and neck at the canter. The rider should follow the gestures back more and follow forward less, keeping the rhythm of the canter until the stride is regulated. An advanced rider on certain advanced horses might set the hand and, when the jaw flexes and softens, instantly soften the hand before going back to following the balancing gestures as the horse holds the new pace; i.e., short canter (see the discussion of half-halt in the introduction).

When returning to the ordinary canter from the short, the rider should use the urging leg at the girth on the side of the leading leg to open the stride of the canter. Encouraging more head and neck gestures as the stride opens up allows the stride to get longer. An educated sport horse at a full controlled gallop in the open is just as much in balance as the same horse trotting a circle in the ring. This point is often missed.

Going to the *gallop* from the ordinary canter requires closing the urging leg at the girth on the side of the leading leg. Just as the canter begins to lengthen, the rider steps down deep in the heel and puts more weight in the stirrup (ankle). This frees up the hind end so that the hind leg can swing under the belly (engage/disengage). The rider's following arm allows contact and more swing of the head, neck, and shoulder so that the stride can extend. "Bridging" the reins while galloping, although frequently done by jockeys and upper-level three-day-event riders, encourages the horse to pull. This technique unfortunately is also used at horse trials with young novice horses. Essentially it teaches the horse to be aggressive and pull. For the tough, often severe, three-day cross-country course, this may be desirable, but the technique is not appropriate to schooling a young horse in this system. When the average jumper or hunter is cantering around a course cleanly, he should not be taught to pull or to set against the rider's hand. Aggressive pullers are difficult to rate (the stride) and are unlikely to produce an athletic, soft, connected performance. It is not a good habit, especially for young horses in training. Some experienced four-foot hunters and jumpers do become somewhat aggressive in competition as they learn the "game," but if they have an educated start they are more ridable or ratable, can be kept tuned, and can go on a decent correct contact.

The horse *backs* ("rein back") in *two beats*. It is like the trot in the sense that the legs function as *diagonal pairs*. Poor backing will result in more beats. The hand should have a little give-and-take action to it. The rider should be careful to soften the hand when the horse softens his jaw and takes a step back (diagonal pair); he may then ask for another step. In this way the horse should not get heavy-headed or behind the vertical when backing. The head and neck should be extended and the mouth closed. After the last step, promptly close the leg and walk forward. Do not halt in the last step of the back.

With the average horse in modern riding, the rider should keep it simple: use the leg to go forward, and use the hand to slow down, stop, and back. Horses should walk forward–halt–back and move forward promptly or trot–walk–halt–back–walk or canter–halt–back and go forward again after the last step of the back. In this way they are alert when they halt. Because they halt with a reserve energy, it is not necessary to use the leg when backing except to keep the horse straight. The head and neck are extended, and the mouth is closed during the back. The fingers/hand should soften with each step of the back.

LONGITUDINAL AND LATERAL AGILITY EXERCISES

Some longitudinal agility exercises are useful in training the rider to develop good habits in coordinating rein and leg aids in cooperation with the horse's movements. It is assumed here that the rider has the fundamentals of a good working position and that the hands are independent of the body. These exercises include transitions to and from all gaits as well as three speeds within the gait; i.e., ordinary trot–slow trot sitting–ordinary trot–strong trot–ordinary trot. In transitions down or shortening at the intermediate and advanced levels, the rider should use the weight aid, give-and-take, and, if necessary, voice for correction of disobedience to shorten to the short trot sitting. Returning, the rider should use a squeeze-release leg. If there is no response, then use the voice (or stick) and return to the ordinary trot. For moving from the ordinary trot to a lengthened trot, posting is preferred, although the advanced rider may either sit or post depending on what the horse needs. The rider should close the leg on the post down and use the two urging legs in rhythm with the horse's efforts. (The horse trots in diagonal pairs.) The technique is a squeeze-release leg, not a driving seat or vising leg. At least most three-quarter-bred and Thoroughbred types are responsive enough to the lower leg to learn to respond to soft aids. If they do not respond, there should be prompt reinforcement of the aids.

Longitudinal agility exercises may also be done at two or three speeds of the canter. For the ordinary canter the rider should sit with a slight angle of the hip and the arms following the balancing gestures. To lengthen the canter the rider should close the lower leg, and when the stride begins to lengthen, take two-point or galloping position using the stirrups, and be careful to follow fully the balancing gestures of the head and neck. Returning to the ordinary canter, the rider should sit down first to use the weight aid. It is not a driving seat; the weight is used as a signal to come back. In rhythm with the balancing gestures, the rider should use give-and-take and shorten the stride (using the voice to correct any disobedience). These longitudinal exercises can get more sophisticated and advanced; for example, gallop–ordinary canter–walk–halt–back–canter. The rider needs to have both an understanding and coordination of the rein aids and leg aids to do the transitions softly and precisely. The horse should remain mentally calm. The head and neck should be extended, the mouth closed, and the body connected as the horse moves through the transitions.

Longitudinal agility exercises that teach the horse agility or coordination in transitions have also been called longitudinal flexibility exercises. However, agility is a concept that more accurately reflects the research on movement, the skeleton, and how horses actually shorten, lengthen, and turn.

Lateral agility exercises should also be practiced in order for a rider to learn the aids, preferably on a horse that is well trained. In this case the rider is learning to use the six rein aids and the three leg aids, the four natural aids, and the techniques of the rein aids and leg aids on each level in coordination with the horse's movements. Lateral agility exercises include large circles, half-circles, half-circles in reverse, and serpentines. On these the rider may practice the inside holding leg, the outside displacing leg as needed, and the inside direct rein with the outside slightly opening direct rein. These aids are also used just before changing direction or approaching a turn.

"Position left/right" can be introduced to an intermediate-level rider. First, to demonstrate at the halt, position the head and neck slightly to the right/left. The rider should be able to see the back of a portion of the horse's eyelid. Be certain to not overbend. Then have the rider, first at the trot, position the head and neck left/right two or three strides before each turn using inside holding/urging leg, outside displacing leg, inside direct rein, outside direct, and as-needed outside opening rein. Keeping the horse moving forward, it can be done at all the gaits. In schooling the horse it can be done in other exercises (see chapters 9 and 12.)

Longitudinal and lateral exercises on the flat will help improve a horse's balance when negotiating a hunter course or a jumper course. However, there are exercises that will inhibit the horse's movement for sport if they are overdone; i.e., the short canter. A horse can be schooled to execute a range of movements through a variety of aids. The question to ask is whether the exercise logically fits into progressive schooling that leads to a calm, efficient performance. The characteristics of the individual horse and the realistic goals of the rider are important considerations as well.

The rider should school and ride on the flat and over uneven terrain using a position based on the stirrup, using a medium stirrup length for jumping up to four feet, six inches, and practicing controls. Most of any jumping course is on the flat, and the quality of the approach and turns often determines the jump. The horse should be schooled and ridden on the flat with the same modern controls and balance as when jumping a course.

THE LEVELS OF CONTROL USED IN JUMPING, STAGES OF THE JUMP, AND MECHANICS OF THE JUMP

There are three levels of jumping that correspond to the levels of control on the flat. When jumping, the rein aids and the leg aids are used in exactly the same way as on the flat in the forward riding system. The turns and approaches to the jump are in the same balance as on the flat. The rein aids and leg aids get the horse straight and regulate the stride in rhythm with the balancing gestures of the head and neck. Maintaining the same position based on the stirrup is essential. Both the position and the controls are the same whether jumping or riding on the flat. This simple idea is one that is often missed if one observes the practice of riding in parts of Western Europe and especially more recently in some parts of the United States.

The objective of the modern hunter or jumper is a fluid, balanced athletic performance achieved through using soft and precise controls with a modern position based on the stirrup. The horse, when given a good foundation on the flat and over jumps, may have the potential to become a show hunter, serious jumper, cross-country horse, or field horse. The controls and schooling on the flat directly correspond to the level and the performance of the horse when jumping. There are three levels of controls in jumping.

ELEMENTARY LEVEL OF CONTROLS IN JUMPING   The horse approaches on loose rein. The rider in jumping position takes the mane early (mane release). This level is used for a beginning rider learning to jump on a made horse, an upper-level rider correcting a position fault, and/or a high-intermediate/advanced rider schooling a young horse.

INTERMEDIATE LEVEL OF CONTROLS IN JUMPING   The horse approaches on contact that is gradually (and in rhythm with balancing gestures) lightened so that the last few strides and the jump itself are off contact. The rider is in jumping position, resting the hands on the neck in a crest release when going over the fence. The purpose of this level is to achieve a softness, precision, and subtle rating of stride between jumps on contact but allows the horse his balancing gestures over the jumps. It is nonabusive to the horse.

The rider who is moving up from taking the mane and the rider whose position when jumping over three feet or three feet, six inches, is not stable enough for following arms should use this crest release intermediate stage as a bridging step to the advanced level. Not everyone can reach the advanced controls level. The intermediate level (crest release) is currently winning in Medal/Maclay hunter equitation classes. It has been commonly used in various forms in the American hunter divisions for generations on green horses. It is also commonly used by international competitors in the jumper division, again in various forms.

Riding teachers need to emphasize correct crest release to avoid having their pupils develop a habit of resting their elbows and upper body on the horse's neck or ducking to one side of the horse.

ADVANCED LEVEL OF CONTROLS IN JUMPING   The horse is on contact throughout. There is frequently an invisible lightening of the feel between the bit and hands in rhythm with the gestures while on the approach and a corresponding strengthening of the lower leg. "Following arms" are used to maintain a soft, passive contact throughout the jump. The rider may use the jumping position or sit deeply in forward position to fit the requirements of the obstacle and horse's jumping effort. The purpose of this level is to develop a quality performance of the horse and rider. Advanced controls or contact on landing gives immediate, soft, precise control. Once expected in an equitation class of national caliber, it is now seen mainly in some jumper classes and in some cross-country jumping. It allows better control on the approach and departure. Having the skill to follow the gestures on the flat at the walk and canter can help develop the technique of following at the jump.

STAGES AND MECHANICS OF THE JUMP   The jump is divided into four parts: approach, takeoff, flight, and landing. (The departure from one jump can be the approach to the next.) See the illustrations.

During the approach, the mechanics of the gait of the approach (walk, trot, or canter) are exactly the same as the mechanics on the flat. In the takeoff, flight, and landing, the mechanics are each different and important to know. The horse has distinct balancing gestures of the head and neck that the rider must follow. The rider must have a hand independent of the body.

The approach to the jump involves the mechanics of the gaits on the flat. Note the discussion of the gaits earlier in this section. It is important for the horse to be mentally and physically stable, straight, and connected in forward balance at the approach to the jump. He will have an extended head and neck. If cantering or walking, there should be balancing gestures. *The approach stops when the true gait of the approach is broken (walk, trot, canter) by the forking of the front legs, the lowering of the head and neck, and the raising of the hind end and legs.*

The takeoff to the jump begins with *the fork:* the lowered neck and head, the forward movement of the horse's body, the forked front legs taking all the weight, the lifting up of the hind end, and the preparation for the double engagement of the hind legs. Next in the takeoff is the *double engagement* of the hind legs, which, when combined with the forward movement of the horse's body, provides the main thrust to help complete the takeoff. The front legs lift off, and, due to the position of the fork, one front leg must catch up to the other. They fold evenly over the top of the fence, but the takeoff is not complete until the hind legs (double engagement) leave contact with the ground.

The illustrations show the phases of the takeoff and how important *the fork* is to the height of the rear end and thrust of the double engagement.

Clearly the stretching down of the head and neck with all the weight on the front two legs should be followed by the rider's hand. The rider keeps the weight in the stirrup and off the back, which will help the horse lift up his hind end as high as he needs to for the spring and thrust of the double engagement. The *double engagement* is important, but it is enhanced and predisposed by a good approach and by a successful fork. In the takeoff phase the fork is missed by some teachers and riders and should be studied carefully. It has significant implications for modern theory development and challenges some old ideas of schooling and riding.

The flight phase is often photographed. There are three main points to look for: (1) The folding of the front legs at or above the horizontal (below the horizontal is often unsafe). (2) Note that the flexibility of the arc in the middle of the flight comes mainly from the balancing gestures of the head and neck. Some believe that the horse is rounding his back, but in fact it is mainly an

The "fork" ends the gait of the approach and starts the takeoff phase of the jump. Mechanics of the jump—approach, takeoff, flight, landing. The approach to the jump can be at regular gaits, the walk, trot, and canter. The takeoff begins with the "fork" and finishes with the "double engagement," and the hind legs leaving the ground. The height of the hind end during the "fork" influences the "double engagement" and the forward thrust through the takeoff into the flight phase. The flight begins when the hind legs ("double engagement") leave the ground. *(Reinhold Tigges, photographer)*

The "double engagement" of the hind legs is the last part of the takeoff. The forward riding position based on the stirrup frees the horse's back while the rider's lower urging leg is efficiently and effectively used at the girth. (*Reinhold Tigges, photographer*)

illusion caused by the head and neck position. (3) In flight the horse begins to unfold the front legs, one ahead of the other, before the hind legs are folding evenly and at their tightest to clear the top of the jump with the rest of his body.

When *landing*, one front foot touches down first, starting the landing phase, and is followed by the other front foot. This is combined with the raised head and neck balancing gesture. The hind legs land one at a time, and the regular mechanics of the gait resume. The reader should note how vulnerable the horse's back is in the landing phase and how important it is for the rider to have a nonabusive position united with the movement of the horse. Again the rider, weighted with spring in the stirrup through the ankle, will have much less chance of banging the back, which, in addition to causing pain to the horse, will affect the horse's jumping effort. Failure to follow this last point often causes a horse to "scoot" after landing. It should be noted that over smaller fences the landing has started while the hind legs are folding their tightest over the top of the fence. After landing, the normal mechanics of the gait instantly resume in the departure from the jump.

Flight phase of the jump. A working hunter on an outside course. The horse's forearm is at or above the horizontal with a balancing gesture of the head and neck. The rider has a following arm. *(Paul Cronin, rider)*

SUMMARY

Modern hunter/American forward riding is more efficient because the same system works in jumping, in the field, and on the flat. It interrelates position, controls, and schooling. Controls taught and used for jumping a course are the ones used on the flat. This concept is easily overlooked, since it is far too common to observe training strategies that work with isolated exercises rather than exercises that are integrated in a system to achieve a complete education of horse and rider.

Modern forward riding on the flat should not be confused in any manner with high school classical dressage, which quite correctly has the goal of full collection (central balance) for performance in the *manège*. In schooling a horse on the flat, the goal of the American hunter system of riding is to produce connected, long, low, ground-covering, efficient movement that is best suited to jumping or covering uneven terrain with agility. The horse is obedient and cooperative. The interacting parts of the forward riding system (position, controls, schooling) each have their own levels and stages for teaching the rider or the horse, but it is one efficient, complete system. Further, the idea of integrating schooling on the flat with jump schooling—i.e., using gymnastics both on the flat (longitudinal and lateral agility exercises) and with jumps (combinations/cavalletti)—is essential for the development of the horse's balance, movement, and agility.

It is important in modern riding to place emphasis on flat riding outside of a ring to develop the mental stability of the horse in the open; to teach the horse to be responsive to the rein aids and the leg aids in the field while remain-

The landing phase of the jump has begun as the second foot to land (left fore) supports the horse. The hind leg is unfolding and will begin the gait (canter) of departure. The rider demonstrates the four fundamentals of a good position and seven physical qualities of the position (see chapter 1). Compare this position to any of the positions on the flat in this text. The closed fingers—not the elbow or body—are rested on the neck (intermediate controls). The importance of keeping the horse's back free of weight and the balancing gestures of the head and neck free of interference is demonstrated here. The position based on the stirrup and practiced on the flat makes educated jumping possible. *(Pam W. Renfrow, rider; Reinhold Tigges, photographer)*

ing calm, alert, and soft; and to teach the horse to work in or near company, especially if that is to be his job. Advanced controls should be taught only to horses that have been given a foundation (stabilized) at the elementary level and then gradually moved through the system's stages of schooling. Applying controls on a level above the horse's education will often lead to mental instability and physical unsoundness. The resulting stiffness is guaranteed, often leaving a lifetime problem with the horse. The commercial direction and pressures in the sport have produced a number of talented professionals who know how to cut a schooling corner to gain short-term success; i.e., a prize or a sale. An uneducated rider (professional or amateur) who, in ignorance, is too hurried and rough can also cause permanent damage.

Gradual transitions and large circles on the elementary level of controls lead to more difficult lateral movements and longitudinal transitions, such as from the gallop to the short canter, from the short canter to the halt, back, and canter. Further, correctly performed half-circles in reverse with flying changes of lead, turns on the haunches at the gallop, and serpentines are examples of more difficult lateral movements on the advanced level of controls. These all develop balance and agility, and they are important for the quality of the

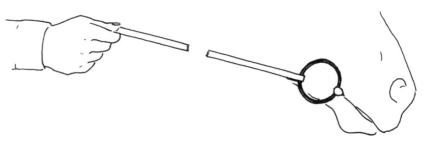

DRIVING REIN
Driving rein is a method of holding the rein that more easily establishes a direct line from bit to elbow. Useful for teaching passive contact to young horses. It is a technique for teaching the rider to follow the gestures of the head and neck first at the walk and canter and then through the arc of the jump with following arms. It can also help a rider adjust to a sensitive horse or soften a set hand. Driving rein was one of the accepted methods of holding the reins in the hunter seat equitation division up until the last part of the twentieth century. It was probably dropped when the crest release (intermediate control) became standard instead of maintaining contact through the arc of the jump (following arms–advanced control).

horse's performance in the open and on a course of jumps, whether they be in a field or in a ring.

On the highest level of horsemanship one is able to evaluate the horse's control level and ride the horse with the appropriate control techniques. At the advanced level the rider can feel the horse's response early and respond softly and precisely with a minimum effort. If the horse has been asked to go from the trot to the walk, the rider begins to close the leg early for the walk forward. To the uneducated eye or to the person on the ground, it is effortless. The rider has been able to feel a horse's response to soft aids even before the actual transition takes place; that feel is a part of advanced riding. Not everyone is able to ride on this level, but to get there it is important to know the three levels of controls and to execute at least mechanically the techniques of the rein aids and the leg aids on the elementary and intermediate levels.

Before one has a chance to have educated controls on the advanced level, all of these things have to be combined with experience on horses with different degrees of sensitivity and in different stages of training. The rider needs to be a fairly mature person with the ability to self-evaluate. The task is considerably simpler if the rider is also well grounded in all levels of modern hunter riding controls theory.

CHECKLIST FOR UNDERSTANDING CONTROLS

The aim of the intermediate controls level is to attain soft, precise transitions.

The two main reasons for riding on contact are to improve the quality of the horse's movement and to improve the controls, making them softer and more precise.

Contact is established on a horse with the foundation of stabilization by feeling the reserve energy in the hand that is created by the rider's lower leg.

The four natural aids are the leg, hand, voice, and weight.

The rider should know the three leg aids and the techniques, exercises, and movements to demonstrate and practice each of them.

The rider should know the six rein aids and the techniques, exercises, and movements to demonstrate and practice each of them.

The rider should know the mechanics of the gaits and how the four natural aids relate to them. The walk and canter, as well as the jump, have balancing gestures that should be followed by the rider's hand.

In the mechanics of the jump, the fork is the beginning of the takeoff. It is where the gait of the approach stops. It, as well as the other phases of the jump, should be studied and understood by the teacher and advanced rider. Modern sport horse riding should be based on the latest research on topics such as the mechanics of the jump.

Program rides should be practiced on a made horse to help the rider improve both position and controls. Please see more on "Program Rides" at the end of chapters 10, 11, 12, and 13.

II THE SCHOOLING COMPONENT

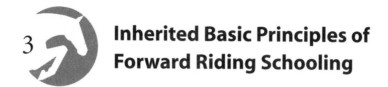

3 Inherited Basic Principles of Forward Riding Schooling

The reader may find it helpful to study the definitions and concepts found in the introduction for an overview of this riding and schooling system before proceeding with schooling.

The main point that was introduced by Caprilli and further developed by Littauer and Chamberlin is that it is more efficient and successful for the sport horse's performance in the field and over jumps to have him in forward balance, not in central balance as is the high school horse in the *manège*.

Some people during different periods in America have used the word *collected* to mean a variety of things, but in this text it is used primarily as a classical dressage term. In modern sport riding the goal is to have the horse in forward balance 90 to 100 percent of the time; that is, *connected;* moving in one piece with a long, low, ground-covering, efficient stride; and exhibiting an athletic agility under the weight of the rider. A horse that is a show hunter, field hunter, hunter trial horse, and/or a show jumper performs these tasks on the basis of ordinary hunter/forward balance gaits. Some sport horses may do some exercises involving a degree of collection for short periods, especially the upper-level jumper, but for the most part the gaits used are connected gaits in forward balance. Therefore, that is what should be practiced in flat training. Further, to be united with this movement and balance, one should be in a position based on the stirrup and use modern controls that yield the desired balance and performance. A harmonious unity of position, controls, and schooling results in a distinct method of modern sport riding.

This system for schooling hunters/jumpers is suitable for the show hunter, the field hunter, the amateur who jumps low courses up to four feet, the competitive jumper, and teachers. Parts of the system should be very useful also to the trail rider and for starting horses for other riding objectives such as dressage. This system is a specialized form of schooling for modern equestrian sport involving jumping, speed, and uneven terrain on horses bred to have the right physical and mental characteristics to do the job.

Different athletic disciplines require the human athlete to develop certain skills and certain body strengths peculiar to that discipline. The same principles apply to training horses. The method of schooling presented here is a form of specialized training and is based on the principle that a successful hunter or jumper moves in dynamic balance with natural ground-covering, efficient gaits most of the time and in a connected forward balance.

THE GOAL OF SCHOOLING

The goal of schooling in modern forward riding is to develop the horse's agility and strength to enable him to maintain his own balance under the weight of the rider with as much assurance as when moving calmly but alertly free.

The first aim of forward schooling is to produce an efficient, pleasant-to-ride hunter, jumper, or field horse that will be cooperative with and enjoyed by its rider.

The second aim of forward schooling is to achieve these results in the most efficient, simple way so that a variety of people can learn to ride a horse schooled by this method and a variety of people can learn to school a horse at least under supervision in part or in whole.

In order to achieve these aims, one can use a combination of flat and jumping exercises in a ring and in a field, progressing from poles to combinations to courses. While utilizing uneven terrain, incorporate group exercises depending on the eventual objectives for the horse. All these exercises should be executed on the basis of a few fundamental rules first set forth by Caprilli, Littauer, and Chamberlin. I am pleased to present V. S. Littauer's early summary here. He was my teacher, mentor, and friend. These rules have been the basis of my teaching and schooling in forward riding. They will be emphasized throughout this book.

FUNDAMENTAL RULES OF SCHOOLING

The neck and head should be extended 90 percent of the time and the mouth closed. The horse has a balancing gesture at the walk, the canter, and the jump. These balancing gestures are essential for the horse's agility. The neck is also used to balance the horse when turning, when shortening its stride, and when performing other movements. Certainly the horse can be ridden at all gaits and turns with its head tied down, just as humans can run with their hands in their pockets. However, their performance is inhibited and less efficient. In order for the balancing gestures of the head and neck to be strong enough to be effective, the neck must be extended and the mouth closed. The degree of extension of the head and neck will depend upon the schooling level of the horse, how far along in the monthly schooling program he is, and the specific movement and transition taking place.

A second principle in forward schooling is the *relationship between calmness and the extended head and neck.* An upset horse will most often carry his head too high. A relaxed, calm horse will carry his head in the natural position, which most often will be extended. In early schooling it can be, to some degree, an exaggerated low extension (a young horse's natural carriage).

A third principle relates to *the attitude of the head and neck during slowing down and halting.* As the horse becomes better balanced and connected under the weight of the rider, the head and neck will be raised, at various times a little more or less for different transitions. Overall it will be carried a little higher as the horse develops more strength and balance under the weight of the rider. In sport riding, whether the horse is just starting as a young horse or is trained, strong, and experienced, the head and neck will most often be lower at the walk than at the trot and lower at the gallop than at the trot. This is true because this is how the natural gestures of the head and neck work in relation to the muscles and mechanics of the gaits. Working on progressive increases and decreases of speed or changing of gaits from slow to fast is one of the basic rules of this schooling system.

Further, progressive, gradual transitions contribute to calmness probably more than any other exercise in riding. The gradual transitions to slower gaits and to a halt can eventually be made a little more rapidly, although still softly through teaching the horse flexions (see chapter 9 for a definition of flexions). Even advanced riders should be cautioned to go carefully with mild forms of collection for more abrupt transitions down. The advanced rider schools the horse physically and mentally to realize its full potential as an agile athlete. This is done by building on natural good movement and jumping ability. Contact with reserve energy can help yield the horse's best performance. This should be achieved with a complete preservation of calmness and relaxation and the corresponding extension of the head and neck with the mouth closed. Full collection is not necessary for most horses in this schooling program, and it is not advised for the success of most horse-and-rider combinations.

Impulse forward is an essential fourth principle. The schooling program should enable the horse, with conditioning and schooling, to develop reserve energy, which makes the natural connection under the weight of the rider possible. Impulse forward (reserve energy) is the alertness with which the horse starts a gait, increases the speed, or keeps the pace. Thoroughbred-type horses can have considerable natural reserve energy, and the trainer's objective is to keep the horse calm while maintaining the amount of reserve energy on the right level for the task. If the horse is a naturally lazy half-bred type, a different approach is needed. The horse will have to learn to maintain some reserve energy, especially if he is to be a jumper or show hunter. If the horse with a lazy temperament is to be a field hunter, work in company will increase the reserve energy. Steady impulse forward should be gradually developed in a young horse, and it is related to the natural, gradual raising of the neck as the horse does correct transitions. The development of steady impulse leads to educated contact.

A fifth principle of forward riding, which concerns contact, is the feel of the impulse or *reserve energy created by the leg.* The rider's hands do not pull back on the mouth. It is a feel of the horse moving forward and taking the rider's hand through the reins. The rider's leg creates the energy, especially when the horse lacks natural impulse. It is taught in stages, which should include the following: (1) stabilization off contact, (2) then a passive contact, (3) next, consistent, soft, precise contact in transitions with reserve energy, and (4) then, if necessary for the objectives and if the horse is comfortably able, riding on soft contact with increased impulse, meaning that the horse accepts the bit and moves forward boldly and with the head and neck stretched forward. When riding on contact, the rider must be certain to consistently follow the balancing gestures of the head and neck, especially at the walk and canter and, of course, at the jump.

A sixth principle is the mental schooling of the horse. The training of the horse involves *the physical and mental education of the horse.* The horse needs to understand the aids and respond promptly and calmly. Once the horse is responding correctly, the rider is relatively passive and feels the movement. It is not constant hold, hold, drive, drive, with the rider overworking every step of the way. The sport horse is developed into an athletic, agile, calm but alert horse through cooperation with the rider's aids. He is balanced under the weight of the rider.

A seventh principle in schooling, that of *cooperation,* is relatively new. It is really counter to the greater part of riding history, which has been based on a principle of dominance over the horse. This last comes historically from the seventeenth, eighteenth, nineteenth, and early twentieth centuries. In the latter two centuries, it has been characterized by a male rider training a fairly tough military horse and, perhaps later, large warmbloods in the classical dressage system.

Before approximately 1910, the educated system of riding, the classical dressage school, was formally taught to privileged aristocrats and to the military. The dressage rider is correctly changing the horse's natural forward balance to central balance, whereas in a sport horse the goal is to develop his natural balance under the weight of the rider. The hope is that the horse will take some initiative and make the most of his natural athletic ability, especially when jumping. The principles of cooperation and the mental schooling of the horse are very important in modern sport riding.

The eighth principle is the *foundation of stabilization,* the ability of the horse to maintain the gait and speed asked for whether alone or in company, on the flat or on uneven terrain, or jumping on a looped rein. This principle serves as a foundation for teaching riders and schooling horses before moving on to contact at the intermediate and advanced training levels. A stabilized horse on the elementary level can be pleasantly ridden for a lifetime. However, if most horses remain only at the elementary level of controls, they will not reach their full potential. Stabilization is a foundation in forward schooling and an important step along the way to higher levels. It can be used throughout an advanced horse's career—to warm up, to reestablish stability at a competition, and to reestablish cooperation after a break, especially with the more energetic and/or sensitive type of horse.

Voice commands are very important in teaching stabilization both on the lunge and when mounted. They are the early lessons in teaching cooperation, the mental part of schooling.

It is important to teach jumping in modern riding emphasizing a good release on the approach and in the air as the horse learns to correctly judge his takeoff. Through a looped rein, the rider is careful not to interfere with any of the horse's balancing gestures, especially when jumping green or inexperienced horses.

Stabilization is also an important tool in reclaiming an upset or spoiled horse. The reclaimed horse is first treated as a young horse learning to balance himself off contact. Through repetition, gradual transitions, and wide turns, he learns to calmly maintain the gait and speed asked for on looped reins, responding to the voice and the other elementary techniques of the weight, hand, and leg aids.

Stabilization requires considerable skill and understanding to teach it efficiently and quickly to a young horse. It takes a rider who sits well, understands the different levels of controls, and has the ability to feel the movement of the young horse and apply the aids correctly. Some intermediate to high-intermediate riders can teach stabilization under supervision to a nicely tempered horse. These same riders can in the same way teach a horse other parts of the schooling program.

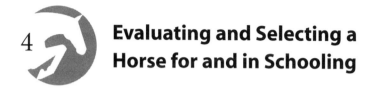

4   Evaluating and Selecting a Horse for and in Schooling

To begin, the rider must decide what the objective for the horse is to be. When schooling is finished, what should the horse be? A show hunter for A-level competition, an equitation horse, a local show hunter, a jumper, a field horse, an event horse, or a dressage horse? These questions should be revisited throughout the selection process and the schooling program.

This schooling system assumes that the rider is using some type of Thoroughbred or Thoroughbred cross. The half-bred or three-quarter-bred traditionally has been used for field riding, hacking, or amateur hunters and jumpers because of its temperament. In general the Thoroughbred type is comfortable, energetic with natural reserve energy, athletic with the ability to jump, and a decent mover. It has suited the advanced rider wanting to compete in show hunter and jumper divisions. Increasingly in the United States, Thoroughbred-warmblood crosses and registered warmbloods are used as well, also with varying degrees of success.

It should be emphasized that the success of schooling efforts depends largely upon the selection of the schooling project. A horse that starts as a naturally poor mover cannot be made into a great mover that will win under-saddle classes in A-level competitions. Schooling can improve the movement, but it will not make a poor mover a winning mover. That same observation also applies to jumping and temperament. The quality of success in this system of schooling and riding depends largely on the qualities and the characteristics of the horse.

After the objectives for the horse are set, the schooling system to be used for the horse must be determined. The modern American hunter system or the modern American forward riding system is best for the sport horse. The horse can be trained under the weight of the rider in a progressive method for work in a variety of settings. The goal is a horse that is performing to the best of his athletic ability while remaining mentally calm and cooperative with the rider. It is a method that will bring out the best in the horse's movement and natural jumping ability, while at the same time keeping him mentally stable and more agreeable to ride.

Bringing a horse up through the American hunter horse show divisions (local "baby green" under saddle and over low jumps through the recognized four-foot division) has given thousands of horses and riders success. A trainer practicing modern riding system principles might use a horse show to evaluate equine pupils on the flat, in company, and over jumps. If the plan is to move from that division to the jumpers, it will be an excellent start for the horse. For a field hunter or a hunter hack, not all of the exercises for a show hunter will be necessary, but other exercises will need to be done more, such as group riding over uneven terrain. For one-day horse trials and hunter pace events, the show hunter division is an excellent start for competition in the schooling plan, along with hunter trials that also emphasize control between jumps, mental stability, and safe jumping form.

In general, if the goal is to have a horse that does upper-level classical dressage, a certain type of conformation, movement, temperament, and breeding that will lead to the level of dressage desired must be chosen. The forward riding system can be selectively used to give a solid start to a dressage horse, with later selection of a system based on the classical dressage school to complete the goals. There are several choices within the dressage system. However, if the plan is to do dressage on the lower levels such as novice, training, and preliminary levels of eventing, and then dressage up through the second and third levels, this system would be a good way to start schooling the horse. When specializing in dressage, there is no reason to do many exercises in schooling such as the jumping and group work, although some uneven terrain might be as useful for the dressage horse as it is for hunters and jumpers. For training a horse that will need to jump, this modern sport horse system is the most efficient one to use throughout the progressive schooling periods.

When objectives for the horse have been selected, an evaluation of the rider is the next step. Is the rider experienced enough in the system to train the horse without professional guidance? Regardless of the answer to this question, having a qualified amateur or professional who will help with schooling at least periodically is a good idea. Evaluations and help sessions should be clearly laid out in the schooling plan and calendar.

Some riders might decide to use a professional teacher for part of the schooling, such as jumping. If the person helping with the schooling is involved in the selection of the horse, things may go more smoothly. Actually, in contemporary commercial riding as it stands in the United States today, most professionals will insist on being involved in the selection of the horse.

Basic information about the conformation of the horse is essential, and the rider should study conformation before going to select and buy a horse. An understanding of the influence of conformation is useful in evaluating a prospective schooling project and can be used to predict strengths and weaknesses that may affect later schooling exercises.

Whether one is purchasing a prospect or taking on a client's horse to school, a sound horse is essential no matter what the objective. If the horse is not sound, it will not be a legitimate schooling project. If the prospect has an unsoundness of the back or joints such as knees and hocks, this will, in varying degrees, lead to problems and possibly unsuccessful schooling. It is vital to determine in advance how to handle the vetting and the soundness check when purchasing or accepting a horse for schooling. After purchase the horse should be checked for soundness throughout the schooling program. If possible, it is a good idea to take the horse home for a few days on trial and then take him from there to the veterinarian of choice.

A veterinarian with extensive experience in equine medicine is essential—that is, a veterinarian who has evaluated many x-rays, has experience with prepurchase exams, and has a reputation for being reputable and ethical. This applies not only to the purchase but also to regular consultation during schooling as problems arise. A careful vetting (prepurchase exam) does not guarantee anything but does yield an evaluation based on problems obvious to an experienced vet. The history of the horse's soundness is very important for the vet to know. Trusting the person selling the horse is still an important factor. The buyer should talk to the vet before the prospect is sent for his evaluation and should be present during the vetting. Furthermore the buyer should clearly understand the pros and cons determined by the vetting. No horse is perfect, but there are certain unsoundnesses that will make reaching the schooling objectives improbable.

It is important to have a routine for evaluating the horse in training as well as for looking at the prospective horse when visiting the seller or a client wanting a horse trained. It is a good idea to run through the proposed routine with a professional or an amateur advisor. It is equally important not to insult or waste the time of the seller. If it is immediately obvious that the horse is undesirable as a schooling project—i.e., poor conformation, performance, or stable manners—then the buyer should politely say "no, thank you," and look at the next horse the person has to show or leave and get on with the search elsewhere.

CONFORMATION AND MOVEMENT'S INFLUENCE ON SCHOOLING

MOVEMENT AS THE TEST OF CONFORMATION

Good performance and movement are the tests for good structure. There certainly is a value to a first impression when looking at a horse. However, keep in mind the old expression, "Pretty is as pretty does." Having a good coat and being muscled can improve the buyer's impression. However, if the horse does not have structure with correct angulation, its movement and soundness will be adversely affected. Conformation may also affect athletic ability relative to speed, turning, shortening, and lengthening (longitudinal and lateral agility). (See the illustrations of the walk, trot, and canter throughout the text.)

Horses that have good conformation can stand longer days of hard work. For example, good feet help reduce the concussion of galloping, turning, and jumping. A good working hunter has limbs that extend freely and a balance for trotting and cantering without tiring easily. Strong hindquarters provide strength for quick bursts of speed in the polo pony or Quarter Horse and are also desirable in the jumper.

The driving horse, the show hunter, the polo pony, the steeplechaser, the Western stock horse, the American Saddlebred horse, and the flat-racing horse all have different definitions of good performance. They have different objectives in their sport, and each requires structures appropriate for its tasks. Some are overlapping and similar, and some are very different from each other. In this text conformation is viewed with an emphasis on the Thoroughbred, the Thoroughbred crosses, and warmbloods, because they are what have proven to be the most athletic and useful horses to become show hunters, jumpers, field hunters, and hunter hacks.

DEVELOPING A KNOWLEDGE OF AND AN EYE FOR MOVEMENT AND CONFORMATION

Conformation is important when selecting a horse to purchase for schooling or in evaluating a schooling project. Having a basic understanding of conformation will help develop an eye for it. In studying a horse's conformation, the rider should be able to predict to a degree the horse's future soundness relative to the schooling objectives. Also conformation determines the type of mover he will become after the schooling program. Therefore, the horse's conformation should be reviewed critically before starting schooling. In devising a weekly and monthly schooling plan for a particular horse, it is important to keep in mind the strengths and weaknesses of his conformation. The characteristics of conformation are as important to keep in mind as the horse's temperament when selecting and training.

To develop an eye or tune up a professional eye to better see conformation and functions, the following suggestions will help. From the beginning the rider must know the *mechanics of the gaits* (see the illustrations in the introduction). A clear understanding of the gaits at walk, trot, canter, gallop, and the back will enable better evaluation of movement and understanding of the concept of dynamic balance. In addition, one must know the *main parts of the horse* and the *important angles* to be evaluated. It is simple for a horseman to memorize these in an evening. It will make breaking the horse up into parts and analyzing the conformation considerably easier. (See the photograph of a conformation horse—the model working hunter—in the color gallery.)

It is important to be able to *recognize movement*—good, average, below average. One way to do this is to study horses and methodically evaluate them, always looking at horses with movement in mind. A rating system (0 to 10) will help in comparing horses seen previously with horses currently under review.

When on a search for a horse to buy or when considering taking on a client's horse for a schooling project, one must be realistic about a horse that might be kind or a lovely color. In favoring a color such as chestnut with white markings, one must be careful. Horse people tend to be a little romantic and are animal lovers and therefore sometimes have trouble seeing through to the important characteristics of the horse—movement, temperament, jumping form, and agility.

Going to horse shows and observing the horses in under-saddle classes helps when learning to recognize and evaluate movement. The winner is not necessarily by any means a 10 mover. He is simply, in the judge's opinion from his vantage point, the best mover in that group of horses that day. With practice, one should be able to eventually pick the top four horses along with most judges. Using the under-saddle class as a study resource, one can rate the movement of each horse. Seeing one's better-rated movers in the ribbons means the rating system is probably beginning to be accurate. Not having exactly the same order as the judge is not cause for concern, because manners and performance, such as taking the correct leads and working in a group, as well as movement, enter into the judge's selection.

When in a stable with a number of horses, evaluate the conformation and movement of each of them. It helps to ask a knowledgeable person to at least pick out the four to six better movers and then compare notes. Splitting hairs is not useful. Someone might give a horse a 6 and someone else a 5.5. The time to be concerned is when one's rating is 8 and a respected colleague's rating is 4. Using this rating teaching/learning exercise for one or two months of regular effort will lead to improvement.

When studying a specific horse, the first things to look for are qualities of movement and conformation. Do not look for faults straightaway. Have a mental picture of what an ideal topline is and determine how close that particular horse comes to the ideal. Having an idea of what constitutes good movement is crucial. Further, memorizing catchy labels such as "wasp-waisted," "swan-necked," or "cow-hocked" is not helpful, but being able to see a long loin, high head set, or crooked legs is. Picking a horse apart and looking for the faults first may mean losing a wonderful schooling project or missing the overall positive impression of all the parts in proportion to each other. The goal is to find horses with good toplines and good angulation in front and behind and who move well. To do that requires implanting the ideal in one's mind and then becoming more familiar with common unsoundnesses.

STUDYING STRUCTURE AND EVALUATING CONFORMATION

After developing an eye for movement by watching and rating different horses in the stable and at horse shows, the next step is to take a closer look at structure in evaluating a horse. A detailed description of good and bad conformation is beyond the scope of this text; however, because a horse's structure affects its schooling from start to finish, it is necessary to discuss here a few essential aspects of structure.

STEPS FOR EVALUATING CONFORMATION   A systematic approach to evaluating conformation, such as the one suggested below, should allow one to form an opinion of the horse's static and dynamic balance and its athletic potential. This procedure is not sacred—you could develop your own plan. The important thing is to have an organized process to follow every time you evaluate a horse.

Step back for an overall impression.

1. Focus the eye specifically to the topline.
2. Move in closer and look at the front end.
3. Then review the topline and side view of the opposite side.
4. Study the horse from the rear.
5. Step back to the beginning spot for another overall impression.
6. Move the horse at the walk and trot, observing him from side, front, and rear.

OVERALL IMPRESSION   When forming a first general impression of the horse, look for overall proportion and a square stance. Consider the agility and balance and how the horse carries himself. Does he look athletic or unbalanced for his age? Does he look "all of a piece"? Does he have "presence"? Does he react suitably to his surroundings?

Perhaps two of the most important aspects of developing this overall assessment are the ideas of angulation and proportion, which will be discussed first, before addressing specific points of conformation in the front and hind ends.

ANGULATION   Angulation refers to the slant of the bones and the size of the angles at certain joints, and it is a very important concept in studying a horse's conformation because of its effect on the horse's athletic ability and soundness. Good angulation results in long, effortless strides; poor angulation creates short, choppy, irregular strides. The main angles to examine are those of the shoulder (scapula), humerus, and pastern in the front end, and the hipbone, femur, stifle, hock, and pastern in the hind end.

The shoulder and hip joints are formed by the largest, strongest bones in the horse's body. These joints correlate with one another as they open and close with the swing of the legs. A horse moves by repeatedly losing its equilibrium as the hindquarters drive the body forward and then regaining its equilibrium as the forehand catches the body to prevent a fall and so forth. The front of the horse normally carries most of the body weight and works like a shock-absorbing mechanism, cushioning the impact from the ground. Whether the horse is viewed from the side, front, or rear, the action should be smooth and harmonious. Problems result when one part of the body has to overwork to compensate for lack of balance, injury, or weakness in another part of the body.

This horse has a long, sloping shoulder and an open angle from the point of the shoulder to the elbow. The cannon bone is short relative to the forearm, resulting in the knees being close to the ground. The angle of the pastern is similar to the angle of the shoulder. He has a balanced topline and correct hind leg as well. *(Keedie Grones Leonard, photographer)*

PROPORTION, COORDINATION, AND BALANCE   Proportioned symmetry is (1) the relative proportion of the horse's topline (head, neck, withers, back, loin, and croup), (2) the length of the legs in relation to the height and size of the body, and (3) the harmony of height and length. Balance depends on the proportion of head to neck, depth of chest to length of legs, overall length of body to height, and a front end that matches the rear end. In other words, when a horse is standing naturally, the angulation of the shoulders and the hip joints should be approximately equal in order to provide the same reach in the front as in the rear. A horse is not in balance if the shoulders and upper arms are steeply set and the hindquarters are well angulated, because he will have a short stride in front and a long stride in the rear. Conversely, good shoulder structure in front with steep hindquarters will lead to a good reach in front but a short stride in the rear. A horse that is equally steep forward and aft can be in balance; however, he will not have the quality of movement and agility that is achieved when balance is combined with good front and rear angulation.

A lack of structural balance is often the reason for unsoundness and poor movement. It can also make for an awkward, unathletic horse.

After studying conformation at the halt (static balance), one should watch the horse move (dynamic balance), keeping in mind what correct, good, sound movement is—long, low, ground-covering, efficient strides. Efficient means movement without interference and without unnecessary vertical action. The hind end should be connected to the front end; he moves in one piece.

There is a simple phrase to bear in mind when looking at conformation: "Short, but not too short. Long, but not too long." This may be a little frustrating to someone who is trying to develop an eye for conformation and movement, but it will make sense with more experience. The only way to come to appreciate this phrase is to systematically rate movement and evaluate the conformation of different horses.

FRONT END: SHOULDERS, LEGS, AND CHEST   A long, sloping shoulder is preferred over a short, straight one. Equally important, however—and often overlooked—is the angle formed by the shoulder (scapula) with the arm (humerus). The ideal shoulder, which allows for a free forward extension of the foreleg, forms an angle of approximately 55 degrees with the horizontal and approximately 100 degrees with the humerus. An animal might have a beautifully sloped shoulder yet be short-strided because of a closed scapulo-humeral angle; on the other hand, an animal with a somewhat straighter shoulder and a good scapulo-humeral joint might turn out to move better than expected. In addition to forming a relatively open angle with the scapula, the arm should be long and should meet the forearm at an open angle.

A long forearm and short cannon are desirable because this places the knee closer to the ground, minimizing knee action and increasing efficiency of motion. A rough rule of thumb is that the forearm should be about one and one-half times the length of the cannon (until one's eye is trained, a string is useful for checking this ratio). Since the forelegs carry so much of the horse's weight, their bones—and especially the cannon—should be substantial, as evaluated by the cannon's diameter. Strong pasterns almost invariably keep company with a good front end, because they are part of the bone assembly that cushions impact from the ground. Good pasterns and strong carpal joints have kinetic spring and resilience.

Ideally, when standing in front of the horse, one should be able to drop a plumb line from the point of the shoulder down to the center of the hoof; most often, however, horses are not straight from the knee down. The most common defects are toes pointing toward or away from each other, but sometimes only one leg is affected, or the two legs can be affected to different degrees. Because such defects stress the legs and interfere with proper motion, one should be careful to watch the horse move both coming toward and going away, at the walk and the trot, to see whether the horse hits his ankles or toes in or out. If the legs appeared to be straight at the standstill but their motion is not straight, they should be closely studied again at the halt. Sometimes horses will move closely at the walk, with ankles nearly rubbing, but not at the trot and vice versa. The trot is the more important gait in this instance. Moving crookedly indicates that the legs really are not straight. Sometimes one needs to decide how crooked is too crooked. Is the chance worth taking? It may compromise movement and lead to unsoundness.

For staying power, the chest should be deep with well-sprung ribs. As an approximation, the depth of the barrel should equal the length between the elbow and the ground.

THE HIND END: CROUP, LEGS, AND QUARTERS   Just as the structure of the shoulder and arm is important to the forehand, so is the structure of the croup and thigh important to the hindquarters. A long, sloping croup, as measured from the point of the hip to the point of the buttock, is as desirable as a long, sloping shoulder; but again, just as in the front end, the principal focus needs to be on angulation. The structure of the hip joint, however, is a bit more complicated than that of the shoulder and therefore a bit more difficult to assess. As shown in the illustration, the shoulder joint is formed of two bones, the scapula and humerus, whereas the hip joint includes three: the ilium, ischium, and femur (there is also a fourth bone involved in this joint, but it is not visible from the side, so we can ignore it in this discussion). The ilium and ischium are fused together, and the socket for the thighbone (femur) is located at that point. The important angle to look for is the one between the ilium and the femur; for a balanced mover, this angle should be an approximate mirror image of the scapulo-humeral angle. Unfortunately, because of the heavy musculature in the quarters, the position of the hip joint is more difficult to visualize than that of the shoulder joint. One aid in determining this position is to observe the croup carefully while the horse is

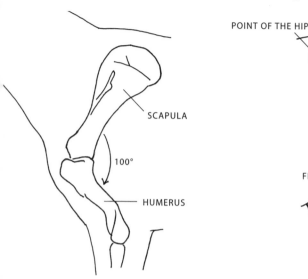

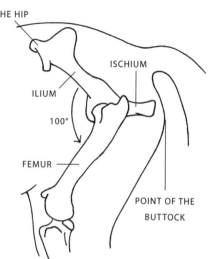

BALANCED ANGULATION
In the front end the scapula (shoulder) and the humerus form an angle that allows the forward swing of the front limbs. In the hind end the ilium and the femur form an angle that allows the engagement and disengagement of the hind limbs. The two angles allow a ground-covering stride and need to be similar in order to have balanced, efficient movement.

walked. As the femur swings forward and back, the approximate point at which it joins the pelvis can be defined. (The motion of the joint can also be felt by placing one's hand on this spot.) The hind legs should be relatively straight, not camped out behind or sloped forward under the belly.

Ideally, standing behind the horse, one should be able to drop a plumb line from the point of the buttock to the cleft of the heel. An easier method of evaluating the straightness of the hind legs is to observe the hocks. If they are parallel and if the width between them is smaller than the width between the points of the buttocks, it is likely that the legs are fairly straight. The hocks should be flat, thick, and clean. Defects include having the hocks pointed at each other (the toes pointing out) or the hocks pointing away from each other (the toes pointing in); these are two extremes. It is, once again, important to watch the horse from the rear as it walks and trots away from you. If the horse interferes with or comes close to hitting himself in the ankle, there is a problem with the hind leg that may have been missed during the initial examination. A vet or more experienced person can help determine the seriousness of the flaw.

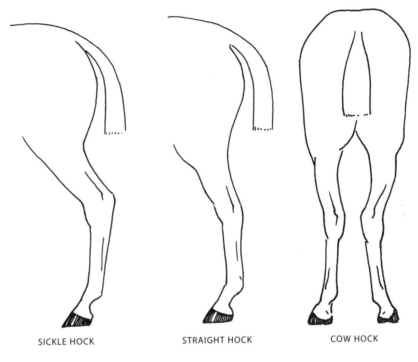

SICKLE HOCK   STRAIGHT HOCK   COW HOCK

For correct hind leg, see photographs in this chapter and those in the color gallery.

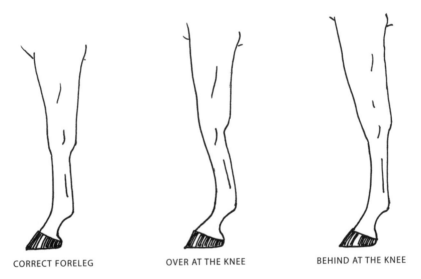

CORRECT FORELEG   OVER AT THE KNEE   BEHIND AT THE KNEE

The hind cannon bones should be substantial and short, and the hocks should be low to the ground, for the same reason that it is good to have the knees low to the ground.

IMPLICATIONS OF SCHOOLING

A horse's conformation influences his level of schooling and determines his job in life. While his performance can be improved through a schooling program, the development of the muscles depends on the shape and angles of the bones to which they are attached. If the horse is built well, a trainer can improve on its natural movements. If a horse is built poorly, a trainer can improve on its natural movements as well but will nonetheless end up with an average or below-average mover. Therefore, one should not select a horse with faulty conformation and expect that certain conditioning and flat work will make it a good mover.

If a horse is coordinated, in harmony, and naturally agile, all of the exercises in this program will be more successful. Teaching the prospect longitudinal and lateral agility will go faster because it will be easier for the horse and, therefore, can result in a better-tempered horse. The reverse can also happen: a willing, cooperative horse that is not well conformed should do the same longitudinal and lateral exercises but must progress more slowly learning to carry himself under the weight of the rider. To stress this horse physically by forcing his development may result in a cranky horse whose good temperament may eventually be lost. To summarize, the schooling objectives for the horse should realistically correspond with his conformation, athletic ability, movement, and natural coordination.

A GUIDE FOR SELECTING AND PURCHASING
A HORSE FOR SCHOOLING

Although this text deals primarily with the schooling of the horse, it is vital that both the amateur and young professional have some guidelines to follow in selecting a horse either for themselves or for a pupil. These guidelines are discussed here so that buyers are prepared, do not get discouraged, and do not buy the wrong horse. Finding and purchasing a schooling project in the very commercialized horse industry takes time.

Keeping a notebook or diary on what prospects have been seen with a rating for each horse's characteristics or important qualities helps keep everything in perspective when looking at many horses. Using 0 to 10 for a personal grading system helps the buyer/trainer be consistent and keep a clear mind while looking at many horses. To find one horse, it may be necessary to look at as many as ten to thirty. A suggested evaluating and ranking system is offered below in this section.

It is wise to have a method you can comfortably apply for evaluating a horse's jumping, movement, temperament, and soundness. These points and considerations will assist in evaluating the prospect before schooling starts and also in reevaluating him at different periods of schooling.

QUESTIONS TO CONSIDER FOR RANKING THE PROSPECTS

What are the schooling objectives for this horse? Local show hunter? A-level show hunter? Jumper? Field horse? Other?

What is the schooling experience of the trainer/rider? First horse or more than ten horses schooled? Will there be a schooling teacher/supervisor?

Depending on the objectives and experience and skill level, decide what specifications are desirable for the horse: age, height, type/breeding, quality mover, temperament, experience, jumping ability, price range. Discussing all of these with a confident amateur friend, a professional horseman, or, if applicable, an instructor, is useful.

Soundness ideally should be a perfect 10, but, in fact, all horses have some defects. The history, vetting, and advice of an experienced person will decide whether the defects are minor or major enough to limit his usefulness. The horse needs to be sound enough to do the job that he is being trained for without any doubts. If he needs drugs to be sound enough to be schooled regularly, then he is not sound enough. Further, it is sad to see so many juniors and their parents being talked into unsound horses without any consideration for the humane treatment of the horse.

Jumping ability should not be below 5 (on a scale of 0 to 10), which equates with just average, in order to be useful. Whether the objective for the horse is to make a lesson horse or a three-foot amateur horse, both need to be safe jumpers. This includes folding; the front legs need to be at the horizontal or above (see photos in this text). A hunter trial or horse trial horse certainly needs to be a steady jumper in good form, because the fences are solid.

Rank each horse seen, 0 to 10, for his *temperament.* A temperament of 8 to 10 is desired. If all else is near perfect and the trainer is experienced, an aggressive temperament will do. This is so especially if the rider/trainer molds this horse into a cooperative, strong performer using this forward riding and schooling system. On the other hand, if the rider/trainer is not experienced, it would be foolhardy to accept anything below a 7 or 8 temperament.

Rank each horse seen, 0 to 10, for his *movement*. What is the horse going to be able to do? If all jumping and temperament factors are strong, what is the lowest ranking that the buyer/trainer would consider for movement?

Many people will present the horse by standing him in a bridle. The buyer/schooler should walk around the horse in the routine steps for checking conformation presented earlier in this chapter. The next step is to test the horse if he seems acceptable. It is important to always watch someone else ride the horse first, observing the horse being mounted and ridden at the ordinary gaits in a flat area (it does not have to be a ring). If the horse trots both ways soundly but is only an average mover and the objective is to have an A-level show horse that will win a decent under-saddle ribbon, that horse is not going to work out for that buyer. The forward riding system of schooling can develop the best in a natural quality mover. However, if the horse is a poor mover, the odds are against his being an A-level show horse.

Next the prospect should trot and canter some single fences, depending upon its experience. The horse should trot a pole and then with wings trot over a small X if he has not really been taught to jump yet. It should be obvious whether the horse picks up his forearms, folding well. The description and illustrations in chapter 2 on the mechanics of the jump should be studied as well as the photographs in this text. If the horse folds loosely four times out of four, he is not necessarily a poor jumping prospect if he is jumping for the first time. However, starting with a horse that does not yet naturally pick up his forearms means taking a chance. A horse's jumping athletic ability can be improved through training on the flat and through combinations and gymnastics over jumps, but a horse that has consistently below-average natural athletic ability cannot be made into an advanced jumper. Training can improve what a horse has, but only within limits.

On this last point, regardless of the schooling objective, a safe jumper that folds in front and behind is needed. If he is made, the horse should have a good "eye" for figuring correct takeoff and enough scope for his job. If it is a field sport horse that jumps cross-country—in hunter trials, riding to hounds, or in horse trials—a safe jumper is still needed. There is nothing more foolish than taking a horse that jumps poorly and rationalizing that no one will score the quality of the jump, as is done in the American hunter divisions. Solid fences cross-country require as good a jumper as a show horse if the horse's and rider's well-being are considered.

If jumper competition is in the plan, ensure that the horse has good scope and form, including folding in front and behind. After time, money, and schooling, he may be only a three-feet, six-inch, horse; but he will be a nicely schooled one that does three feet, six inches, well. He can then be sold, and the seller can try again for a jumper prospect.

Temperament is also a major consideration. Is it a horse that can be taught to be cooperative with the rider? Does it have a temperament and level of sensitivity that is suitable for the objectives? If the answer is yes to each of these, then the horse is a good choice. However, if the temperament is not good, the horse should be passed up.

There are other suitability factors to consider as well, such as the size of the horse for the rider.

People selling horses or presenting a horse for the first time often have them groomed for the buyer's convenience and time. However, if the horse seems desirable, it is important to watch him in the stall as well as being groomed and tacked and to notice whether he pins his ears viciously or whether he is kind while being handled in the stable. If a well-mannered horse in the stable is required, carefully consider his learned manners. Some otherwise good-natured horses may pin their ears while being groomed but do not bite or kick. These behaviors can often be handled in an experienced setting.

If the horse seems to pass all of these tests, it is a good idea to change the setting in which he has worked. Ride the horse down the driveway and away from the stable to be sure that he goes willingly and bravely. To be fair, the test selected must be suited to the educational level and age of the horse. If it is a young horse, it is good to go out on a minihack or walkabout with an older horse to get a feeling of how he responds and how cooperative he is when he comes across something strange.

If that works well, the next step is to take the horse home or to a professional's stable to get him into a strange setting. The seller should be willing to put the horse into a van and meet the buyer at a show ground or farm mutually agreed upon. It is wise to watch the horse load as well.

At a strange place, if the horse is young, it may be possible only to see him walk and trot in an enclosed ring. However, if the horse is older, it should be possible to see all of the things that he does well at home in the new environment. It is also useful to watch him at a horse show from the moment he unloads.

In a sale situation, it is critically important that drugs masking an unsoundness or calming the horse are not used. A plan for checking out that aspect should be developed prior to looking at the horse. The vet relies on the

Trot-lengthening at the advanced level for a hunter or jumper. Connected, ground-covering movement in forward balance. The rider demonstrates well the four funda-mentals of a good position and a direct line from bit to elbow, feeling a soft contact created by the leg. The hands and legs are in position to effectively and efficiently apply rein aids and leg aids. At the end of the long wall the horse returns to the ordinary trot, completing a longitudinal agility exercise (see chapters 9 and 10). This horse also demonstrates the angles of both the front end and the hind end opening and closing to produce good movement (see chapter 4). *(Louise W. Serio, rider; Mandy Lorraine, photographer)*

Adult Amateur Hunter. Correct design of position based on the stirrup allowing spring in the ankle, knee, and hip. Crest release with a good loop to the rein is allowing the full balancing gesture of the head and neck during the flight phase of the jump. The horse is folding well with the knees above the horizontal. *(Jamie P. Martin, rider; Flash Point Photography)*

Pony field hunter. Good jumping form over a drop stone wall following horses downhill in a tandem team. The young rider's position based on the stirrup allows him to stay with the pony and to be nonabusive on the downhill landing. *(David R. Cronin, rider; Teresa Ramsay, photographer)*

Pony show hunter. The pony's knees are above the horizontal, and he is just leaving the ground from the double engagement of the hind legs. The pony is mentally stable jumping through the arc of the flight phase. The rider's crest release (intermediate controls) allows the full use of the pony's head and neck balancing gesture. The rider has a good traditional forward riding position based on the stirrup. Whether a horse or pony, adult or child, the system can be used successfully integrating position, controls (three levels), and schooling (three levels). *(Elizabeth Coughlin, rider; Pennington Galleries, photographer)*

The trot (two beats) with head and neck extended, mouth closed, accepting contact created by the leg. Good horizontal engagement of the hind near leg and extension of the outside shoulder, humerus, and foreleg. The horse demonstrates advanced-level soft contact with reserve energy. The rider demonstrates a correct design of position including angles at the ankle, knee, and hip. *(Anne Kursinski, rider; Reinhold Tigges, photographer)*

Show hunter. The rider demonstrates correct weight distribution through the angles—ankle, knee, and hip—and crest release with a good loop to the rein, encouraging the balancing gesture of the head and neck. The horse's knees are above the horizontal, and he is folding at the ankle as well. Compare this position with the timber horse ridden by this rider. *(Mike Elmore, rider; Judith Buck Sisto Photography)*

Timber race. The rider demonstrates correct design of position as well as unity, non-abuse, and security. The horse at speed has a long arc in the flight phase over the timber fence. There is a good balancing gesture of the head and neck, with the forearm above the horizontal. *(Mike Elmore, rider)*

Leg-yielding at the trot off the left leg to the right. The head and neck are slightly positioned left. The left foreleg is crossing in front of the right foreleg. The aids are soft, and the horse is responsive. *(Liz Callar, photographer)*

Model working hunter. Note the topline and the balanced conformation be-tween the front end and the hind end. The correct angulation allows ground-covering athletic movement. (See chapter 4.) *(Kenny Wheeler, handler; Teresa Ramsay, photographer)*

The walk (four beats) on contact. The horse's head and neck are extended, and the mouth is closed. The rider demonstrates the correct design of position at the walk, connecting the horse from leg to hand. The weight in the stirrup increases when the gait and speed increase. There is a direct line from bit to elbow, allowing the rider to follow the balancing gestures of the head and neck. These gestures are similar to the balancing gestures of the head and neck at the canter, gallop, and jump. *(Cindy R. Prewitt, rider; Brant Gamma, photographer)*

Lateral agility cantering (right lead) through a narrow turn. The horse is connected and moving in one piece. The rider's aids are inside holding leg, outside displacing leg, inside direct rein, outside neck rein. *(Winn R. Alden, rider; Liz Callar, photographer)*

Flight phase onto a bank. Rider has a united, nonabusive, and secure position based on the stirrup. *(Ramiro Quintana, rider; Liz Callar, photographer)*

Flight phase off the bank. Rider has a united, nonabusive, and secure position based on the stirrup. *(Ramiro Quintana, rider; Liz Callar, photographer)*

Forward riding on the advanced level. The schooling has helped the horse develop to the best of his abilities. Even folding through the arc of the flight and good use of the head and neck. The rider is using advanced controls with a direct line from bit to elbow and has a solid forward riding position. The four fundamentals of a good position include unity of horse and rider and efficient and effective aids; i.e., the leg is at the girth ready to apply the leg aids upon landing, the hands on contact following through the jump and into the first stride of the departure ready to apply the rein aids. Some of the seven qualities of this position include correct weight distribution, spring, and even grip with the inside thigh, inside knee, and inside upper calf. This position is not just a style of riding on the flight phase of the jump but a part of a system of schooling and riding the horse on the flat as well as over fences. *(Joe Fargis, rider; Janne Bugtrup, photographer)*

A connected, ground-covering trot in forward balance on soft contact with reserve energy created by the leg (advanced controls). The rider demonstrates a united position with efficient and effective use of the aids. The stirrup length is approximately at the rider's ankle, which is recommended for efficient, ordinary flat riding and jumping up to four feet, six inches. In advanced riding over higher fences raising the stirrup one or two holes increases spring, and on the flat a longer stirrup by one or two holes will give a stronger leg but less spring in the three angles. *(Christi Rose, rider; Al Cook Photography)*

Short turn at the connected canter in forward balance. Note at this instant all of the weight is on the horse's right fore (dynamic balance), and the rider's position is based on the stirrup, allowing unity of horse and rider through this lateral movement on a course. This photo demonstrates the practical and efficient qualities of the forward riding system with its integrated parts—position, controls, and schooling—on the flat and jumping. *(Joe Fargis, rider; Liz Callar, photographer)*

Young hunter. The horse's forearms are at the horizontal. The head and neck balancing gesture is extended over the arc of the jump (flight phase). There is soft contact in the following arm (advanced controls). *(Paul Cronin, rider; Rick Photography)*

Amateur Owner Division. The horse is folding well with a good balancing gesture at the head and neck. The rider has a good leg position based on the stirrup, which is used for flat riding as well as jumping. Practicing flat exercises in a position based on the stirrup and controls based on softness and cooperation helps riders develop the four fundamentals of a good position and the seven physical qualities. (See chapters 1 and 2.) It is more efficient to have the same basic position and controls for both flat riding and jumping. *(Pam C. Dudley, rider; Pennington Galleries, photographer)*

Lengthened canter. (Three beats.) Leaving the diagonal pair (second beat), moving forward to the support of the left leading leg. The rider is on soft contact with reserve energy in two-point position. The inside leg is efficiently and effectively used at the girth to urge and hold as needed. The correct weight distribution creates the spring in the three angles: ankle, knee, and hip, which allows the unity of horse and rider. The position and controls on the flat in the forward riding system are a foundation for riding courses. This horse's movement demonstrates a ground-covering, efficient stride, which is the result of both angulation (see chapter 4) and mental and physical schooling (see part 3). *(Louise W. Serio, rider; Mandy Lorraine, photographer)*

Advanced control in forward riding. The horse is folding well and is allowed a full balancing gesture of the head and neck with following arms, a direct line from bit to elbow. The rider's correct design of position allows correct weight distribution and spring in the angles at the ankle, knee, and hip. Compare this position to other photographs on the flat in this text. The jumping position represents a complete forward riding system with three interacting parts—position, controls, and schooling—for flat riding, uneven terrain, and jumping. *(Joe Fargis, rider; Tish Quirk, photographer)*

horse's history the seller provides. Since it is not possible for the vet to catch all masking drugs, blood can be drawn at the vetting and saved. The blood can be analyzed later if there are soundness or temperament changes.

If there is anything about the horse's movement, jumping ability, temperament, or soundness that the buyer does not like or cannot live with, the horse should not be purchased or taken on for schooling without making conditions with the seller. Hoping to change a serious habit or problem after he is bought or taken into training can be risky. If change is a necessity, such as the way he folds while jumping or the way he acts when he is asked to do something new, then the horse should not be bought or taken on. Most field hunters do not have to be good movers; show horses do. Both of them have to be safe jumpers.

When buying a very green prospect, an experienced horse person can offer an educated guess as to its future temperament in company or the height he might finally jump based on what that person sees and possibly on the horse's breeding.

FINANCIAL CONSIDERATIONS

The success of a schooling program will depend largely on the characteristics of the horse relative to the goals of the rider. Further, it is difficult in this twenty-first century to find suitable prospects. After some encouragement from a number of amateur pupils and some professionals, I have included this section on financial considerations. The author, however, has some reservations about putting commercial values on a horse. Each horse as a living creature is important, and what might be to some a less-fancy horse will be to another an invaluable equine friend.

Also bear in mind that the real price of the horse includes the purchase price, traveling expenses, a professional or amateur friend advisor's daily fee and/or a finder's fee, the vetting for soundness, the insurance policy, and the shipping home. Most of the expenses of finding a horse will be incurred even if the horse is ultimately rejected because of soundness or because it fails a test at the very end. It is vital to have both the funds and spirit to move on and find another horse.

There is no standard method used in pricing horses. Some are overpriced, and if the buyer wants them, he pays the price or possibly risks offending the seller by offering less. Some prices include a commission, and a seller will not take an offer for less but will pay a commission. It is sometimes better to have the seller pay the commission to the professional as a method of getting a horse for less money. It is very important to avoid paying a finder's fee to a professional who is also receiving a commission from the seller. Ensure that all such transactions are known to you. A good professional will keep the client clearly informed and will welcome any questions about pricing, commissions, and so on.

With the financial considerations, there are three rules of thumb in purchasing a horse.

RULE 1   The buyer should develop and follow a general understanding of the current horse market. This can be checked out by current pricing of a variety of horses during the search. The following is a rough guide that can be helpful in categorizing as price research for the prospect is done. If the plan is to sell the horse after schooling him, this guide will give an idea of what might be gotten at resale. An estimate of resale value can also help in determining whether a fair price is being asked before the cost of schooling begins. A professional should develop a pricing guide both for personal reference and for keeping clients informed. The following price range descriptions are from the least expensive to the most expensive group.

Price Range I
A two- to five-year-old in a field or a racetrack reject. It trots its first crossrail satisfactorily (ranking 5 to 6), is an average mover (ranking 5), and seems to have average temperament (ranking 5). Variations might include a 15.2-hand gelding that is attractive and athletic or a 16.2-hand in poor condition and a less-than-average mover (ranking 4).

Price Range II
1.   An attractive horse started in schooling with good form over low fences at home
2.   A finished green horse starting to win at local shows (three feet to three feet, six inches), respectable in some low divisions at A-level shows
3.   An excellent amateur horse at three feet in the show ring or in the field, with a temperament ranking of 9, with good experiences, a safe jumper, and a ranking of 5 for movement

Price Range III
1.   A talented jumper, well-started in good local competition

2. A lovely, green prospect, ranked 8 to 10 in temperament and movement, with starting jumping potential
3. A made, good show horse or good field horse with a ranking of 5 in movement but sound and with a good temperament

Price Range IV
1. Quality in all respects (jumping, movement, temperament), well-started green horse
2. Quality in all respects, hunter/jumper prospect just broken, purchased off the farm
3. Made horse that wins at A-level shows with quality in all respects; may be very expensive if proven in good company and if an amateur can ride it at three feet, six inches, or higher

The asking price, however, is not by any means the actual price, as the seller may be testing the market, may think he has more horse than he actually does, and/or may have included inflated commissions.

RULE 2   The buyer should not pay more than he can get back with a normal effort barring major changes in soundness and performance. If a horse is overpriced but the buyer decides he must be had anyway, the buyer cannot expect to resell him at the purchase price.

RULE 3   The buyer should not spend more than he can afford to lose.
It is important that the buyer stay focused. Writing a check for a horse that is not sound enough or a horse that is missing a key quality means losing track of the original goal. That is the time to stop and reconsider purchasing this horse either personally or for a client. The pressure of time and a skilled salesperson are factors that can lead to the purchase of an unsuitable horse.
In general, disliking something significant about the horse's temperament, jumping ability, soundness, movement, or looks means the horse should not be purchased. One should never count on correcting a significant fault in schooling, because, if it cannot be done to a satisfactory degree, a poor selection has been made. If the fault can be corrected later, that is fine, but one should not count on being able to do so.

5 Preschooling Preparation
Handling the Foal to Age Two

The rider should not assume that the schooling project, whether three, four, or eight years old, has been started or handled well in its earlier life. It may be helpful to review information about handling the foal, yearling, and two-year-old. The rider/trainer can then incorporate earlier and possibly bypassed training sessions into the schooling of a three- to four-year-old horse.

It is wise to give the prospect a complete review of handling and lessons in cooperation with a ground person, working thoughtfully on areas of the horse's resistance or nervousness. He may need to learn or relearn how to cooperate with a ground person. Some horses do come with undesirable habits that will need to be positively corrected.

ON-THE-GROUND TRAINING

When dealing with a foal from the early days, during and after weaning, and through starting it as a two-year-old, it is important to know that cooperation, good manners, and confidence must be instilled long before the actual mounting begins. On-the-ground training should be horsemanlike, consistent, and kind. The foal should be handled as soon as possible after birth. Imprinting is strong during the first twenty-four hours. Imprinting can prevent a natural suspicion of people. A soft sheepskin-covered leather halter should be fitted to the foal's head and slipped on and off several times. The halter must be adjusted frequently as the foal grows. As he is being touched all over, make sure he accepts handling of his ears and head. This avoids later head shyness and facilitates bridling and haltering. The foal should accept general grooming, which accustoms him to humans and their touch. His legs should also be handled and his feet picked up in order to make later trimming and shoeing easier. The trainer should always remember to consistently reward the foal for good behavior and gently but firmly correct him for any negative behavior.

When the foal is about one month old, he can be introduced to leading, making use of the foal's natural inclination to follow his mother. He can be led by her side and gradually tempted away. If the foal is allowed to follow his dam on and off vans and trailers several times, loading problems may be eliminated. The trainer must be sure the foal moves forward freely, willingly, and without fear so that he does not learn forms of resistance such as pulling back or rearing. If the foal shows signs of fear, immediately slow the training process. Never punish a foal for reacting out of fear. The punishment can convince the young horse that his fear was well-founded. This point should be kept in mind throughout the schooling program.

The groundwork with the foal or a young horse should include leading at the walk, halt, trot, and a few steps of turn on the forehand, using voice and a hand in place of the leg for the turn on the forehand. While being led, the horse can be exposed to a variety of situations such as cars, trucks, machinery, playing children, dogs, and horses being clipped. They become common occurrences to him. It is much better to have the foal or the young horse experience these things before he is ridden. The foal or young horse new to a stable should be put first in a quiet area and later moved to a paddock or stall nearer the center of activity, thus gradually exposing him to new noises and sights. He will learn to accept tractors and bicycles as facts of life. The young horse should learn to stand quietly on crossties as well as in his stall while being groomed. This will later make him easier to clip, trim his feet, and pull his mane. The latter should be done over a long period of time, making it a painless memory. Use crossties that will give a little, stand a calm horse beside a youngster that might give trouble, and be sure that if he does pull back on the ties he goes against a wall, not a wide-open aisle.

INTRODUCING THE HORSE TO THE HALTER, LEADING, THE SADDLE, AND THE GIRTH

In the summer of his two-year-old year, it is time to introduce the horse to a saddle. Prior to this, pads and towels may have been carefully placed over the youngster's back so that he begins to accept the feel of something on his back. Some people use a surcingle and later a saddle; others might lunge or "long-line" him first. If correctly done, long-lining is a good experience and a good building block for future training.

It is not a good idea to stand young horses in the stall with a bit and side reins. They learn to resist the bit—overflex/go behind it—and some learn

Demonstrating starting a horse lunging at the walk and halt with experienced people lunging and leading. Next drop the leader and lunge without tack at the walk and trot in an enclosed area. *(Keedie Grones Leonard, Megan S. Proffitt; Reinhold Tigges, photographer)*

to grind their teeth. It is a negative way to introduce the bit. Unfortunately, average and well-conformed horses can easily learn to be behind the bit, and the rider will spend hours undoing that bad habit. With progressive educated schooling, they will learn to flex easily at the poll.

Some people prefer to "pony" or lead the cooperative two-year-old. Led by a rider on an older equine stable friend, the young horse becomes comfortable with seeing the rider above him and may also be less easily spooked by strange animals and new objects.

Some people do the first mounting in a stall, others in a small enclosed area like a lunging ring, with someone holding the horse. Much depends upon the facilities at hand, the experience of the person mounting, and, of course, the temperament of the horse.

When dealing with a two-year-old or a young horse being reclaimed, it is important to tighten the girth very slowly. If the horse has had a bad experience in the past with the surcingle, doing up the girth may trigger that memory, and the trainer may then have a great deal of work to do before mounting him.

Handling and leading to teach willingness and cooperation is an important place to start. Especially if the horse is large and awkward, it is better to delay lunging rather than risk an injury. Protect the legs with boots when lunging. Voice commands used early on while grooming and leading the foal will carry over to the lunging lessons.

One must keep in mind the young horse's short attention span; five to ten minutes is long enough for any type of lesson. It is sometimes necessary and more effective to have two short lessons in a day than one long one. If a young horse is worked too long, he will become sour, irritated, and uncooperative. This would be a poor beginning to a training program.

The foal or young horse should not be asked to do something unless the trainer is certain that the horse is both mentally and physically capable of doing it. With horsemanlike groundwork, the young horse can learn the habit of cooperation, a key to schooling in this system.

When rewarding the young horse with food, put the treat in a bucket. Foals can nip and do not need to be encouraged by treats fed by hand.

STARTING LUNGING THE YOUNG HORSE

The yearling can be gradually introduced to lunging at the walk for short periods of time to avoid boredom. The person doing the lunging should be skilled in lunging techniques. To give the yearling a notion of how to lunge, two people are needed. One should be in the center of the lunging circle, and the other person should lead the horse from the outside. The lesson should be short, clear, and pleasant. Once he has had a few of these lunging lessons at the walk, ideally in the fall of his yearling year, stop lunging until the summer of the two-year-old year.

Later lunging teaches the horse good manners, responsiveness to the voice, cooperation, and beginning stabilization and balance. Some muscle strength and coordination can be developed. The young horse should learn to respond to the voice commands of "walk," "whoa," "trot," and "good." He can learn two speeds of the trot—ordinary and slow—and perhaps the canter departure on either lead from a trot. The voice can be reinforced with a whip pointed at the girth and a tap below the hock. Verbal praise is important. The developing horse should be lunged on as large an *enclosed* circle as possible with good footing. The size of the circle is a function of the coordination of the young horse. He will indicate if he is becoming uncomfortable. The trainer's response should be to enlarge the circle. If the horse has a difficult, uncooperative temperament, it is possible that more lunging for shorter periods might be advisable. Incorrect lunging could lead to both mental and physical impairment.

It may be useful at this point to note the late-twentieth-century popularity for schooling all ages of horses in "round pens" using "horse-whisperer" techniques learned in texts and special clinics that have been heavily marketed. Some horsemen have had notable successes with this method of schooling founded on basic animal behavior theories. However, if the trainer is not educated and sensitive to the horse, round pens can be abusive and harmful to the horse's schooling. For example, exhausting a muscle-sore horse into submission while traveling crooked—i.e., haunches in, head out—can be a negative start to the schooling program. If the round pen is in your program, first teach lunging as suggested in this system (chapter 7).

Late in the summer when the two-year-old is lunging reasonably well at the walk and with some trotting, first the saddle and then a rider can be added. The first time the rider mounts might be in the stall, but the rider can also mount the two-year-old in the lunging area and be led about there. The lunger's voice and the rider's voice used at the same time as a tapping leg will help the horse get the idea of moving forward from the leg. In mounted lunging, the horse can learn to calmly accept the weight of the rider. The sessions on the lunge circle should be short, only five to ten minutes for six to twelve times. The horse can then be turned out until the spring of his three-year-old year.

It is a delight to start up a young horse after his fall/winter off and find that in one or two lessons he has remembered nearly everything done with him in the summer or early fall of his two-year-old year. However, the rider/trainer must be prepared to repeat basic lessons before moving on. When starting cold with a new three-year-old or reclaiming a poorly started four-year-old, do not assume he has been taught the basics. Lunging is discussed in more detail in chapter 7.

All young horses are different. These suggestions will be helpful depending on the trainer's experience, the weather, the facility, and/or the horse's temperament. One thing is certain: correct, careful, gradual horsemanlike groundwork teaches a horse to behave cooperatively and will promote good manners in the stable and paddock; at the same time, it strengthens, conditions, and helps him develop coordination, all in preparation to be ridden.

6   The Philosophy for Schooling in the Modern Hunter/Jumper System

Throughout training the rider needs to keep in mind that exercises must be introduced slowly. The results may seem at first a little crude and not go smoothly, but by working on them gradually and repeatedly, performance will improve over time. A horse cannot be schooled as though it is a machine. Various things will go wrong, requiring a change of plan in the schooling calendar. Repetition and timely rewards are critical. It may be necessary to go more slowly in some areas than implied by this plan, but it may be possible to progress sooner in other areas depending on the trainer's skills and the horse's mental stability and physical condition. For example, once the horse is stabilized, combination work might progress faster than work on contact. All the lower-level exercises should be seen as progressive steps, one building to the next. For example, the transition from the walk–halt–walk is a step moving months later to canter–halt–back–canter. The four natural aids should be used with the correct techniques, and the six rein aids and the three leg aids used on a level suitable to the horse's age and training. For example, the technique of a tapping leg for the green horse moves to a squeeze-release leg for the more experienced horse.

The rider/trainer has approximately three seconds following a behavior to cue the horse whether that behavior was correct or not and to reward or correct the horse. If you wait longer, he may not understand. Use the voice in the appropriate tone, and a carrot can be used. Further there is a "teachable moment" that not only needs to be recognized by the rider/trainer but also needs to be planned through progressive steps leading up to it.

Capt. V. S. Littauer in his teaching and in his work *Common Sense Horsemanship* (2nd ed., 256–57) gave simple but insightful advice that represents the traditional approach basic to educated forward riding schooling. This advice continues to be pertinent in the twenty-first century for riders, teachers, and trainers.

BE TACTFUL

While the horse is upset, the trainer should not ask anything or try to teach the horse a new movement. Choose a moment when he is in a cooperative mood. The trainer must always be the sympathetic teacher and not the conqueror of the beast. This last is still erroneously promoted today—dominance, attacking if the horse is working against the rider, "making him do it."

BE PATIENT

The trainer should try every means of explaining to the horse what is wanted. If the horse refuses to cooperate, it may be because the trainer did not explain clearly enough to him what is wanted. The rider has to learn to interpret what the horse is saying. When riders train their first green horse, this is often a problem. The rider feels the horse is being disobedient and must be punished, when in fact, either through a previous week's riding or something that day, the person has not explained it well enough to the horse. The horse is confused, not disobedient.

BE MODERATE

One must never forget to consider the horse's mental and physical fatigue. Every lesson is a step in the gradual development of the horse, and every lesson must be only slightly more difficult than the preceding one. A successful horseman with progressive schooling creates the "teachable moment."

BE ANALYTICAL

When resistance is encountered, its cause should be determined. Perhaps it is an off day for the horse. At the same time, it is not appropriate to always rationalize the horse's faults. Two or three bad days in a row could mean trouble, not just an off day, and it is time to get some help. On the other hand, resistance may have a physical cause. Some of the horse's muscles might hurt after too much of any one exercise on a previous day. Possibly the horse cannot concentrate. He is too young, or he has never had instruction before. If it is only his second month in schooling, he should not be treated as though it is his first year. Perhaps the horse is sick, has a temperature, is not eating well, or has a tooth problem. Each of these conditions will require different actions on the part of the trainer. Further, the habit of mentally reviewing the lesson after it ends is very helpful in developing sound analytical skills.

BE PERSISTENT

If analysis leads the trainer to believe that there are no legitimate causes for the horse to misunderstand or resist, then the trainer should calmly insist on the execution of what is asked. Be certain to reward promptly. If he is a kind, willing horse, it is probably better to be less stubborn about it and to get some outside help. Another key aspect of persistence is regular, consistent school-ing. Riding three days, having two days off, and on the fourth day starting a new lesson simply does not work. The horse will be confused, and training will have to begin anew. One also cannot work a horse for six weeks (giving him a day off once or twice a week), take a week's break, and then expect to take up exactly where training left off. Too many breaks can mean not being persistent enough. Lapses in schooling are not to be confused with planned breaks. However, a horse can learn in the interval and can come out a little better as long as he has sufficiently learned the lesson before the break.

BE JUST

A horse should never be punished merely because the trainer is irritated. One should never punish in anger. When feeling generally angry with the horse, the best thing to do is forget about schooling or go for a hack or ask someone else to ride him. Correction should be educated cues and should be the result of cool judgment and not hot emotion. Both discipline and reward cues must be administered very rationally and consistently. Only then will the horse learn to know what is good and what is not acceptable in his behavior. No one can ruin a horse faster than a short-tempered person. Horses, especially tough ones (many of the best ones are a little tough), will accept discipline if they understand what it is for, if it is moderate, if it is timely (within three seconds), and if it is suitable to the disobedience. Littauer offers serious advice to the rider/trainer that is important to repeat here: "Stop to consider what your horse thinks of you."

BE GRATEFUL

It is important to give the horse frequent rests and to reward him consistently with a stroke or kind words in a soft tone or sometimes a carrot after he has done something better, each time he cooperates, and after he has learned a new lesson.

Reminders: Before continuing to chapter 7 and part 3 of the text:

Review the Definitions and Concepts of the American Forward Riding and Schooling System, which are found in the introduction.

In part 3 of this text ("A Progressive Schooling System of Seven Periods"), you will refer to and need to be familiar with Program Rides for Different Levels of Riding and Schooling, as well as appendix 1 ("Setting Combinations and Jumps for Different Levels of Schooling").

III A PROGRESSIVE SCHOOLING SYSTEM OF SEVEN PERIODS

7 Establishing Cooperation, Starting Stabilization
Schooling Period 1

Establish cooperation through ground handling, lunging, mounted work at the walk on the flat, and hacking with an experienced horse.

Begin to teach *stabilization,* including responsiveness to voice commands in coordination with the lunger/rider's techniques.

Lunge at the walk and trot. Teach voice commands.

Begin *mounted work,* walking with some trotting, carrying over the voice commands from lunging to teach elementary leg and hand signals.

Hack at the walk with a well-mannered horse.

The pace and direction of the first four to five weeks of schooling depend on the horse's experience and the general conditions. The schooling plan for the first period assumes that the horse has been prepared on the ground and is mentally cooperative and that he is sound, an average or above-average mover, and naturally athletic. He shows potential for good jumping form. Horses come from different backgrounds. It is useful to be aware of what the horse has done in the past. For a young horse, a serious schooling program should not be started before age three or preferably four, with light, consistent riding and pleasant experiences up to that point. Ideally, for the first schooling period the horse should be a three-and-one-half-year-old gelding that has been well handled since foaling. (See chapter 5 again for reviewing how to handle the foal/young horse.) It should be noted that mares can make exceptional horses, but they tend to be more sensitive and may require a more experienced trainer.

This program relies on starting with a horse that is essentially obedient, trusting on the ground, and nicely started under tack. Ground work with the foal is essential from the first day. It builds confidence in humans and establishes cooperation. If the trainer is reclaiming—that is, working with a three- or four-year-old or older horse off the track or elsewhere—it will probably be necessary to redo some of the groundwork to ensure that the horse will stand nicely for the blacksmith and can be groomed comfortably, led in and out of the stall, turned out in the paddock, and led down the driveway with passing cars and activity, being obedient and cooperative with the handler.

It is necessary to develop a mental attitude in the horse that encourages him to cooperate with the trainer. The trainer needs to be able to teach the aids and the proper responses, the first steps, and then progressively use them in a sophisticated system to obtain a good performance from the horse.

Unfortunately, even today there remains notable influence from the nineteenth-century cavalry, which worked with a less sensitive horse. There was emphasis on discipline, force, and getting the horse to perform quickly. There was not much emphasis, quite understandably, on having quality transitions and movement in the field, jumping a barrier, or making a turn after a jump. The latter came only at the end of the mounted military's history and only in certain countries such as Italy, France, and the United States, especially at Fort Riley. Modern riding on the flat and over jumps became more sophisticated. Unfortunately, in some organizations and competitions today, driven primarily by commercial pressures or lack of education, there is still an element of force and a reliving of the nineteenth-century cavalry objectives. It is one of the chief differences in the mental part of schooling between modern American hunter/sport horse riding and what has been the traditional wisdom.

The concept of cooperation in this system leads to an attitude that sets the stage for the rest of the schooling program.

A young horse travels with a low head carriage in the first stages of lunging and training. The long muscles of the back and neck should be relatively relaxed, and the joints should swing. When reclaiming an older horse, the idea is to return him to the green horse carriage, getting him to stretch his head with his neck down. He will be carrying himself, to the uneducated rider's eye, a little long, with the head carriage too low and the long muscles of the head and neck too relaxed. However, this is desired in this period. By no means should this carriage be corrected by overriding the horse or by applying gadgets. When the horse learns to make the transition from the trot to the walk and from the slow to the ordinary trot to the slow trot, he will begin to be a little better balanced whether he is being lunged or being ridden in a large area. There are many lessons in balance for the horse learning to carry the weight of the rider. The idea is to gradually move the horse up, establishing cooperation between the horse, rider, and lunger. One should not try to artificially change the balance of the young horse, especially in the early lessons of the first period of schooling.

Having facilities that allow turnout is essential for this schooling program. Allowing the horse to be calm in the field, to relax, take a deep breath, and let down will make the schooling plan much better than if limited turnout is available. No turnout is a difficult situation, especially in cooler climates. Horses that are only turned loose indoors or are turned out next to heavy traffic face more stressful circumstances than those that are free to eat a little grass in a quiet setting, look off to the horizon, or have a little canter, if possible, over uneven terrain. Turnout is important to the mental stability of the foal, young horse, or reclaimer. It will make him much easier to handle and start, and he will be more cooperative during the first period of training. It will also help the training go more smoothly throughout the seven-period schooling program.

If the horse is really frisky or too fresh, it is much better to have him turned out for a long time. He does not have to be galloping but just grazing and occasionally moving around the paddock, all day or all night, depending on the safety and availability of turnout.

If the project is a former racehorse or a reclaimed jumper or event horse and he is very fit, it would be wise just to turn him out for a few months and then start handling him like a three-year-old; that is, essentially starting again, as though the horse knows nothing, after he has been completely let down at pasture. If he knows a little of the positive responses, progress will be a little faster than with a young horse. If the reclaimer has some bad habits, he is going to have to unlearn them and start again. This is often a longer process than starting with a three-year-old. A careful, complete start for the young horse or the reclaimer shortens schooling time in the long run.

During the first period of four to five weeks, the objective is to establish a good mental attitude. This is the concept of cooperation with the ground person and the rider and having the horse learn the voice aids. Methods used include leading and handling on the ground, lunging in a large area, simple transitions mounted in the same area as lunging, and hacking with an older horse out of the ring or the equivalent.

LUNGING TO TEACH COOPERATION AND BEGINNING TO ESTABLISH THE FOUNDATION OF STABILIZATION

There are three reasons for lunging: (1) as a way to teach a young horse co-operation and to begin to establish the foundation of stabilization, (2) as an important technique in the retraining of an upset horse or a horse being reclaimed, and (3) as a useful technique in exercising a made horse when it cannot be turned out on a particular day, in preparing him at a competition, or in assisting in "stabilizing" a sensitive horse on a cold day. (This is not to be confused with lunging to exhaust a horse.)

The horse has learned to lunge well enough for the first schooling period once he has learned to walk and trot with a long, low head and neck carriage and to obey the commands of the lunger in both directions, staying on a nice, even, large circle, cooperating fully with the trainer. Once learned, if he tends to have a docile temperament, lunging can be dropped to once a week or less,

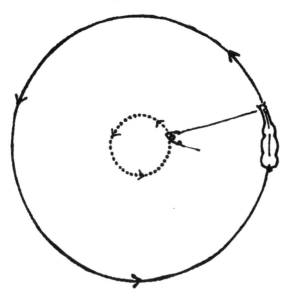

THE WALKING LUNGER
If the lunger walks an inside circle it allows the horse's track to be larger and especially a green horse to be comfortable. It also helps the lunger to stay opposite the horse's withers for communication and safety. The lunger is at the point of the moving triangle, with the horse at the base. The lunge line should be semi-loose. Cue the horse with voice, followed by a check-release on the line. The whip is pointed down and toward the hocks. Teaching the horse the voice cues and establishing cooperation is the goal of lunging in this system.

coming back to it when it might be needed to fill in, such as on an icy day when the horse cannot be turned out, when legging up slowly, or at a horse show where the horse has to be without turnout and needs a bit of exercise. If, on the other hand, the horse seems to be sensitive, high-strung, or very cheery, it may be necessary to continue to turn out and then lunge before starting any new mounted lesson or to lunge on all jumping days. In some schooling periods with some horses, it may be necessary to lunge every day. This will establish cooperation and the foundation of stabilization before mounting and will help prevent the horse from learning bad habits like bucking under tack. The main objective in teaching the horse to lunge is to teach cooperation with the trainer in the center and to teach the horse to become accustomed to the use of the voice aid, which will be used when the horse is mounted, making the transference of the leg and rein aids simple. It can also be used when the horse is older in reestablishing the foundation of stabilization. If a horse has been taught correctly, it will be a lifetime benefit for the trainer/rider as well as the horse to know sophisticated voice commands used appropriately.

In this program lunging a horse to fix special problems caused by conformation is not discussed. If the project is an average or above-average mover and athlete, fixing or training on the lunge for any purpose other than to teach cooperation and stabilization is not recommended at this time.

HOW-TO POINTERS FOR LUNGING

To get off to a good start, pick a lunging time to prepare the horse for a successful lunging session in much the way as would be done for a mounted lesson; for example, not just before feeding or while other horses in the stable are being fed. Do not try to teach lunging when the horse has not had his regular turnout. "Equestrian tact" and common sense apply to lunging, riding, and training a horse in all areas. Keep in mind the mental and physical condition of the horse. Proceed slowly with a young horse. Try to avoid cutting a corner for a quick fix in lunging. It will not be beneficial to the horse's future. Take it slowly, using many short, repetitive sessions and doing one step at a time. Through repetition and interval learning, the horse will make the associations and will be lunging well. If the horse develops the habit of behaving well on the lunge line, he will have it for a lifetime. If he develops the habit of bucking, running off, and resisting on the lunge line, that will most likely be what he carries on to other times that he is lunged in his adult life.

If lunging is to work, the trainer must be skilled at basic lunging. Riding pupils should practice first on a made horse if they need to learn or fine-tune skills in lunging.

The lunging area should ideally be a large, enclosed circle with good footing on which the green horse is comfortable turning. Therefore, large or awkward young horses will need a larger circle. If a complete lunging ring is not available, one can be built by using two sides of a normal ring and jump poles and standards to close in the other two sides. The footing should be safe; that is, firm with a soft spring to it. It should not be slick or deep. Avoid, especially with a young horse, tripping, slipping, or pulling a muscle while trying to turn or travel on a circle too small to comfortably perform transitions. Also if the footing is too hard, it will not be pleasant for the horse. Avoid dust, which is clearly unhealthy for the horse and the lunger as well.

The lunging equipment needed is simple: (1) a standard lunge line, (2) a standard lunging whip, (3) a lunging cavesson or a leather halter with sheepskin, and (4) protective boots for the horse's legs. A standard lunge line is made of either linen or nylon webbing, about one and one-half to two inches wide and thirty feet long. The lunger should wear gloves to protect her hands. Using a halter, slip the lunge line under the nose and clip it on the opposite side. Be certain that the halter fits correctly so that it is not bumping into the horse's eye. Especially, at this time do not use gadgets, such as a bit with side reins. The lunge whip should be seven to eight feet long, including the lash at the end. The lunge whip should be thought of as an aid to the schooling and by no means as something the horse should fear. It is important not to crack the whip and get the horse scooting from that kind of noise. It is another reason why teaching lunging with a vocabulary and emphasis on tone is preferred. Sometimes people can be seen at competitions throwing sod at a kind horse to get him to go faster, because he has gone numb to the cluck or he is so frightened of the whip that the trainer cannot get near him to tap behind and below the hock or point at the girth. The whip is an aid to move the horse out and forward. It is similar to the leg aid. When the whip is used as an aid at the girth, the lunger steps out to the horse and does not reel the horse into the center. The whip here is used as reinforcement to the words. Teach the young horse to lunge without a saddle first and then add the saddle.

The lunger stands at the point of a triangle, with the horse as the base of the triangle. When going to the left, the lunge line should run over the palm of the lunger's left hand. The extra length of the line should be in the right hand, safely folded, along with the whip. The line should be easily reeled in or out should a horse spook. The whip should be pointed down and toward the horse's hind end unless it is being used at the girth to point and move the horse out. The lunger stays approximately opposite the girth area. To ask the horse to go forward, get behind the girth area. To ask the horse to slow down, step up opposite the shoulder. To ask the horse to stop on the circle, move out in front of the horse. Do not reel the horse into the center either intentionally or because the lunger halted or did not walk a large enough circle.

The initial goal is to have the horse obey signals of the lunger: voice, leading rein of the lunge line, check-release of the lunge line, the lunge whip tapping or pointing, and the body position. In both directions the horse should be able to perform the gaits at even speeds (walk, trot; wait until next schooling period to canter). Such exercises should be performed calmly and obediently, including transitions. Begin with walk–trot–walk exercises with, perhaps, longer periods at the trot if the horse is not stable. Depending on the horse's age, size, and condition, ordinary trot–short trot–ordinary trot can be considered, or ordinary trot–walk–halt–walk–trot without allowing the horse to come to the center at the halts. Later, canter departures on either lead and then canter departures on the correct lead from the trot can be performed. Avoid letting the horse learn to depart at the canter by lifting his front end. The goal is a smooth, flat canter departure. The leading lunge line and the check-release of the lunge line tie in with the opening rein and the check-release of the reins when mounted, combined with voice aids. The pointed, tapping whip at the girth combined with the voice relates to the tapping leg combined with the voice when mounted.

The voice is an important natural aid, especially in the first months of schooling. If the trainer and handlers used it on the ground, the horse already knows "whoa" and might possibly have been taught the word "walk." The horse knows the tone of voice as well: a calming, slow, low voice to reward, as in "good," or a sharp voice, as in "no," to correct a disobedience. In undertaking lunging in this system of schooling, the trainer should have a vocabulary as large as the horse's capacity to understand it. He should be able to use the words "walk," "trot," "sloooow trot," "canter," "whoa," "good," and "no" in the right tone. He should use a sharp tone to make the horse go forward, especially if it is a lazy horse, and a slow tone for transitions down. In lunging, reward with the word "good" in a low, slow tone; at the halt use the voice in conjunction with a stroke on the neck; and correct disobedience with the word "no" sharply used for discipline combined with a jerk-release of the lunge line on the nose. Save the cluck for such special occasions as hacking and passing a rock in the woods or a spooky jump. The cluck reinforces the leg. Do not "overcluck" the horse for all forward gaits and numb him to this signal. Also, say "whoa" only when you want the horse to halt. If the horse is cantering and you want him to trot, say "trot" in a low, slow voice.

Do not scream at the horse or cause unnecessary noise. A sharp tone is needed, but it does not have to be loud. Many horses will be more attentive and listen more closely for the next cue if there is not noise pollution from shouting or constant clucking.

Once the horse really knows voice commands, use "whoa" in an emergency. For example, if the horse is quickening or about to buck, say "slow" or "whoa" at that moment. Just as with the cluck, too much use of the word "whoa" for all transitions down will eventually cause it to be ignored by the horse. Have a vocabulary of seven words ("walk," "trot," "canter," "whoa," "slow," "good," and "no"). Use them accurately and with the right tone.

It is important to combine the words with the use of the other aids. Use the voice for lunging with a check-release of the lunge line or with the pointed tapping whip at the girth area and with the body position. With a rider in the saddle, the carryover from the handling on the ground and the lunging will be easier for the horse. Using the voice preceding all weight, leg, and hand aids and correcting any disobedience to these aids will be understood by the horse without jeopardizing his mental stability by an overcorrection. In general, the lunger should be passive when the horse is performing correctly. For example, when he has been asked to do an ordinary hunter trot and is doing it, there is no reason to keep using the whip or voice. If constant use of the voice does seem necessary, it is likely that the technique and correction system are breaking down. The horse should maintain the gait and speed asked for without constant regulating from the lunger and later the rider.

Once the cooperative young horse lunges well in its regular location, it is a useful training experience to change locations. At first the horse will probably be distracted and not so cooperative in the new location. It may be necessary to start again patiently with the simple, slow, short sessions. It is a good learning experience for the young horse to cooperate with the trainer in a new, distracting setting.

If a horse has a good temperament, has had positive handling experiences on the ground, and is working with a trainer who knows how to lunge, the horse should easily learn to be stabilized on the lunge line. He should maintain the gait and speed asked for and execute fairly smooth, cooperative transitions within a four-week period.

PROGRESSING FROM LUNGING TO MOUNTED WORK

The mounted rider continues the training and education of the horse in this program. In competitive disciplines, where some trainers no longer ride, a great deal is done—often too much—on the lunge line. Unfortunately, damage to the horse can be done on the lunge line as well. The horse can become mentally uncooperative, unstable, unsound, resistant, or bored and will sometimes develop a mean streak because of the intensive work he may be getting on the lunge line.

This schooling program assumes that the person training can ride, and the next consideration is to teach the horse to carry the weight of the rider, to be balanced, and to move straight. Having a professional teacher/trainer on the ground periodically assisting the rider in the schooling could be an ideal combination.

After lunging the horse, take him for a hand walk or mount him and do simple exercises in the lunging area on the flat or go for a hack with an older horse. Be certain to relate all of the mounted sessions to the lunging sessions by carrying over the voice with leg, weight, and hand aids, using elementary-level techniques such as opening rein and check-release.

Keep the mounted circle larger than the lunging circle, because the horse will be less balanced and coordinated with the weight of the rider. In the first schooling period after lunging, mount and do at least walk–halt–walk on a large circle using voice reinforced with the leg and hand. If the horse is older, after lunging the mounted session can include the trot and the weight aid combined with the voice in transitions down.

The mounted rider can also walk–trot–walk using the voice, tapping leg, and check-release rein. Young horses may not be ready for the canter–trot–walk transitions as abruptly under the weight of the rider as they can do them without a rider on the lunge line, so avoid them. Some young horses may not be able to take the ordinary trot–slow trot sitting–ordinary trot until they are stronger. At the beginning consider posting to the slow trot.

Early mounted flat sessions that follow lunging should last about five to ten minutes. End these sessions with a pleasant, positive exercise as well.

In this period, the tasks are to teach cooperation and to establish the foundation of stabilization.

OTHER POINTERS ON LUNGING

When lunging, the trainer should keep the horse's circle even by walking a small circle himself. The horse will then stay out on his circle. Lift the whip and point it at the shoulder or girth if he is popping his shoulder or falling in. Often a horse will repeat this action on the same part of the circle, so be alert and anticipate it. This is one more reason why the lunger should be experienced and skillful with the equipment.

If the horse bucks, give a short jerk-release on the line, which will put the haunch out away from the lunger, and at the same time use the voice ("no"). Do not hold or hang on the head.

If a horse being reclaimed has had poor experiences with the whip, try holding it pointing back and down rather than forward and down toward the haunch. If he has been abused by lunging, it may be necessary to skip it. In such a case, at a later time lunge the horse mounted without a whip and have the rider give the horse many strokes. Over a period of time, this might make it possible for him to trust the lunger.

Early on, the trainer may find that the horse is more agile and moves more easily in one direction than the other. If the horse being reclaimed or the young horse is mentally too excited lunging, then starting with the easier, softer, more comfortable side is better. Once the horse has learned to calmly obey and cooperate with the voice commands and the rider's body position to walk, trot, and canter, introduce two speeds of the trot (ordinary and slow) and walk–halt–walk. The less agile side should gradually get more lunging. Eventually most of the lunging will be in the harder direction. It is especially important that the circle be larger on the stiffer side so that the horse is not forced and uncomfortable, assuming that the horse is sound and that the lunging will not provoke an unsoundness.

In recent years many riders have used equine chiropractors quite successfully. They have discovered injuries in racehorses and upset jumpers that were being reclaimed to be hunters or sane, stabilized jumpers. They may have been injured at the starting gate or in some way in riding, such as being halted and backed roughly from the canter or from incorrectly used draw reins. Certain injuries will be made worse by lunging, especially when the horse is wearing gadgets.

Teaching the horse to halt from the walk or trot on the circle without walking to the center seems to be a problem for some less experienced trainers.

Lunging the rider at the walk. Starting to ride a young horse. The rider is on passive contact, as the horse is not yet stabilized on a loose rein. The objective is to teach the voice aid and cooperation at the walk and trot and later at the canter. Both the lunger and the rider use voice. The lunger walks a small circle to keep the horse on a large circle. *(Keedie Grones Leonard; Megan S. Proffitt, rider; Reinhold Tigges, photographer)*

In going from the walk to the halt, the lunger should say "whoa" but should not halt until the horse obeys. Repeat the voice command often while moving up and out toward the horse's shoulder, checking and releasing with the lunge line as it is folded in to the opposite hand. In halting, make certain not to have a steady tug on the nose or get behind the girth. The latter will move him forward. The lunger should keep walking with the horse until the horse halts. If not, the horse, still walking, will inadvertently get pulled back into the center, toward the halted "post" of a trainer. Instead of halting early, the lunger should walk a little faster, getting in front of the horse's shoulder. Saying "whoa" and giving several quick check-release signals with the lunge line should get the job done. Then walk out and stroke the horse and praise him by voice. To discourage the horse from coming to the center, do not feed the horse rewards until out of the lunge ring.

Do not make jumping on the lunge line part of the young horse's normal schooling. Instead, lead a horse over a pole or, once a horse has learned to lunge, perhaps trot the horse over fixed poles in both directions. Walking over single poles in a straight line might be especially useful for a horse that is anxious about poles. Being led or ridden at a walk over poles can be done just as easily as lunging and with less risk of any injury to the horse. Just as in jumping pens (Hitchcock pens), horses lunging over jumps can learn to favor a side. When starting out a young horse, do not create a jumping problem that will have to be corrected later.

Do not lunge for too long at one time. Lunging times vary with the temperament, age, and experience of the horse and the purpose of the lesson. Five minutes can be sufficient. Always end lunging on a good note, on an easy task. Depending on the season and weather, short lunging periods can be done from three to six days each week if the horse needs it.

Avoid putting the extra length of the line in the same hand that is facing in the direction that the horse is going. This can be very unsafe because the line cannot be moved in and out as quickly as when the line is between both hands. The lunger in the center should be certain to move, walking a small circle. Do not stand like a post for the horse to lean against. This will be a little less likely if it is a small enclosure, but if it is a large enclosure, it is important not to get the horse leaning out against the line. Move with the horse in order to be able to move him to the outside of the circle. So doing ensures that he will not be inadvertently pulled in, which, most of the time, causes horses to come to the center to say "hello" to the lunger in the middle of the lunging exercise.

When first teaching a horse to lunge, have an experienced assistant lead him on the outside. That assistant must be certain to follow the commands of the person on the inside doing the lunging. It should be possible to do walk–halt–walk safely without exercising the assistant too much.

Again, inexperienced riders who do not know how to lunge correctly should start with a made horse that already knows how to lunge. Spend four or five sessions learning to handle the lines and whip and position the body correctly. Know how to use the voice in the right order with the whip, which is tapping or pointing. Develop the habit of using the check-release of the lunge line on the nose in coordination with the voice. An inexperienced lunger or one who does not understand what his body language and the techniques applied with the equipment communicate will do more harm with the young horse than can be imagined. It may also be unsafe for the inept lunger.

In general, trainers must be very alert to avoid an accident, especially lunging young horses on cold mornings and lunging horses that are not known to them.

HACKING OUT

After lunging, hack out in the company of an experienced, well-behaved horse for ten to thirty minutes, depending on the condition of your horse. This is an important exercise in the first four to five weeks of the training program. If he is a horse being reclaimed, he should have a longer walk and have a long trot with a quiet companion. The reclaimed horse may have to be in front to start, but a green horse might be more confident following. Encourage the horse from the beginning to keep the correct distance from the other horse by using voice and the check-release technique. If the young horse going behind travels too closely, without prompt correction he will quickly develop an unsafe habit. He will then have to be retrained. Without too much fuss, teach the horse to keep a distance from the start. When out with a well-mannered, short-walking horse, improvise. Go abreast except when anticipating an obstacle—for example, a rock—or find a horse that walks a little faster than the one being trained so that the "spacing" lesson can be taught without cramping the walk.

Establish good habits in hacking from the start. Pick a nice, calm setting to hack. Avoid potential troubles such as a steep stream crossing or traffic.

If the accompanying horse is obedient and brave, the horse being trained will have a better chance of becoming obedient and brave. If the young horse goes out with a horse that shies, then he may well learn to shy by mimicking. It is easier to start with a well-mannered horse for the younger horse to copy. If one is not available, it is better not to go out with a poorly mannered horse.

If the horse passes a rock and is afraid at this early stage of training, do not *further* traumatize him by making him go close enough to sniff the rock. Making him face the spooky obstacle may set up resistance to the lower leg. As he is forced straight toward the object he might resist by going backward. Both are to be avoided.

Insofar as possible, ride the horse past the object as straight as you can. Keep his mind on where he is going and his head looking forward, not sideways at the obstacle. The point is to develop the habit of boldness in the horse and the habit of responsiveness to the lower leg. Using the brave older horse to start with on the ride is simply a method of putting the odds of success in the trainer/rider's favor. Horses learn by habit and have good memories. The habits of obeying, cooperating, and exhibiting boldness while hacking out carry over to a course of jumps and other activities.

EQUIPMENT

It is important to stop here to discuss martingales, side reins, and bits. Lunge with the saddle after the horse has mastered the idea of lunging. Remove the irons or at least tie them securely so that they do not flap on the horse's side and complicate the lesson. No gadgets (this includes side reins) are recommended, especially in schooling periods 1 through 3. The lunging equipment that should be used is discussed earlier in this chapter under "How-to Pointers for Lunging."

BITS

Ride with a smooth snaffle bit through the first two schooling periods and into the third. Later, especially when field riding in company, more bit may be needed. A soft, short-shank rubber pelham can be useful. This bit is sometimes called a "Tom Thumb." Riding with the rubber bit, which is very soft, will not toughen the mouth. Do have the curb chain on the bit to correct the young horse if he disobeys the soft, straight rubber bit. In some situations a "slow" or soft twisted bit, instead of a pelham, may work suitably. Do keep the bitting as soft as possible. School regularly at home in a smooth snaffle or in the softest bit you can use on the flat and over fences. If a horse is regularly schooled in a strong bit, something even stronger may be needed on a cold day or at a competition when the horse is frisky. The mouth gets toughened over time by a strong bit, and then the only recourse is to add further hardware as the months pass.

Unfortunately, many riders beginning to learn about schooling or training the horse think all they need to do is change the bit to solve the problem. Be suspicious of trainers who make much of their skilled suggestions for different bits, gadgets, the amount of tranquilizers for different objectives in the horse's training, or the amount of painkillers to improve the movement. Be alert not to fall into a trap, the latest hardware or pill, to make the world better instantly. People should consult their veterinarian and use medications sensibly and ethically.

Using a comfortable bit and noseband is the best way to teach cooperation and acceptance of the bit and a better way to work through solving an acceptance problem.

To keep the mouth soft and educate the horse, practice soft and precise transitions over and over using the correct techniques of the weight, hand,

and leg reinforced by the voice and ensuring that the horse remains calm throughout transitions and turns. If necessary, use a loose martingale on occasion, and periodically upgrade the strength of the bit cautiously and relative to the task at hand.

STANDING MARTINGALES

A loose standing martingale for hacking out is fine and in some cases may be necessary, but if a martingale is tight and holding the neck down, the horse is not learning to accept contact created by the leg and to carry the weight of the rider in a connected, united way. He may not accept the hand without pulling up. Standing martingales cover up faults in the rider's hand and the horse's balance, especially in transitions. Incorrectly used standing martingales can cause a horse to be upset by distorting the natural head and neck carriage.

Horses develop correct head and neck carriage through gradual progression from the stage of the low green horse carriage to the stage of the connected horse balanced under the weight of the rider. Further, if the martingale is too tight, a horse can learn to lean on the martingale for balance. Often the muscles under the neck will develop incorrectly so that eventually, without the tight martingale, they are strong enough to carry his head above the bit. He is almost looking to feel the end of the martingale for balance as he sticks his nose in the air. In reclaiming such a horse, it may be necessary to prolong Schooling Periods 1 and 2 exercises. However, martingales can be used if adjusted loosely and used infrequently during schooling on the flat and in combinations and other jumping in this program. A martingale can also be used out hilltopping or hacking with a group of people, at a horse show, or in strange places where the horse might unexpectedly shy or raise his head too high.

RUNNING MARTINGALES

In general, the less equipment one needs to use in training the horse, the better the results. In some situations, such as a schooling project or competing with jumpers, a running martingale may be preferable to a standing martingale and/or required by rules. Further, in the hands of an advanced rider, it can be less restrictive and preferable to a standing martingale. It should be adjusted loosely; the rings should easily reach the withers. A correctly adjusted running martingale pulls the reins down the moment the horse resists by raising his head too high. Provided that the running martingale is loosely adjusted, the direct line contact from bit to elbow should be easily maintained when the horse is not resisting.

CROPS AND SPURS

In general, it is better to always carry a crop when schooling. Have the habit of carrying it in both hands or on both sides of the horse. It often works well if you switch the crop to the inside when working on the flat. Spurs should be used by riders with a strong leg position. The spurs should be short, in most cases turned down, and never cause the slightest injury or damage to the skin. The crop and, if used, the spurs reinforce the voice on the elementary level and the leg on all levels. The crop and spur are used near the girth with one tap to cue the horse. (See chapters 1 and 2, tables 1 and 2, and the leg aids illustration.)

SAMPLE MOUNTED WARM-UP

To prepare for these important simple sessions, ensure that the horse has been turned out in a paddock to relax mentally and to exercise while free. Calm, consistent handling while leading, grooming, and tacking will help establish cooperation, responsiveness to the voice, and trust.

During this first schooling period the mounted sessions are short and simple, teaching cooperation and voice signals. These will become a warm-up routine for early schooling. Lunge at the walk and trot; do mounted walking, halting, and trotting; and ride in company at the walk. Older horses being reclaimed should be ridden longer under saddle.

8 Developing the Balance of the Young Horse
Schooling Period 2

This period should last four to five weeks, depending on the horse's mental and physical maturity and how well the horse achieved the first period's objectives: establishing cooperation with the rider and beginning to demonstrate the foundation of stabilization through the lessons and methods of early lunging, simple mounted flat work in the lunging area, and hacking out at slow gaits with an older, well-mannered horse.

KEY CONCEPTS AND EXERCISES FOR THE SECOND SCHOOLING PERIOD

Stabilization of the mounted horse off contact (looped rein) is a primary goal of the second schooling period, with an emphasis on *cooperation* and *calmness.*

Elementary controls including the voice and loose rein and the four natural aids (weight, voice, hand, and leg) are integrated into mounted lessons using the appropriate techniques; for example, opening rein and tapping leg for turning and check-release for slowing and stopping. Study the elementary controls in chapter 2. Repetition in such areas as long periods at the trot, large circles and turns, and gradual transitions (trot–walk) are important for establishing the habit of a good performance with a pleasant attitude.

Preparation for jumping is done by simply stabilizing the approach to single poles on the ground and stabilizing the departure. A series of poles may be added. Integrate this exercise with the elementary flat exercises. (See appendix 1, the section on "Starting to Teach Jumping," Steps 1 and 2.)

Introduce two speeds at the trot (ordinary–short–ordinary) when hacking out with a suitable equine escort. Practice lengthening the stride at the walk.

Throughout the period in the different settings and exercises, teach leg aids to go forward and to increase the speed. Teach the weight and hand aids to slow and halt. Use voice cues in coordination with the leg, weight, and hand aids; frequent halts to teach obedience; and wide turns to teach steering.

STABILIZATION

Stabilization is the chief objective of the second schooling period. Stabilization means maintaining the gait and speed asked for whether alone or in company, on uneven terrain or on the flat, or jumping, using elementary control techniques. In modern riding in the early part of schooling, cooperation has come to replace discipline and domination. Keep this in mind during training. Disobedience must be corrected in a timely manner, and the degree of correction must be appropriate. The trainer must also ensure that the horse

Loose rein walk in a field on a calm but alert horse demonstrating correct head carriage for a young horse starting schooling, the goal for an upset horse being reclaimed or an older made horse on elementary control. The rider is sitting forward in the saddle with a stirrup short enough to allow an angle at the knee and ankle. The rider, without adjusting stirrups, is ready to trot, canter, or jump. The position allows efficient use of the leg at the girth. (Jill Randles, rider; Reinhold Tigges, photographer)

was prepared and that he was given a fair request. Stabilization becomes an important tool and foundation in the mental and physical schooling of the young horse throughout this program as well as in mentally and physically reclaiming the older horse. In the second schooling period, riding is still off contact. In the third period, looped reins will gradually be replaced in the majority of schooling on the flat with riding on passive contact.

Stabilization is also a valuable foundation for the intermediate and advanced horse. These first lessons in schooling that establish cooperation will stay with the horse as a foundation. For example, when riding or competing on a cold morning or at a different location, the rider can begin warming up off contact on a large circle to establish stabilization.

By the end of the second schooling period, the horse learns leg and hand aids, and they can gradually replace voice commands. It is important that specific techniques of the rein and hand signals are used in this second schooling period. The horse should be able to stand, eventually on a looped rein, without being held in place. Correct a disobedience to the tapping leg and voice with a stick (tap) at the rider's boot. Certain lateral exercises such as large circles, large half-circles in reverse, and large half-circles at the walk and possibly at the trot can also be done (see the illustrations at the end of chapter 9).

Especially in the second schooling period, for calmness, keep the speed of the trot a little slower than ordinary. As soon as the horse is maintaining the trot and an even speed asked for on the lunge line, then the trot under the weight of the rider can begin to be stabilized. Consistently add the voice to the hand and leg aids in exactly the same sequence; for example, going from the trot to the walk (downward transition), use weight, voice, hand, and leg. The horse should catch on to this quickly and will begin to cooperate.

ELEMENTARY CONTROLS

Little by little during this period, transfer the horse's lesson from the voice commands on the lunge line to the leg and hand aids on the flat and on trails. Unless he is an unusually calm horse or the weather is warm, throughout the second schooling period plan to lunge the horse first for five minutes, or as little as the horse requires. If he is calm, begin to select the direction in which he needs more work in these short sessions. If he is not calm, take the softer, more agile direction. Do work in both directions, but avoid making work unpleasant.

When first starting to teach the canter, teach the voice command for the departure on the lunge line. Make the lunging area as large as possible, and do not insist on a full canter circle if the horse is too young or too large for a small lunging area. Ask for the departure from the trot with the voice ("canter"), and accept either lead. When mounted, repeat the same steps. If possible use the same lunge area but double the size of the circle, because the horse now has the weight of the rider to carry. Give the aids for the departure from the trot (voice: "canter"), inside direct or slightly opening rein, outside displacing tapping leg, and again accept either lead at this time.

Leg and hand aids are taught more seriously in this second period. Use the three leg positions with a tapping technique. Not all of the six rein aids are used in the second period. The opening rein and two direct reins of opposition are used. The first combination rein aids are an inside direct rein and an outside opening rein to help guide the horse to track "on the line" whether straight or turning. All the rein aids are used in coordination with the legs. However, using corrective rein aids (the indirect rein of opposition both in front and behind the withers) this early is considered overriding the young horse that has so far developed only an elementary understanding of rein aids. It can be confusing to the horse to use more sophisticated aids before he is ready. If the leg and hand signals are combined with the voice learned on the lunge, the horse will understand them and cooperate more quickly and efficiently.

Always begin with gradual transitions and large circles throughout this period; for example, walk–halt–walk–trot–walk–trot–walk–halt. Avoid exhausting the horse. Just ask him to cooperate with the rider's cues. Ensure through the voice that the horse understands what is being asked of him with the legs and hands. Correct any disobedience to the aids but be alert not to ask too much—for example, an abrupt transition or a hard series of exercises. If the rider listens, the horse will usually indicate when he is getting frustrated or not understanding. Start and finish the lessons with something easy, thereby creating a pleasant note and a positive experience.

After he has had a warm-up and is doing the simple things well and conditions are right, then start to introduce a new movement or exercise.

In the second schooling period, integrate frequent halts for the horse's mental stability. Turns should be wide, using the leading or opening rein. The guiding rein/opening rein relates to the lunge line and is successfully used in this period for turning the horse.

It is too early to start jumping in the second period, but practicing trot-

Stabilized horse on loose rein trotting evenly spaced ground poles. The rider is in correct two-point, with even grip with the inside lower thigh, inside knee, and inside upper calf. *(Jill Randles, rider; Reinhold Tigges, photographer)*

ting mounted between standards without quickening can be done. Individual poles placed throughout the working area may be walked and trotted. The young horse should maintain the gait and speed asked for passing over the poles off contact; i.e., the walk or trot. If the horse is ready and if a ground person is available, put several poles in a row, at first walking (three feet to three feet, six inches, apart) and then trotting (four feet to four feet, six inches, apart). Adjust the distance to make it comfortable for the individual horse. If the horse gets rattled by a series of poles, avoid them until he is stable over a single pole and further along in training. By the end of the second schooling period and at the beginning of the third period, a horse should be able to walk and trot about six correctly spaced poles on a looped rein. (See appendix 1, the section on "Starting to Teach Jumping," Steps 1 and 2.)

Reclaiming ruined hunter/jumpers or timber/steeplechase racehorses often takes longer for stabilization in this simple exercise over poles because they may be unstable at the jumps due to previous riding experiences. The only thing related to jumping being taught here is an even gait approaching and departing the pole. Do not raise the rail to an X or a low vertical until the approach and departure from a single ground pole are straight and stable, with an even gait and speed and with an extended head and neck, mouth closed.

Continue to hack out to further teach stabilization in unfamiliar settings and to establish cooperation with the rider's aids. Get the horse in the habit of obeying the leg to move forward, cooperating with the rider, and passing boldly through new sights. Doing this with a sensible older horse makes it much easier to accomplish successfully. At all costs, think ahead and avoid an argument with the animal.

Going out on the trail with an older foolish horse is unwise. If a sensible older horse is unavailable, try talking a pedestrian friend into walking down the trail ahead of the horse at the walk, crossing streams, passing a rock, and passing potentially frightening places with the person on foot leading the way. Or if there is only one rider, try ponying the young horse while riding the sensible one. Or vice versa, if it works better. This will work with some horses. It is necessary to be creative if an older sensible horse with a second rider is not at hand to demonstrate the habit of boldness and cooperation. Be certain to carry over the same rein and hand signals at this elementary stage to the trails and to the field. Educated riding is not just for the ring or for jumping. Be consistent with voice, weight, leg, and hand aids in all settings.

In the second schooling period, hacking out may be the day's only lesson, or lunging to teach or reinforce stabilization and cooperation. Introducing a few steps of the canter on the lunge line may also be done. Then mount and go for a hack with another horse or mount and do some flat exercises in a large area, preferably an enclosed ring. These would include simple transitions from the trot to the walk, two speeds of the trot (ordinary–slow [posting or sitting]–ordinary), and walk–halt–walk.

COMMENTS ON SCHOOLING DURING THIS PERIOD

The experienced amateur who is beginning to school horses should find this discussion about schooling useful. An experienced professional rider may use this section to develop fresh ideas and to teach pupils to school horses.

The weather, the ability to turn out the horse, and the horse's temperament will help determine what part of a day's plan gets done or dropped and in what order to do things: lunge, flat work, hack.

Although each of the lessons for each week in this second period should be planned out ahead, it is important to remain flexible. For example, on the East Coast, the weather may be cold and inconsistent, and the training might have to be delayed until March or early April. While in schooling, turning out should be fairly regular, and if March weather was pleasant the lunging should have gone well. The horse should have developed cooperation and begun to be stabilized. However, if it was a cold and windy March, it may be necessary to continue work on the lunging into April.

It is very important at this stage that the young horse be allowed to carry his head and neck low and extended in a natural carriage until he has learned to carry the weight of the rider with more coordination through transitions. At first the rein will be semi-loose. Starting lessons with a floating or loose rein may not be possible until the horse has been completely stabilized. The rider should work toward being completely on loose rein.

Most horses are not physically or mentally ready to accept educated contact in the second schooling period, so it is introduced in the third schooling period when the horse is stronger and more stabilized. A passive contact with a driving rein could be used for controls in this period if the horse is steady and the rider very experienced in forward riding theory and skilled in the saddle. However, it is more efficient in schooling to have a short looped rein that does not interfere with the low natural head and neck carriage at this stage. When the horse is stabilized the rein can be more looped or loose.

THE IMPORTANCE OF HEAD CARRIAGE

The head and neck carriage cannot be emphasized enough. It is with this carriage that many trainers make a serious schooling error. Many people hurry the horse to market or a competition. With gadgets and forced upper-level aids, one can get the young or uneducated horse to make an abrupt upper-level transition or sudden halt; however, doing so predisposes the horse to stiff muscles and to resistances such as grinding the bit, fear of the rider, nervous attitude, and, with horses of certain temperaments, stubbornness or sourness. Some of these horses may be seen later at a competition being lunged to exhaustion in order to be quiet enough to compete. Others may be drugged and competed locally. Others may find a new owner and be reclaimed.

In reclaiming an older horse, the work in the second schooling period may take longer, six to ten weeks, but it will be vital to success. The reclaimer

BEHIND THE BIT

The horse escapes a forceful hand and discomfort or pain by rolling under and behind the vertical. The rider cannot achieve soft, precise control. These horses are often mentally unstable or have upset reserve energy. Heavy use of gadgets such as draw reins and tightly adjusted side reins can produce this carriage as a habit. To reclaim this horse he will need to return to a young horse head and neck carriage and have reschooling, starting with stabilization.

ABOVE THE BIT

The horse escapes a forceful hand and discomfort or pain by pulling up to escape each time the reins are used. This can be a habit of carriage. Horses that are ridden in a tight martingale or draw reins often escape up as soon as the "tie-downs" are taken off. To reclaim this horse he will need to return to a young horse head and neck carriage and have reschooling, starting with stabilization.

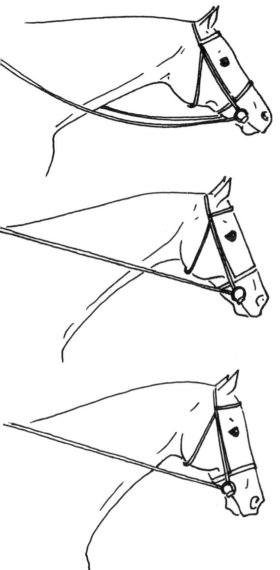

YOUNG HORSE HEAD AND NECK CARRIAGE
This is the approximate carriage of a young horse on a looped rein starting schooling on the flat and over ground poles and jumps. It is the first objective in reclaiming and stabilizing an upset horse and is similar to the carriage of a trained horse first warming up to work on contact.

HEAD AND NECK CARRIAGE OF A HORSE SCHOOLED FIRST TO PASSIVE CONTACT
Appropriate for most trained horses in hunter under-saddle classes, hunter over-fences classes, basic flat work for young horses, amateur riders on the intermediate level, field riding, and for a specific goal or function that can be better achieved on this level of connection and contact.

HEAD AND NECK CARRIAGE OF A HORSE SCHOOLED TO EDUCATED CONTACT WITH RESERVE ENERGY
On this level of contact and schooling there is more reserve energy created by the leg. The head and neck carriage changes as the horse's balance under the weight of the rider develops over months of schooling. On the flat longitudinal and lateral agility exercises, jumping through combinations of varying distances and going over uneven terrain help the horse achieve connected forward balance. The horse's training moves from loose rein (elementary control) to passive contact, and to soft contact with more reserve energy—the latter only if appropriate for the horse, his owner, and his function or sport specialty. Gadgets can produce a fake frozen frame for some gaits and movements for short-term objectives. However, they cannot produce the mental and physical development needed for a sound, athletic, calm, and useful horse.

will have setbacks in the program as he recalls unhappy experiences and repeats old habits. It is therefore necessary to return to stabilization regularly to reestablish the foundation before moving on again. The trainer should take the older horse being reclaimed to the point that his head and neck carriage is nearly returned to his three-year-old stage. This will help the horse establish both mental and physical stability.

The horse's mental stability and movement are closely related to the head and neck carriage. If an error has been made by introducing something too soon or too harshly, return to simple exercises that he knows in order to restore mental calmness and physical relaxation.

The horse will begin to become better balanced under the weight of the rider through simple exercises and gradual transitions. Eventually the head and neck position will be raised, especially in transitions down. Avoid the temptation to force the head and neck to come up in the transitions.

The rider is passive but not permissive. Each lesson must be planned out, but little is accomplished relative to an advanced lesson. The horse's physical and mental progress needs to be evaluated regularly, although at this period, for some riders not much exciting is taking place.

If the rider is used to riding only upper-level horses, then it may be difficult to feel the changes or to understand the role interval learning plays in training the young horse. Given time, the horse becomes more naturally connected, remains calm, and develops the best qualities in his movement. The importance of stabilization as a foundation to the future training of the horse as he develops mentally and physically may not be fully realized until a rider/trainer has achieved it successfully on at least two or three horses.

In the second period of schooling it becomes clearer that the ideal conformation of a hunter or jumper works best in this system. Accommodate any serious conformation faults, especially head and neck carriage, as training progresses. Horses are built differently. If a horse is lower in the front than behind (assuming he has finished growing), this will lead to problems in schooling, specifically teaching contact and establishing a good connection. If a horse has a very high head carriage, mental instability may be a consistent problem as well as shortened gaits. Further, a horse with above-average natural agility will be able to handle all of the lessons (lunging, gradual transitions, wide turns) more easily than a horse that is less coordinated. The latter horse will require more practice with wide turns and very gradual transitions.

Do not go on in the schooling program until the objectives of the second schooling period have been achieved; that is, the horse is stabilized and maintains the gait and speed asked for, whether alone or in company, on the flat or in a field, or "jumping," with the rider using elementary control techniques. All of these are achievable at this stage of development provided they are on the beginning level; for example, "jumping" here means calmly approaching and departing from poles.

Allowing the horse to learn to balance himself under the weight of the rider with an extended head and neck through a series of gradual transitions and large circles and turns is the key to schooling the young horse in this period. When pupils are learning to school, these first two periods or eight weeks are very difficult for advanced junior and amateur riders who are used to riding upper-level horses, especially with accuracy and promptness. The aids, transitions, and turns are made simple for the unbalanced green horse. The rider should use controls that are on the horse's level of education. The training goes slowly and takes considerable patience and thought. Consider often what the horse thinks of the rider and what he is doing.

SAMPLE MOUNTED WARM-UP

At this stage, the following could be a day's schooling in itself, or it could be used in preparation to go on a walking hack with an older horse. It is done on a looped rein off contact as much as possible.

Lunge for approximately five minutes if necessary. One may also lunge with the saddle.

The girth should be tightened gradually in three steps: (1) loosely when first saddled, (2) after walking toward the mounting area (after tightening, stretch the skin under the girth by pulling each front leg forward or having the horse walk), and (3) again after five to ten minutes of mounted walking.

Mount softly. After standing in the stirrups for the first few steps of the walk, sit softly in the saddle.

Walk for ten to fifteen minutes before considering trotting. With some horses, it may be necessary to keep the walk simple, steady, and calm. With others, some exercises can begin early at the walk. Either after fifteen minutes of walking or during the walk, try the following. Walk in one direction until the horse is calm. Work in many short halts with check-release reins and voice, and reward with a stroke. Then change direction and repeat the halts. Walk over ground rails and between standards. Take two-point or jump position at the walk to get the horse used to the rider shifting weight in the saddle. Walk half-circles to change directions.

Trot in one direction on a large circle until the horse is reasonably stable. Include walking breaks and halts. Change direction and repeat. Be intentionally repetitive to calm the horse (it is a little boring).

Then go on a walking hack with an older horse. The amount of warm-up necessary in order to undertake the hack will depend on the mental stability of the horse. An inexperienced horse should be prepared to go on a hack in this way in order to avoid possible exciting mishaps.

In leaving the second schooling period and looking toward the third period of schooling, the horse begins to become stronger and better able to carry the rider through gradual transitions and wide turns. He develops a reserve energy, and he begins to become naturally connected carrying the rider. When teaching stabilization off contact, there should be an impulse or reserve energy developing that will be important as the horse moves on to a passive contact in the next schooling period.

9 Achieving Stabilization and Introducing Passive Contact
Schooling Period 3

This period includes four to five weeks of active schooling exercises on the flat, over low jumps, in the open, and in company.

The success of the horse's training in this important period will depend upon the horse's level of cooperation and stabilization achieved in simple exercises in lunging, doing flat work, going over ground poles, and hacking out at the walk during the previous schooling period.

KEY CONCEPTS AND EXERCISES FOR THE THIRD SCHOOLING PERIOD

Stabilization in its full meaning should be well established in the young horse during this period. The horse should consistently maintain the gait and speed asked for on loose reins whether alone or in company, on the flat or on uneven terrain, or jumping. The natural carriage of the *extended head and neck,* with the mouth closed, is maintained.

Introduce *passive contact* when the horse is stabilized on looped rein at the walk, trot, and canter, at least in the ring or an open, flat area. The important gradual change from the elementary controls to the intermediate controls is begun in this period. For example, weight, hand, and leg aids are used mainly, gradually dropping the voice commands, which are then used only for reinforcement. The techniques change as well; for example, the tapping leg becomes the squeeze-release leg for responsiveness to the lower leg. Check-release becomes give-and-take for slowing or stopping, and riding on passive contact gradually replaces riding on loose reins. The concepts of connection, engagement/disengagement, and impulse or reserve energy begin to be emphasized.

Canter on loose rein, stabilized horse. The horse's weight is on the outside hind leg (dynamic balance). The rider is sitting forward in the saddle with some weight distributed to the stirrup with a correct design of position. *(Anne V. Swan, rider; Reinhold Tigges, photographer)*

Longitudinal agility exercises to slow down or halt and to move forward are taught, including trot–walk–halt–walk–trot and three speeds of the trot.

Lateral agility exercises on wide turns include circles and half-circles. Short turns at the walk can be practiced.

The first, *combination rein* (inside direct rein of opposition, outside opening) for turning replaces turning on the opening rein.

Jumping cavalletti poles in a series with an X is introduced. Stabilization in jumping continues to be emphasized, trotting single Xs and low verticals, with possibly a low, one-stride in-and-out. (See appendix 1, the section on "Starting to Teach Jumping," Step 3.)

Hacking out at the walk and trot in the company of two or three kind horses and *hunter exercises* develop stabilization in company. Begin cantering in company one at a time on a large circle in the open while the group walks and later trots on the same pattern.

Moving to the third period of schooling requires a reminder that this plan must be adjusted to the horse's mental and physical condition. Further, the plan assumes that a good place to regularly turn the horse out is available and that the weather for riding is fairly even. Sudden changes in weather require an adjustment to schooling plans. The plan also assumes that the horse is getting consistently ridden, that a large, flat, enclosed ring is available, that a fairly flat space in a field for schooling without too many distractions is at hand, that there are some trails for walking and trotting, that an older well-mannered horse to escort the green horse is available, and, if necessary, that mounted sessions are preceded by lunging.

Continue the lunging to teach cooperation, especially if the weather is suddenly cold, if the horse tends to have too much reserve energy or to be a nervous horse, or if he is a horse being reclaimed.

If some of these schooling facilities are lacking, consider alternate resources at hand. Try trailering a green horse to a friend's ring or open space or field and/or to a nearby woods where there are trails. Continuing to go to the same places in these early periods of schooling will allow the horse to develop the habit of cooperation and learn the foundation of stabilization. For experience and to develop boldness, some people have made up little trail "rides" around their paddock and stabling area on the days they could not trailer to a better trail-riding area. Start the mounted lessons with something simple. Use the appropriate sample warm-up plans. Reestablish the foundation of stabilization. Some horses may need to have their lunging and a gradual warm-up done on elementary control, including looped rein, every time they are ridden. This may be six out of seven days of the week.

Horses need at least one day off a week. Many horses are better if they have two, consecutive or separated, days off.

The more placid horses need to have the lunging sessions kept short and most probably need lunging only once or twice a week during this third period just to keep refreshing their memory on the voice commands and reestablishing the foundation of stabilization.

A horse that is unstable is not only one that wants to go too fast at the gaits but also one that will not keep an even pace because he is too slow or lazy.

It is essential that the rider have a correct and well-balanced position, using the four fundamentals of a good working position, which include efficient and effective use of the aids and being able to stay united with the horse's movement throughout the transitions, thereby using the hands independent of the body. It is also important that the rider/trainer have a very clear understanding of theory and concepts and skilled use of both the elementary and intermediate controls levels, including leg and hand aids and techniques.

At the end of this third schooling period, the young horse should be able to perform well in at least one setting on the elementary controls level and, to some degree, in the beginning intermediate controls level. This would include a stable, connected walk–trot–canter in both directions, three speeds of the trot (ordinary–slow–ordinary–strong–ordinary), trot–canter–trot transitions, gradual transitions to the halt, trotting single low fences and low, one-stride in-and-outs, performing in company at the walk and trot, staying coordinated over slightly sloping terrain at the walk and trot, performing a short turn at the walk leading to a turn on the haunches, trotting large circles and half-circles, and accepting passive contact at the trot and parts of the canter. By the end of the third schooling period, if the program has gone smoothly, some horses should be able to maintain passive contact through transitions.

SCHOOLING AND RIDING ON PASSIVE CONTACT

Stabilization was the goal of the last schooling period. Teaching the young horse to consistently accept passive contact is the chief goal of this third period. Passive contact gradually begins to replace riding on loose reins, although warm-up is done off contact, on loose reins, and the lesson is finished off contact, on loose reins. Some elementary exercises may be performed in the middle of the lesson, depending upon the horse and its needs. The jumping will continue on the elementary level of controls, while the flat work is starting on passive contact with intermediate controls. Initially the goal is for a passive, consistent acceptance of the bit with an extended head and neck in a natural young horse carriage. It is not the time to go on soft contact with more reserve energy or impulse with a young horse.

Once again, at least 90 percent of the time, the head and neck should remain naturally extended and the mouth closed. Do not force a change in the balance or head and neck carriage. The transitions should be gradual and the circles and turns large while riding on contact in this third schooling period. Try very hard not to hurry this natural progression. As the young horse learns to be connected and balanced under the weight of the rider, transitions eventually are less gradual, and turns become less wide as the young horse can more easily handle them.

There are two reasons to teach the horse to go on contact. The first is that it improves the rider's control over the horse. The controls become softer and more precise with contact. That goal must always be kept in mind: soft and precise transitions. The end result is a cooperative horse with a good attitude toward the hand and leg signals and a balanced, agile horse. If during schooling, anything is done that physically distorts the head and neck carriage or mentally upsets the horse, it is time to try something else or talk it over with an experienced person.

The second reason to teach the horse to go on contact is that riding on contact improves the quality of the horse's movement. This third schooling period is just the beginning stage of teaching contact; there will be a significant difference after seven periods of schooling in this method.

The trot is normally the best gait to use to start teaching the horse to accept a passive contact. Ensure that the horse is stabilized off contact at the walk, trot, and canter before attempting to ride on contact. By no means should it be "leg, leg, hand, hand," constantly holding and driving.

In general, when riding on contact and especially when teaching it, the faster the gait, the more energy or impulse. Therefore, in the third schooling period, the rider should be feeling very little, if any, reserve energy at the walk. This will occur later when the horse is in better condition, stronger, and more experienced on contact. Most Thoroughbred-type horses will have enough reserve energy at the trot for contact. Also, because there is no balancing gesture at the trot, it is a little easier to keep consistent contact. Some more placid horses might need to canter off contact and then return to the trot and establish contact. Although the canter is faster, the young horse at this time is normally not naturally connected enough under the weight of the rider to be in consistent contact. Further, the balancing gestures of the head and neck and the three-beat gait at the canter make it a little more difficult to keep consistent contact.

If the rider's hand at the walk or the canter is set against the natural balancing gestures, whether on a looped rein or on contact, a distorted position of the head and neck is produced that throws the horse off balance. Further, some stiffness and pain will result, leading to problems in future months. Setting the hand against the balancing gestures and rough, abrupt transitions destroy calmness at this stage of schooling. It slows the development of the natural athletic agility of the horse under the weight of the rider and often leads to an ill-tempered, unbalanced horse. This is especially true if the horse is predisposed through breeding and/or early handling to being a little feisty, hot, or oversensitive.

Some cross-country riders bridge their reins against the neck. This is a riding expediency or technique to deal with a very fit, pulling, aggressive horse. It is not desirable for a trail horse, field hunter, show horse, or hunter trial horse, and it is not necessary for horses competing in horse trials on the lower levels. The bridged rein is unwise to apply to a young horse, especially in his third period of schooling. Teaching a horse to pull is contradictory to the soft flat work goals of this system. An educated horse person will recognize the difference between a coping technique and techniques that progressively build within a concept and a system of riding. A schooling technique should both solve a problem and potentially prevent others.

When first teaching the horse to accept passive contact, the aim is good engagement and disengagement; that is, the swing of the hind leg under the belly and the horizontal thrust forward. This helps connect the horse and, of course, provides the reserve energy or impulse the rider needs for the feel of contact. A rhythmic lower leg in the squeeze-release technique establishes the gait, speed, and degree of reserve energy desired for passive contact.

Engagement and connection are interrelated concepts. In the first stage of teaching contact it is important that the horse stretch his head and neck forward and reach for the bit. The rider's leg helps create the energy, and the hands feel this gentle pressure or stretching forward. Avoid pulling or heavy force. If the horse is green and unbalanced, he will tend to lean on the rider's hands for support. Setting the hand at this time will teach the horse to be heavy-headed in the bridle and thereby disconnected; that is, moving in two pieces. This used to be called "heavy on the forehand," but it is, in fact, an inaccurate description and misleading to the rider. Nonetheless a heavy-headed, disconnected horse is to be avoided. Well-intended riders who try to correct the heavy-headed, disconnected horse with a constant holding hand will actually train the horse to be heavier and more unbalanced. Some horses learn to be behind the bit at slow gaits and others become pullers.

To teach passive contact, start at the trot on looped reins, gradually taking up the slack. Depending on the natural impulse or reserve energy of the horse, use the lower leg to urge the horse forward and to stretch his head and neck forward into the bridle. This is asked just for a few minutes; then give the horse a stroke and try again. If conditions permit, have short periods of riding on contact in an open, flat space or on the trails. The latter might be essential where a more placid horse will become a little more animated. The text on later schooling periods discusses some disadvantages of riding fully on the bit. In this third schooling period the goal is a passive, following, even feel of the horse's reserve energy created by the leg. It develops more precise controls and a better-moving horse. These lessons must be repeated many times. By the end of the third or into the fourth schooling period the horse will be accepting passive contact at all gaits for at least short periods of time. The horse should happily accept passive contact, with an extended head and neck and closed mouth. The horse's natural carriage will change as he learns to balance himself under the weight of the rider through gradual transitions and over uneven terrain. Especially in teaching schooling, the "driving rein" is a useful technique to ensure a direct line from bit to elbow and to help keep a soft, consistent feel. Carry the reins in the hands, palms up, between the thumb and index finger with all fingers closed (see the illustration in chapter 2).

When riding on contact, one of the chief hand techniques is *give-and-take* to shorten the stride or to stop the horse. On contact, the rider takes for a fraction of a second and gives back to contact. It is repeated as necessary. This builds out of check-release at the elementary level, short checks with a looped rein. At the intermediate level, gradually drop using the voice except as a reinforcement. (For more information on give-and-take, see "Concepts and Definitions" in the introduction and the discussion of "Contact" in chapter 2.)

In transitions down, for example, from the trot to the walk, the idea is to stop posting (weight), use give-and-take with two direct reins of opposition, and then, as the horse begins to walk, close the lower leg in an alternating leg technique to encourage the hind leg to swing under the horse's belly. Hands follow the balancing gestures of the head and neck at the four-beat walk, maintaining consistent, passive contact. Avoid sitting behind and driving the horse forward in the transitions down or bumping on the horse's back. The hand must always be independent of the body. The horse needs to consistently respect the soft cues given by the rider's lower leg and to consistently trust the rider's hand by accepting a passive feel of the bit. At first it is a passive contact, and later in the horse's education it is a soft contact with reserve energy. (See tables 1 and 2 in chapter 2.)

FLEXIONS

Flexions are a relaxing of the muscles of the lower jaw. As the tension of the reins is stronger, the mouth softens while the lower jaw flexes. The rider's hand instantly softens as the horse's jaw responds. Reserve energy created by the leg is essential to quality flexions. The rider must be experienced, educated, and talented to teach good direct and lateral flexions. Most riders should start with the give-and-take technique to achieve soft, precise controls. The give-and-take with more reserve energy and two direct reins of opposition could, in time, prepare the horse to learn direct flexions (see chapters 10 to 13 on the fourth through seventh schooling periods, and particularly the discussion of flexions under "Advanced Schooling on the Flat" in chapter 11).

From the beginning of teaching passive contact, develop an understanding of flexions in order to avoid teaching a fault to the horse. Any bit acceptance faults will become lifetime habits that will follow the horse and rider like a cloud on a sunny day. If the horse is well connected and has balanced conformation of the topline, avoid having too much flexion of the poll in the third and fourth months of training. It will come naturally to horses with this conformation. This is one of several reasons to keep the transitions gradual and use the weight before the hand, and, to reinforce, use the voice before a "nip" or stronger fixed hand.

During the third schooling period, the horse on passive contact begins to turn on a combination of rein and leg aids. The first is an inside direct rein of opposition and an outside opening rein as discussed below. The result will be a softening of the inside lower jaw and slight bending of the neck laterally, particularly in the upper third of its length. *The horse should first develop a flexion of the lower jaw and have a habit of it before being taught the flexion of the poll.*

Depending on the horse's natural athletic ability and natural reserve energy or impulse, it is possible to now begin doing the lateral and longitudinal exercises suggested earlier at the elementary controls level (loose rein) and at the intermediate controls level (contact), as well as the exercises presented in this schooling period. At first, use very gradual longitudinal transitions: canter–trot–walk–trot–canter–trot–walk. The horse begins naturally flexing the poll very slightly as a result of increased tensions on both direct reins. This requires a great deal of tact and understanding from the rider to avoid having a horse that is overflexed or behind the bit. Basic flat exercises correctly ridden in this schooling program should progressively develop flexions in the horse. Therefore, many hunters and jumpers that respond to the intermediate controls and that have good conformation may not need the lesson. Flexions are taught, if necessary, in the fifth schooling period and are further discussed in chapter 11.

LONGITUDINAL AGILITY

These exercises are continued in the third schooling period. An excellent exercise is working on three speeds of the trot on the flat provided it is done in a large area and with gradual transitions. In addition to agility these exercises help teach responsiveness to the lower leg and consistent acceptance of the passive contact. A faster trot or strong trot at this stage normally has more impulse. Be certain that in coming back the horse does not get heavy-headed on the bit or disconnected. Use consistent give-and-take with two direct reins of opposition, reinforced with voice, in rhythm with the leg where needed, when shortening from the strong to the ordinary trot. At this point do not make the transition abrupt. Keep the horse's head and neck naturally extended through this stage of his training. Teach ordinary trot–slow trot sitting–ordinary trot first, as it is physically easier for most horses, mentally relaxing, and they can learn it quickly. In the short trot with some young horses, consider posting to protect the young back.

Eventually the three speeds of the trot can become a very useful gymnastic. Later in the fifth and sixth schooling periods in moving from strong trot to the short trot, you should be able to ask for a prompt longitudinal transition involving a sophisticated light contact with an educated horse responsive to the hand and leg aids.

LATERAL AGILITY

This continues to be taught on large circles and large half-circles to change direction. The horse is taught to bend softly laterally through the head and neck, to maintain connection on the line through good engagement on the turns, and to maintain a steady reserve energy or impulse on the turns.

As mentioned earlier, *the first combination rein is the inside direct rein of opposition with an outside opening rein,* combined with an inside holding leg (squeeze-release). This is to keep the horse straight and on a large circle moving forward, engaging and disengaging the hind leg. At this stage of schooling, enlarge the circle when correcting a popped shoulder. Late in this schooling period or into the fourth schooling period, if a horse pops the inside shoulder, consider using a corrective rein, the inside indirect rein of opposition in front of the withers with an outside slightly opening rein, and, of course, the corresponding leg (inside at the girth, outside displacing). The indirect rein of opposition should not replace the inside direct rein and outside opening rein combined with an inside leg to keep the horse on the line in normal turns. Turning regularly with an inside indirect rein of opposition will destroy the lateral contact on turns and teach the horse to cock his nose. This is counterproductive to straightness and connection.

In this third schooling period, turning with an inside direct rein of opposition will begin to help teach the horse lateral flexibility of the jaw, which is necessary to develop the lateral agility of the horse.

Short turns at the walk (wide) can be used early in the schooling to teach the horse to yield from the outside leg without increasing pace. Walk on the long wall, reverse direction, and return to the track on the long wall. Use inside opening rein, outside neck rein, outside tapping leg (elementary technique) at the girth to start, and finish with an outside displacing leg. Position the head and neck to the inside. These are discussed further in the next schooling period.

Neck bends are used in warm-up to stretch the muscles of the neck. These are done softly, slowly, and progressively. Forcing or jerking the lateral stretching of the neck will cause injury and stiffness. Use the leg to walk straight a certain number of steps and an opening rein alternating first on one side and then on the other repeatedly to softly stretch the neck on both sides.

As the schooling progresses on the flat, ensure that the horse remains mentally calm with his head and neck extended appropriately for his natural stage of development under the weight of the rider. Always keep in mind the horse's balancing gestures or oscillating gestures. Ensure that the passive contact with the naturally extended head and neck is consistent with the balancing gestures at the walk and canter and that the reserve energy felt in the contact is created by the leg.

JUMPING

Jumping progresses more dramatically in the third schooling period. At this point the horse has learned to approach the standards and the ground rail while maintaining the gait and speed asked for on a looped rein at the walk and trot. Avoid cantering single rails this early, as the green horse may not be ready for them without too much rating from the rider. It is much easier to teach a horse to canter a low fence by trotting to a low combination after cavalletti poles, an X to an X with one stride of the canter between the two. Once the horse is trotting the approach to the jump and maintaining the gait and speed asked for, cavalletti poles are no longer needed to regulate the speed of the approach. Eventually he will be able to handle an X to a low oxer with one cantering stride.

In setting schooling fences, there are two basic types of jumps: a vertical and an oxer. The latter is a spread fence of at least two elements that can be ramped or square depending upon the objective. Properly set, an oxer can encourage a horse to develop a consistent form. The horse folds earlier and holds its form longer than when jumping a vertical. Oxers encourage the use of the head and neck as a balancing gesture as well.

Looking ahead to the schooling that follows, working with the combinations opens a new door. At first, a one-stride combination (trotting approach) is used, then a simple triple combination, and eventually a quadruple with different distances between each jump. However, at this stage in the third schooling period, keep the jumping simple. (See appendix 1, the sections on "Starting to Teach Jumping," Step 3, and "Starting to Teach Combinations," Step 4.) Reinforce the stable approach and departure, and ensure that the horse is straight and jumps in the middle of the jump. Both now and in future schooling it is very important that the distances to all combinations be correct (see appendix 1). Adjust the distances for the stage of schooling and balance of the horse and the size of the horse's natural stride. Avoid causing the horse to quicken in combinations or to jump flat, getting out of distances set too long, or to swing to the left or right to find more room to jump out of a tight distance. Setting the correct distances in the combinations is very important to teach correct jumping habits.

Ensure that the pupil/rider knows how to pace off a distance and set simple combinations. In the event of unsureness, practice with a made horse first, and, of course, obtain outside help.

Months later, make three, four, or five cantering strides to the jump, *always at the correct takeoff.* Americans have been schooling hunters with combinations since the 1950s, before it became popular on the international jumper levels. However, currently in parts of this country and Western Europe, combinations are still not often used in the ordinary teaching and schooling program.

Combinations will help horses develop the habit of correct takeoff. The main combination is a trotting approach to an X approximately twelve to eighteen inches high, with an eighteen-foot distance between the X and a small ramped oxer at about two feet. The oxer should be twelve to eighteen inches wide, and eventually two feet wide. Later the width helps develop some flight to the jump. It is preferable that the combination is down the center of the ring or in a flat area. However, if a wing is needed or limited space requires being along the fence line, then change the direction of the combination daily so that the landing and approach are alternated. Placing rails and flat work between jumps will help as well. Do not always land and turn in the same direction when jumping. This will teach the horse to land on one lead and drift in the air. From the start, develop both sides on the flat and encourage landings on either lead.

Good habits early on in jumping and on the flat will lead to successful schooling results later on in the seven-period schooling program. Do most of the jumping at the trot during this schooling period. Using a two-beat gait with no balancing gesture, the horse stays fairly balanced under the weight of the rider at the trot. It is a slower gait, so he has time to look the jump over and make an adjustment. Horses starting should be jumped on a looped rein with a supporting lower leg so that they are clearly stabilized to the jump and can learn to judge the takeoff on their own.

When reclaiming a horse that lands on one lead all the time, analyze the situation. Be sure the horse is sound. If he is sound and remaining calm in the favored direction, then mainly work in the stiff direction or the side he does not favor. If he is always landing on the right lead, try turning to the left, being alert to other unwanted habits that might start. Use placing poles to ensure that he jumps straight on the approach and landing. However, if he does object to more work on the hard side by scooting on landing or quickening on the approach, start out on the easier side. He needs to understand the desired calm approach and departure to the jumps at this stage. Slip in considerable flat work on the stiffer side on large turns, especially during the jumping sessions. Periodically double-check the problem with a vet or an experienced equine chiropractor.

When teaching the horse to be stabilized on the flat and over jumps, stay in one setting until training is going well before moving to a new setting to test what he has learned. Then repeat the flat and jumping lessons in the new environment.

By moving simple combinations to different places in the regular working space and building a one-stride combination in a field with good footing, the location of the jumping lessons can be changed without much effort. This will help the horse to be more stable jumping in different settings and to develop boldness while also encouraging straightness when jumping and turning in either direction after the jump.

HUNTER EXERCISES

In the third schooling period, *hacking out* with a quiet older horse continues, but now it is done at all gaits. Hacking out teaches agility and boldness. If the hacking out with one or two well-mannered horses is going well, begin to teach hunter exercises to further develop stability in company. These exercises help prepare the horse for under-saddle classes, busy warm-up areas, riding to hounds in company, and general group riding.

Hunter exercises are best done in a large field or a wide dirt road. Improvise if the ideal facilities are not available. Working in a line of three to six horses, the horse halts and is passed by two or three horses at the walk, and each, in turn, halts at the top of the line. If there are only three or four horses, allow a wider distance between horses to make the line longer. Another routine is to have the line walk while the horse from the rear trots to the front and

Hacking out at the trot on passive contact (left) and on a looped rein (right). Riding out develops boldness and cooperation. At first, ride at the walk with a trained, calm horse and gradually move to faster gaits. Ride both behind and beside a calm horse. Integrate hunter exercises with trail riding. Eventually ride out with more horses if the horse's future requires work in company. Double-file, especially in a larger group, can help keep horses calm. *(Mr. and Mrs. James Young, riders; Keedie Grones Leonard, photographer)*

1

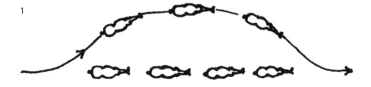

2

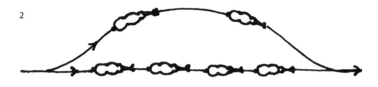

3

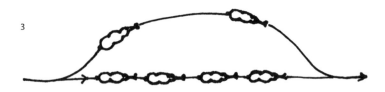

HUNTER EXERCISES

Pattern 1, the line is at the halt; passing horses walk to the front and with spacing halt. Pattern 2, the line is walking; passing horses trot to the front and then walk. Pattern 3, the line is trotting; passing horses canter to the front and then trot. Start with a small number of horses in a large flat field or area and progress over several months through these patterns. In later schooling increase the pace and space, add uneven terrain, add one or two horses, and create different patterns; i.e., include jumps. This exercise is used to stabilize a horse in company and for teaching riding in company (under-saddle classes, riding to hounds, competition schooling areas, and trail riding).

returns to the walk, asking the horse being trained to remain walking while being passed at the trot and then pass the other horses and go bravely to the front with good spacing. In this system, the same rein and leg aids taught on the flat and used in jumping and the same position based on the stirrup used on the flat and while jumping are used in riding outside in company.

There are many creative variations on these hunter exercises involving speed, jumping, and head-on approaches. The main point is to teach the horse to cooperate with the rider's aids and pay less attention to the other horses in the group while keeping a safe distance. Be certain to use the same system of riding in the field—for example, position and control techniques—as in flat schooling and jumping courses. If a horse becomes upset with an exercise, return to a slower routine to restore mental stability.

SAMPLE MOUNTED WARM-UP

The warm-up should be done off contact as much as possible in preparation for early lessons on passive contact.

Walk for ten to fifteen minutes before trotting. Work at walk–halt transitions. Change the direction on large half-circles and half-circles in reverse. Walk three or four loops of a wide serpentine. Walk in two-point over single ground rails between standards. Use gentle neck bends to stretch his muscles. The walk warm-up could be done on a trail or in an open space, carrying out some of the same exercises.

Trot on a large circle in one direction until the gait is stable. Do several trot–walk transitions. Change direction and repeat. Trot single ground poles. Take two-point at the trot to accustom the horse to the shift in weight.

Avoid "pressing" for the correct lead. Work on flat simple canter departures beside a fence before the turn in both directions from the trot. Work on the same large circle used for stabilizing the trot. Keep the canter until the horse is maintaining the speed or is stable.

Next teach a new lesson such as beginning passive contact at the trot, a short turn at the walk, and ordinary trot–strong trot–ordinary trot; teach jumping in progressive steps; or reinforce elementary controls techniques in gradual transitions. Do whatever is on the schedule or whatever needs to be improved or picked up from the past weeks.

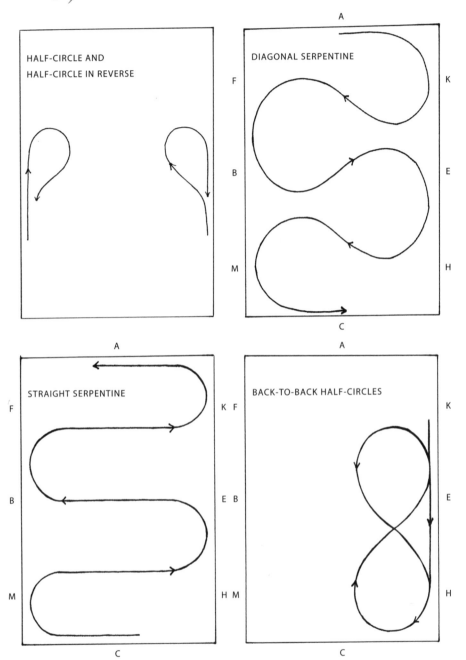

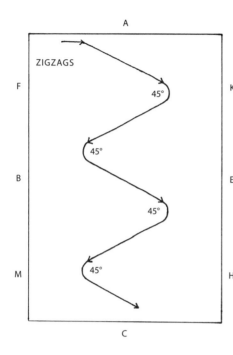

A

ZIGZAGS

F

45°

45°

B

45°

M

45°

K

E

H

C

SCHOOLING MOVEMENTS

Like the program rides, these movements should be done in a large level area (100 feet x 175 feet to 125 feet x 250 feet). Letter markers will make them easier to do, as well. The size of a standard dressage ring is too small, especially for a young, developing horse. These varied lateral movements are preferred to repetitive work on circles. Use position left/right preparing for all turns. Teach one thing at a time. First walk, then trot enlarged parts of the movement before putting it together. The goal is to teach lateral agility to a hunter or jumper, not to perfect a performance on a particular movement.

The capital letters at the perimeter of these diagrams are keyed to the Program Ride movements outlined in tables 3 through 7 (see chapters 10 through 13).

Introduce these schooling movements in the following periods:

Second/third schooling periods, chapters 8 and 9
—Half-circles and half-circles in reverse
Fourth schooling period, chapter 10
—Serpentines
—Back-to-back half-circles
Fourth/fifth schooling periods, chapter 10 and 11
—Zigzags

Introducing Lateral and Longitudinal Exercises, Jumping, and Fieldwork

10

Schooling Period 4

Schooling Period 4 lasts four to five weeks depending upon how strongly the young horse or reclaimer enters this period from the third period's lessons.

SCHOOLING ON THE FLAT AND EXERCISES FOR THE FOURTH SCHOOLING PERIOD

Work at the canter becomes a focus or priority. Develop canter departures on the desired lead, counter-canter off the half-circle, three speeds of the canter starting with ordinary–long–ordinary, and large circles and half-circles at the trot and now more at the canter.

Use smaller circles and half-circles at the slower gaits, trot and slow trot sitting.

Improve short turns at the walk and begin one or two steps of the turn on the haunches.

Introduce half-turn on the forehand to further teach the displacing leg aid.

Jump simple combinations to teach correct judgment of the takeoff at the canter and improve the horse's jumping ability, straightness, and form. (See appendix 1, the section on "Starting to Teach Combinations," Step 4.)

Jump slightly higher fences. Introduce color.

Practice trail riding/hacking out over uneven terrain at the trot and canter.

Perform hunter exercises at slow gaits.

Moving into approximately the fourth period, or fourth to fifth month of schooling, things become a little more interesting for the active rider. However, competitive-oriented riders need to continue to exercise patience and to move toward the goals slowly.

Based on the evaluation of the first three to four months, it may be necessary to go back to fill in any gaps. Horses have ways of telling the rider when things are not going well. These signals—scooting, unnecessary shying, pinning the ears, or acting cranky in other ways—differ from horse to horse and even with the seasons. Identify and solve any mental or physical problems before going on to new lessons and experiences. If there is even the possibility of a problem, repeat the early lessons more slowly, but continue some variety. Have a professional or capable amateur watch the horse go and possibly give a schooling suggestion for the problem(s) or, if a problem persists, check for soundness.

However, if the schooling has gone well, introduce less gradual transitions, less wide turns, more variety in jumping locations and distances, and gradually increased jump spreads and heights.

Further, as the flat schooling progresses, passive contact will gradually be replaced by a *soft contact with more reserve energy.*

LONGITUDINAL AGILITY EXERCISES AND TRANSITIONS

Up to this point the rider did not insist on a specific lead, and when the outside lead became awkward, the horse was allowed to trot and just slip into the inside lead. Now it is time to ask for the desired lead each time at the canter departure and have a simple change of leads off a half-circle, returning to the rail with an interruption at the trot. Be careful to use exactly the correct aids each time (inside holding leg, outside displacing leg, inside direct rein). Avoid punishing or making a scene if the horse takes the wrong lead. Double-check to ensure that the rider is not inadvertently giving the horse the wrong signal. Especially in the beginning, plan ahead. Select a direction that is comfortable for the horse and ask for it before a turn with a fence on the outside.

Changing leads off a half-circle will begin to teach the horse the meaning of the specific combination of the leg and hand signals. Cantering, trotting, changing leads, and continuing the canter is a useful longitudinal agility exercise and can eventually be done in different places and on different patterns.

THREE SPEEDS OF THE CANTER   In Period 3 an objective was three speeds of the trot; in Period 4 the focus is on speeds of the canter. Start with the ordinary–long–ordinary canter, as it is easier on the horse mentally and physically. He needs to be longitudinally agile before doing the short canter

Riding on soft contact at the end of the second beat of the short canter with the head and neck positioned right. At the third beat the weight will be on the right leading leg, and the balancing gesture of the head and neck will be at that moment the most forward. The rider's seat is in contact with the saddle at the short canter, with less weight in the ankle. The leg position (design and angles) at the sitting short canter is similar to the position at the posting trot, gallop, and jump, but with less weight in the ankle and stirrups. *(Jill Randles, rider; Reinhold Tigges, photographer)*

well. Work on the trot began with the ordinary–short–ordinary trot, because the lengthened trot can be too strenuous as well as exciting to some young horses and horses being reclaimed at that period of schooling. To lengthen the canter from ordinary canter, the rider should close the lower leg and take two-point to free the back for the lengthening. The inside leg, or the leg on the side of the lead, is the urging leg. To shorten, sit down so that the weight aid alerts the horse before using the hand in rhythm with the balancing gestures to make the transition from the long to the ordinary canter. Use the give-and-take signal, rating the stride in rhythm with the canter back to the ordinary canter. The voice may be used here to help teach or remind the horse what the weight and hand aids are asking of him. This transition is made without the horse opening his mouth or becoming heavy in the bridle, and it should be soft and correctly balanced at this point, if not precise.

Do not press for the ordinary to short canter, especially if the horse is large or just learning to carry the weight of the rider at a comfortable ordinary canter that the rider can sit to. Pressing the short canter at this point may lead to one or more of the following undesirable characteristics: an overflexed horse or a horse behind the bit, a heavy-headed horse in the bridle that is also disconnected, or an uncooperative, cranky horse. These resistances are learned and sometimes develop slowly, sneaking up on the rider/trainer. Some trainers use gadgets and muscle (hand/leg) to get the short canter. However, winning the skirmish of the short canter with such tricks may mean losing much of the calmness, softness, and quality of the horse's performance. Some horses learn the short canter more easily on uneven terrain. Be patient. Develop a whole athlete progressively.

UNEVEN TERRAIN   Uneven terrain at the trot and canter helps the young horse learn to shorten and lengthen the stride in exactly the same way that longitudinal agility exercises do in the flat schooling; i.e., ordinary trot on the flat, short trot downhill, and lengthening trot uphill. Uneven terrain helps the horse have a better attitude toward training. It puts the lesson in a more natural setting. It also develops condition and better coordination.

In schooling over uneven terrain, shorten the stride on the more level area before starting down the slope. For example, post the short trot before starting to trot downhill. If the horse quickens, walk. Eventually the horse will shift his weight and shorten on his own or balance himself going down the slope. When the horse is stabilized over uneven terrain at the trot, begin to teach the horse to canter on slightly uneven terrain. If the horse becomes unbalanced going downhill, walk or return to the trot. Repeat this until he can maintain the shorter canter down the entire slight slope.

BACKING   Walk–halt–back–walk is a longitudinal agility exercise. It also teaches responsiveness to the lower leg. Put off teaching backing as long as possible, especially with a difficult horse. All young horses should learn to go forward and halt before they learn to back. Horses back correctly with their head and neck extended and mouth closed, obediently, softly, and straight in diagonal pairs with even steps. This goal should not be compromised.

The mounted rider asking for the back after a forward walk and halt uses a give-and-take of the reins. As the horse takes a step, the hand should soften, and with each step soften and take. When first teaching backing, take just one step, walk forward, and stroke; another day, do two steps; later, three steps, and then four. This is all done over three weeks. Do not halt on the last step of the back; always walk forward promptly and then, if desired, halt. Moving forward from the last step teaches the horse to go forward from the lower leg and helps avoid teaching the young horse to resist by backing hurriedly to escape the rider. It is very important to teach backing correctly and at the right moment in the lesson as well as in the right schooling period. In this system the leg is used only to keep the backing straight. Keep it simple for the young horse. The hand is used to slow, halt, or back; and the leg is used to go forward or move over.

For a horse that is particularly resistant to backing, consider having someone on the ground tap the horse on the coronet band with their toe or a crop just as the rider is taking and giving with the hand. This is to give the horse the idea of what you expect. After one or two of these sessions, the

Lengthening the trot uphill on passive contact. The rider is in two-point position to free the back, allowing better engagement and disengagement. This photo shows the swing of the shoulder-humerus angle (see chapter 4). On level terrain the gait shortens to the ordinary trot in a longitudinal agility exercise. *(Jill Randles, rider; Reinhold Tigges, photographer)*

Short trot downhill. The rider is forward in the saddle with the correct design of position and the weight in the stirrup to free the horse's hind end. The horse's head and
neck are raised slightly for the short trot. The mouth is closed, and the horse is lightly
accepting contact while balancing itself downhill. The horse returns to ordinary trot
on the level. Uneven terrain is a longitudinal agility exercise. *(Jill Randles, rider; Reinhold
Tigges, photographer)*

person on the ground should just need to point to the horse's hoof to correct
any disobedience to the hand. Try to avoid resistance to the hand, causing
the head to be fixed above or behind the bit. Keep in mind that the head and
neck should be extended and the mouth closed. Teach the habit of correct
backing from the start, and the horse will back correctly for a lifetime. Being
able to get him to move back and take steps is not worth anything if he backs
with his mouth open or with his head in the air or rolled under, or if he rushes
back any number of steps he chooses. Reclaiming the backing is much more
difficult than teaching backing slowly and correctly from the start.

LATERAL AGILITY EXERCISES

In the fourth schooling period, there is a gradual diminishing in the size of
the circle and half-circles, especially done at slow gaits such as the trot and
the short (slow) trot sitting. There is also a gradual increase of speed on the

larger turns. It is simpler for the horse to stay coordinated at slower gaits on the shorter turns and, until he is physically and mentally comfortable, it would be foolish to try anything more difficult.

On the other hand, horses develop agility turning at speed by only practicing turns at speed. By the end of schooling, a horse should be able to gallop through a fairly short turn, but he must work up to this task. By practicing turns at the canter and then later (Periods 6 or 7) at the gallop, the horse learns to develop this agility. Trotting circles will help the horse become coordinated in stages and will teach him the movement and aids, but they cannot take the place of cantering circles and galloping turns. The exercise of galloping turns at speed to develop agility is important for the sport horse. The horse must remain calm mentally, of course, and be prepared for the exercise taught later in schooling. It is time to start gradually moving toward this objective.

SHORT TURN AT WALK   It is preferable to teach what is informally called by the author a short turn at the walk before teaching the actual turn on the haunches or the turn on the forehand. This can be done sooner with success. Walk the horse energetically along the long wall. Using a combination of an inside opening rein and an outside neck rein (pressing toward the inside but not crossing the wither or the mane) and an outside tapping leg at the girth, keep the horse walking a wide turn. The head and neck should be bent slightly to the inside or position left/right. With practice, as he understands the turn and it becomes shorter, he ends up yielding to the leg and neck rein to the rail. The younger horse catches on to this quickly because he can more easily and naturally anticipate the change of direction and going somewhere. The horse moves forward and over from the tapping (elementary) or squeeze-release (intermediate) technique of the leg and begins to learn more about the lateral aids. If the horse starts to quicken, simply use check-release or give-and-take if on contact and the voice ("walk"). This exercise should be done in both directions and should be wide at first. Eventually it becomes much tighter and closer to a turn on the haunches from the walk.

TURN ON THE FOREHAND   This movement serves to reinforce or teach the lateral aids. Some riders can inadvertently confuse the leg and hand aids, which can upset or frustrate the young horse. The horse has been taught go forward from the leg, and now the rider is asking him to yield laterally. Just as in backing, in teaching the turn on the forehand, take one step at a time from an outside displacing leg, tapping technique, then stroke the horse, then take one more step, then stroke, and so on. The half-turn on the forehand is done in four steps and it is a 180-degree turn. When schooling, walk forward after the last crossing-over step of the hind leg. The front legs mark time in place as the anchors for the turn. In teaching the turn on the forehand, if the horse is tense walk forward after the second step, then the third, and, over a period of time, he will get to the fourth step and a complete turn. Be alert to a heavy hand or a nervous horse that might lead to resistances. The hands are used to prevent the horse from walking forward instead of yielding laterally to the leg. They should not ask the horse to turn in front. The horse's eye should be in the direction of the turn. In equitation competitions and later in schooling remain at the halt after the fourth step.

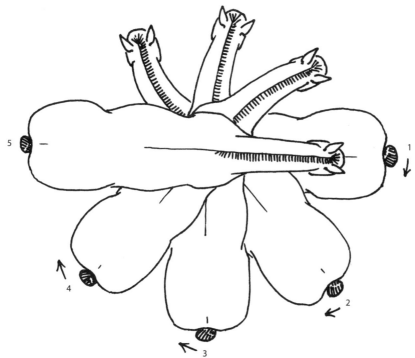

TURN ON THE FOREHAND—RIGHT
The head and neck are positioned (right), slightly in the direction the horse is turning. The right displacing leg moves the haunch to the left, with the right hind leg crossing over the left hind leg. It teaches the horse lateral leg aids. Avoid using an inside indirect rein in place of the leg.

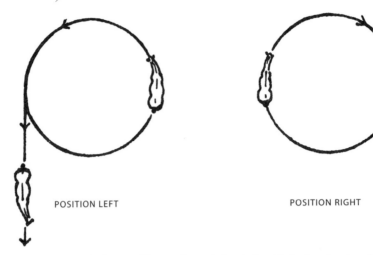

POSITION LEFT   POSITION RIGHT

The horse is on the line, tracking up through the circle with the head and neck correctly to the inside. It becomes an exercise after the circle, as the slight bend or position of the head and neck to the inside is maintained on the long wall. The inside holding leg and the outside displacing leg help maintain straightness, connection, and forward energy. It should be done at all three gaits. Follow the gestures of the head and neck at the walk and canter.

Avoid an argument over the turn on the forehand. Turning on the forehand is not, in itself, a lateral agility exercise. It teaches the horse the aids. Especially in the fourth schooling period, if it looks like it will cause a confrontation, skip it. Use a short turn at the walk to teach beginning yielding to the leg in both directions.

POSITION LEFT AND RIGHT   On half-circles and on the serpentine, begin to use "position left" and "position right." Position the head and neck slightly in the direction of the turn before getting to the turn. Very softly, not forced, the aids are an inside direct rein of opposition, a slightly opening outside rein, and especially an inside holding leg. The rider can also do the position left or right on the straightaway. It is just as though the horse is about to circle left or right, but the rider's inside holding leg and the outside rein ask the horse to track straight while positioning the eye softly to the inside. This exercise can help both the horse and rider learn to turn softly and straight.

SERPENTINES   In the fourth schooling period, begin to teach the serpentine at the trot. Serpentines should have been walked in earlier schooling. A serpentine consists of three or four very large loops to start. They can be a series of half-circles with a diagonal line coming back through the middle to start again. This is often a good time to teach a little leg-yielding off the inside leg through the center. If the horse has learned to yield on a short turn at the walk, it will come easily. Alternatively, do a serpentine with a straight line through the center. In this schooling period, trot the serpentine at an ordinary hunter trot, keeping the pace even through the turn. If the horse starts to lose the haunch to the outside or the horse in any way begins to become uncoordinated, enlarge the size of the loops, making it simpler to teach him to be on the line. Be sure to ride on correct contact, feeling the reserve energy created by the leg, and make sure the horse is connected and moving in one piece on the line through the turns. Consider doing a short trot sitting or posting on the serpentine with wide loops if the horse is large and awkward, or with the loops a little smaller for an athletic horse. It may be useful to do a short (slow) trot sitting on one loop and ordinary trot posting on the next loop. Ensure, especially at first, that the loops are large, and, if advisable, reduce the number of loops. (Teaching the serpentine at the canter is discussed in chapter 11, which covers the fifth schooling period.)

A serpentine can be done down to the end of the ring. Then change directions back across the diagonal sometimes at a strong trot, or return to the starting point at an ordinary trot, and then repeat it. Or one can do a serpentine down the ring and then a serpentine back up. Later in the fifth period if the horse is ready, improvise on the serpentine, such as cantering on the right lead, trotting to the left, trotting to the right, cantering the last loop to the left, or any combination of these. Try to keep the horse soft, connected, straight, and mentally calm with his head and neck extended and his mouth closed. (See the two line drawings at the end of chapter 9.)

COUNTER-CANTER   The counter-canter is an exercise that teaches balance and lateral agility. It is a useful lateral exercise for both the young well-conformed horse and the horse with a head and neck carriage problem. The lowered head in the direction of the lead helps a high-headed horse stretch down softly on contact and encourages a stronger balancing gesture. It can be a lifetime regular exercise for many horses.

In the fourth schooling period teach the counter-canter on a half-circle or, if it is easier for the horse, change direction at the canter across a diagonal line. Be certain not to confuse the young horse during this period by teaching the

The counter-canter exercise is used in developing lateral agility and later in teaching the flying change. It can also be useful in schooling to encourage a horse to lower his head and accept contact. This horse is finishing the second beat (diagonal pair) of the three-beat canter and is bent slightly left in the direction of the lead with his head and neck extended, mouth closed. The rider demonstrates a united and efficient position with a soft, passive contact following the balancing gestures of the canter. *(Lorraine H. Stanley, rider; Reinhold Tigges, photographer)*

desired lead and the counter-canter at the same time. Avoid overdisciplining a young horse for taking up an undesired lead regardless of which exercise is being undertaken. Other horse/rider combinations may prefer to get the counter-canter from the trot on a straightaway in a large space or field or on the rail with haunches out.

LEG-YIELDING   A hunter or jumper should be able to yield laterally to the leg without increasing the speed while being schooled on the flat and when jumping a course. The horse should remain calm and connected with ground-covering, agile strides. The trot is the best gait to begin to do this exercise because it has reserve energy, has just two beats, and the head and neck are steady. It helps teach straightness and helps make the horse more rideable especially over a course of jumps. It is not presented here as a step toward collection but as a practical exercise done in natural balance for a hunter or jumper. This exercise can benefit the rider by developing coordination of the aids.

Many horses have one side that they yield to more easily. When first teaching any new lateral movement, consider starting on the softer side in order to introduce it more easily. Then tactfully emphasize the stiffer side.

If the horse responds to the aids for a short turn at the walk, a turn on the forehand, and a large serpentine or half-circle, it is ready for this exercise. The same holds for teaching the rider. In the leg-yield the horse travels both forward and sideways, crossing his legs. The horse moves with his eye slightly away from the direction of travel. Ideally the shoulder should always lead the quarters.

The following three patterns can be used in teaching leg-yielding.

1. Leg-yielding from the quarter line to the rail; i.e., right to left: The horse is looking right and yielding left from an inside right leg. Before the end of the ring or sooner, if a resistance or the loss of impulse occurs, straighten and go forward.
2. Leg-yielding from the center line executed as described above in 1.
3. Leg-yielding on a circle spiraling out to a larger circle—i.e., on a twenty-meter circle gradually move out to a thirty-meter circle—using an inside leg with the head and neck in the direction of the circle. This pattern is too difficult for this fourth period.

More advanced leg-yielding exercises are discussed in chapter 13.

ZIGZAGS   Long zigzags can be done at the walk during this fourth schooling period if the horse is yielding well at the individual short turns at the walk. They are 45-degree turns, more like short turns at the walk, or beginning turns on the haunches. At the trot they are too difficult for most horses at this time.

Leg-yielding at the trot off the right leg to the left, the head and neck positioned slightly right, with the right fore crossing in front of the left fore. The horse is calm and comfortable. *(Liz Callar, photographer)*

In the beginning the horse may quicken a little from the lateral leg. Use the voice ("slow") and the hand softly, giving and taking, telling him not to go faster but just to yield away from the leg. The zigzag should be started at the walk. The short trot sitting can be added if the horse is progressing easily at the end of this fourth schooling period. (See the line drawing at the end of chapter 9.)

TRAIL RIDING AND HACKING

Quiet hacking and cross-country work continue during the fourth schooling period. Hunter exercises are done at faster gaits, such as passing at the trot and passing at the canter while the group walks or trots. The horse listens to the rider's aids and cooperates with the rider while other horses are working at different gaits in different directions. Hunter exercises are generally useful in schooling a show hunter or jumper to become used to company. Some trainers and riders go to a warm-up area at a horse show to teach the horse to "go along and get along" in company. However, the hunter exercises at home are more efficient, for if they start to go wrong, the direction, pace, or exercise can be changed to suit the young horse's needs. Reestablish stability and try again. Everyone in the hunter exercise is there to adjust to the green horse. Hunter exercises at faster gaits will, of course, prepare the horse for hunter trials and riding to hounds. When teaching schooling to riders, organize the right combination of horses, and conduct the early sessions from the ground. This exercise can also be used to teach a rider to control a horse in company.

JUMPING AND COMBINATIONS

The X as a teaching and warm-up fence has been used in America for more than fifty years. It is low, inviting, and encourages straightness. However, a low vertical should also be used to encourage even folding, especially with lazy horses.

Combinations become more important as jumping is taught more seriously in the fourth schooling period. Continue to combine longitudinal and lateral agility work on the flat and over uneven terrain with trotting poles and a variety of combinations. (See appendix 1 for information on setting combinations for different levels of schooling.)

Each jumping day, review the jumping preparation exercises. In any specific day proceed only if the simple exercises over poles, single X, a low vertical, and a one-stride in-and-out are going well; that is, the horse is stable and straight on the approach and departure.

If the jumping is off to a good start and the horse is hacking out boldly and seems to be brave around the stable, begin to change the variety of the low obstacles. Raise the low poles up to eighteen inches. Add a little color to the low jumps. The horse should respond to the same squeeze-release leg to the jumps that are used with him on the flat. Remind the rider to allow the freedom of the head and neck, step down in the heel, close the lower legs in rhythm with the gait, and ask the horse to go forward to jump bravely. In this system of riding, a position based on the stirrup is used that carries throughout both the flat and jumping work. Integrate the jumping with the flat training. (See appendix 1, the section on "Starting to Teach Combinations," Step 5.)

DEVELOPING AN ATHLETIC JUMP

Begin to change the focus of the jump lessons from stabilization, boldness, and obedience to teaching the horse to develop the skill of figuring correct takeoff at the trot and canter in the next three schooling periods. Trotting to the single low jumps and using a one-stride in-and-out are preparation for this goal. Continue to trot into combinations because it is easier for the horse to jump from the trot. (The trot is a slower two-beat gait without balancing gestures.) Continue to trot new or strange single low jumps, which will develop the horse's agility, confidence, and boldness. This will make it simpler when more color is added to the combinations and later during cantering courses with a variety of jumps.

When jumping at the canter, the correct takeoff can be consistently produced with combinations; i.e., the triple combination (one-stride to one-stride). This is done by adding on to the one-stride combination that the horse knows well. Make certain the horse is jumping straight and in the middle of the fences. Be alert for any quickening or instability. Be sure that he is prepared for the jumping lesson by the previous day's work. He should be sound and consistently brave when jumping. A horse can have many good sessions, but one negative session will last in his memory longer than one would imagine.

Look for correct figuring of the takeoff, good use of the head and neck, athletic folding, straight jumping, and landing on either lead comfortably. As the horse becomes braver, jumping single jumps with color, begin to add a little variety to the fences in the combination. In the next schooling period, when adding a third jump or one with color, if a ground helper is not available to change jumps, first jump the third fence as a single fence. Angle it very low, by itself. It can be as low as a foot or six inches, if need be. Thus when jumping the entire triple, the horse will have already jumped the new fence at a lower height. Anything that prevents the possibility of refusing, scooting, or ducking out should be planned. However, do not regularly let the horse see or sniff the jump before jumping it, as it will become a habit.

Responsiveness to the lower leg emphasized in flat schooling and learning boldness through hacking out are two ingredients that help prepare the horse for this stage of jump schooling.

If the young horse jumps ten jumps ten times, all straight, with correct takeoff, folding well, and with calm, alert approaches and departures, he is developing the habit of good jumping. If, on the other hand, only four or five are correct, he may be learning something else. Habits, good or poor, can be learned quickly. After dismounting and at the end of the day consider, without rose-colored glasses, how things actually went and how they might go tomorrow. Plan the next several sessions accordingly.

Later when the young horse or reclaiming project has mastered the triple in-and-out at simple one-stride distances, consider doing other types of distances in the combinations, especially in the fifth, sixth, and seventh periods. They can be longitudinal agility exercises such as one-stride to a three-stride to a one-stride to a bounce.

Looking ahead, gradually use combinations to move a horse toward doing courses. Trot into a vertical to a three-, four-, five-, six-, or seven-stride line. Also trot into a one-stride in-and-out and then three to six strides to a simple one-stride in and oxer out. Continue to trot to the first fence. This makes figuring the correct takeoff from the landing of the first fence easier, as well as making the first jump more accurate. It ensures learning correct takeoff at the canter. Later in schooling, canter into the lines, but do not rush this process. First develop more miles at correct takeoff with distances set for the canter stride. Throughout the schooling and for other suggestions for combinations refer to appendix 1 ("Setting Combinations and Jumps for Different Levels of Schooling").

It is possible but not always productive at this stage to hire a skilled professional rider to canter single fences, rating the horse's stride to the correct takeoff. It can look simple, but do not be deceived. When even an advanced amateur rides the prospect, it may become obvious that the horse has not learned to figure correct takeoff but is depending upon the rider to rate and place him for the jump.

The objective is to teach the horse to jump with minimum direction from the rider, including correct judgment of the takeoff. Much later, when difficult courses are ridden and the horse has been taught to be rated softly on the flat and to figure correct takeoff, the rider and the horse together will negotiate these courses. If necessary, in certain situations a skilled professional rider may be more useful at this point.

PROGRAMMED RIDES AND EVALUATION

As one comes to the end of the fourth schooling period, which is approximately four to five months into schooling, it is time for a more formal evaluation of progress. Prepare a small programmed ride or a warm-up routine. This is not a dressage test as in the classical dressage school, but it is a schooling flat test for the sport horse in a large arena where the horse is connected and on soft controls.

For example, ask the horse to perform a mini-program ride by entering the center line of a large ring (100 to 125 feet x 175 to 250 feet) at the trot on contact, tracking left, doing a half-circle along the left wall, picking up the right lead canter on the diagonal line, doing a half-circle along the other long wall, having a simple interruption at the trot, picking up the left lead canter, and cantering down the center line, trotting, and then walking. There should be considerable distance between transitions and movements, so the size of the ring will be very important in planning the ride. These program rides for the sport horse could also include a turn on the forehand, several halts, gradual transitions from the canter to the walk and halt, backing, half-circles in reverse, serpentines at the trot and integrated throughout the flat ride, trotting single Xs and single verticals, and trotting into a one-stride. Plan it so that the horse turns in different directions on landing. In this evaluation ride, designed for your horse, do not emphasize precision. Go for quality of movements and transitions. The horse should be responding cooperatively, staying balanced under the weight of the rider through the gradual transitions and on wide turns and circles, connected (moving in one piece with energy) on the turns, traveling on the line, and engaging the hind leg by swinging it up under the belly. Either passive contact or soft contact with impulse should be maintained throughout the gaits and all transitions, with the head and neck extended and mouth closed. Also include some work off contact, demonstrating that the horse has remained mentally and physically stable after the work on contact.

See the end of the chapter for a sample formal program ride and additional suggestions for using a program ride in a schooling program.

Work over uneven terrain is part of the evaluation. Trot at least a low vertical and/or a simple one-stride combination in a field or open space.

Consider videotaping the evaluation. In using the evaluation, be realistic in planning future schooling. That which went well should be emphasized as well as what needs to be improved. Does the horse have a good attitude toward the rider's aids? Is he cooperative? Is he stabilized, maintaining the gait and speed requested? Does he consistently accept the contact? Is he demonstrating some form of lateral and longitudinal coordination and agility? Once again, emphasize the quality of the movement and the soft controls and transitions over precision. Getting it done at the letter should be less important than the quality and balance of the movement.

SAMPLE MOUNTED WARM-UP

Walk off contact for ten to fifteen minutes after mounting. Go on a walking hack with an older horse to a different flat schooling area or walk in the schooling area on different patterns such as the serpentine, the half-circle in reverse, the center line, and the diagonal line. Work in some soft neck bends, halts, short turns at the walk, and several ground rails. For the rider, exercises such as two-point, rotating the arm to stretch the muscles of the shoulder, rotating the toe and ankles, rotating the neck, and dropping and picking up the stirrups at the walk should also be useful.

Start on looped reins, emphasizing elementary controls and stabilization. With calm horses, move to passive contact early in the trot warm-up, such as four minutes. With an energetic horse, spend a longer period ensuring the horse is stabilized before moving on.

Begin trotting and stabilize the gait on a circle in one direction and then the other. Include two speeds of the trot (ordinary–slow–ordinary) and transitions from the trot to the walk. Incorporate trot poles and individual small verticals. Trot a half-circle and a half-circle in reverse as well as other large

TABLE 3

PROGRAM RIDE

FOUNDATION SCHOOLING RIDE FOR YOUNG HORSES, HUNTERS, AND JUMPERS

Review elementary controls and have a clear understanding of stabilization. A good working position is essential for successful schooling. To be performed on a looped or loose rein and, where noted, passive contact. (See part 1 of the text.)

The capital letters noted for each movement refer to positions in the diagrams of Schooling Movements in chapter 9.

		Movement
1	A-C	Enter ordinary trot; loose reins
	C	Turn right
2	B	Walk
	F	Ordinary trot
3	H	Half-circle; on the diagonal line approaching the rail, left lead canter
4	C	Canter to C
		Large circle (approximate width of arena, suitable for young horse)
		Canter to E
5	E	Ordinary trot
	K	Walk
6	A	Halt; half-turn on forehand, walk to K
7	K	Ordinary trot
	H	Canter, right lead
8	A	Canter to A
		Large circle
		Canter to E
9	E	Ordinary trot
	H	Slow trot, sitting
	C-M	Ordinary trot

patterns to change directions. These might include the serpentine. Do many gradual walk–trot–walk–halt–walk transitions.

Begin cantering on a looped rein. Do not change directions until the first direction is stable. Do several simple changes of lead with long interruptions at the trot on the circle. Move to passive contact and then soft contact with more reserve energy if it is going well. A flat, straightforward canter departure on the desired lead is expected. Also, if the horse is ready and can do it easily for a warm-up, canter half-circles to change direction with a long period of the trot before taking the new lead.

10	C-M	Leave track to approach fence
	M-F	Take trotting jump
		Ordinary trot to A
11	A	Large circle to establish passive contact
	KXM	Lengthen stride at trot
	M	Ordinary trot
12	C	Halt; back four steps; walk forward
13	H	Ordinary trot
	K	Canter, left lead
	A	Large circle
14	FXH	Change direction over jump. Elementary or intermediate controls. Simple change of leads, if necessary
15	F	Half-circle; simple change of leads on the diagonal line approaching the rail
16		Canter to E
	E	Walk, gradual transition through the trot
	K	Gradually go to loose reins
17	A	Turn down center. A-X establish passive contact
	G	Halt, stand quietly five seconds; leave ring on loose reins
18	Stabilization of horse	_____
19	Contact/impulse/quality of performance	_____
20	Position of rider	_____
21	Efficient use of aids	_____

• Large space; minimum of 100 feet x 175 feet.

• Large comfortable circles and wide turns (i.e., approximately 60 feet) before smaller circles and turns.

• Gradual, soft transitions are more important than precision or accuracy.

The jumping should be on elementary controls. Do the low, simple jumping before finishing the canter warm-up. If a horse is young or tends to be placid, he may jump better if he has a little more energy. However, if the horse is overendowed with reserve energy, do some warm-up jumping after all of the canter work.

Then start the lesson of the day. It might be longitudinal agility exercises such as two or three speeds of the canter or lateral agility exercises such as trotting a serpentine, trotting less-wide turns, or cantering wide turns. It may be teaching jumping or the short turn at the walk, or it may include working over uneven terrain and doing hunter exercises in a group. The warm-up should have gotten the horse listening, loosened up, cooperative, and stable so that the lesson of the day will go well.

USING THE PROGRAM RIDE IN SCHOOLING

Beginning in this schooling period, sample programs for different levels of riding and schooling will be provided at the end of each chapter. Review the earlier section in this chapter on "Programmed Rides and Evaluation." Do not press your horse to do the more advanced program rides if they do not meet your schooling objectives. Some may want to use portions of the advanced rides. Adjust the rides to suit your horse's level.

The rider needs to be able to coordinate the four natural aids using the techniques suitable to different levels before training a young or inexperienced horse. These program rides may be used to evaluate riders as well as the horse. See the line drawings at the end of chapter 9 for the location of the letters used in these sample program rides.

Program rides can be an important method of schooling the horse and evaluating his progress beginning in this fourth schooling period.

Practice the movements individually as an integrated part of a progressive schooling plan. Start with elementary controls–level techniques and aims and gradually move to passive contact and then to more impulse on soft contact if the horse's ability and temperament allow it.

The equine and human pupil should remain calm but alert in performing these individual movements. If there is any concern expressed, lower the level of the movement until a good performance is achieved on that level. Do not force or progress faster than common sense and horsemanship dictate.

11 Progressive Combinations, Uneven Terrain, and Flat Work without Sacrificing Softness
Schooling Period 5

The fifth period lasts four to five weeks, depending on the horse's progress as gauged by the rider's evaluation at the end of the last schooling period.

Regular riding with a consistent method and techniques is essential to progress. Be sure that the horse continues to be calm, sound, and cooperative as his education is stepped up.

Any advance planning or program set down must be flexible and vary with different horses as well as with different riders. Riders schooling horses need to be careful that their own riding position and aids, as well as their understanding of schooling theory, are up to par. They must be able to communicate clearly on the horse's schooling level and correctly interpret the response of the horse to the rider's requests.

Progress may seem to be slow, and the "quick fix" for short-term success is always tempting in schooling. Enough trust can be gained so that a horse can be stepped up in one or two areas of schooling such as jumping. In these situations, it is a question as to whether such riders are giving the horse a good foundation for his future schooling and new experiences. Is the horse learning to figure correct takeoff for himself while at the same time learning on the flat to be softly rated by the rider?

Later in the seventh period and beyond, the courses and challenges may become more difficult, requiring the rider and horse to figure the correct takeoff together and to ride difficult lines as a team. Therefore, at this stage in the fifth period, the advanced rider schooling the horse must be very careful to teach the horse a proper foundation, which requires the rider to be passive at the correct moments.

The horse should be comfortable with different riders. Part of the test or evaluation at the end of this fifth period might be to have a good amateur rider do the program ride that was used to evaluate the prospect at the end of the fourth period. This will ensure that the horse really is learning the correct leg and rein aids for longitudinal and lateral movements and that the horse is stabilized; that is, maintaining the gait and speed asked for on the flat, over jumps, on uneven terrain, alone, or in company.

On the other hand, if the rider schooling the horse is at the intermediate or advanced level, it may be appropriate to select a professional not involved with the schooling of the horse to ride and evaluate him at the end of this fifth period. Actually just watching a different rider with the horse for a half-hour on the flat and a little over jumps is in itself valuable. In teaching schooling in a group, it is a useful exercise for the teacher to have pupils change horses and evaluate the strengths and weaknesses of the new mount. The regular rider can also observe the horse's reaction and performance with a new rider.

KEY CONCEPTS AND EXERCISES FOR THE FIFTH SCHOOLING PERIOD

For *jumping* use more combinations to develop the natural athletic ability and to give the horse positive experiences in finding the correct takeoff from the canter.

Use simple, low trotting courses with some color in a flat area.

In *fieldwork*, stabilize the canter and hand gallop over uneven terrain. Use longer periods at the canter in the open.

Include individual low, inviting natural fences with schooling in the open. Integrate them with lateral and longitudinal agility exercises over gently rolling terrain.

Perform exercises in company at the right level of difficulty for the young horse.

Integrate longitudinal and lateral agility exercises into all fieldwork. Use the same position of the rider based on the stirrup, the same aids or controls, and the same schooling principles and techniques used in the flat riding and jumping.

During *flat work,* require more precision without sacrificing softness, back from a halt after the trot and return to the trot to further develop coming back and to encourage impulse forward and responsiveness to the lower leg. Practice changing leads with fewer strides at the trot or walk, rather than a longer period of interruption as encouraged in the earlier schooling periods. A half-turn on the haunches develops cooperation with the lateral aids. If the horse is ready, serpentines at the canter and zigzags at the trot further develop lateral agility.

Start to introduce specialized schooling on the flat primarily for the jumpers and some hunters. Many horses can skip this schooling and be quite successful show hunters in the four-foot working division, and many riders will be more successful in their schooling if they do not undertake a specialized level on the flat. In other words, a horse schooled to be stabilized off contact (Schooling Periods 1 and 2), then schooled to passive contact (Schooling Period 3), and then educated to *soft contact with more reserve energy* (Schooling Periods 4 through 7) may be more than sufficient for most successful horses and riders. A young horse being introduced to specialized schooling on the flat must have an experienced rider. The rider inexperienced in specialized schooling on the flat should first learn the method and techniques on a trained or made horse.

Gradually develop riding on a soft contact with more reserve energy and connection. If appropriate, in short periods practice the short gaits with more impulse. This is done with some horses to improve movement and performance on some jumping courses.

Increase the degree of reserve energy–impulse at the slower gaits.

Develop the lengthened trot from the strong trot.

Practice canter departures from a walk.

Practice soft, abrupt halts from a trot and from a canter, always moving forward after the halt.

JUMPING

Jumping progresses with more combinations to develop ability and to teach correct judgment of the takeoff from the canter. In this schooling period and the next, go from triple in-and-outs to quadruples and quintuples. For example, ask the horse to trot into a combination consisting of five jumps (low vertical, canter one stride to an oxer, two strides to an oxer, three strides to an oxer, one stride to an oxer) followed by a change in direction. *If this begins to upset the horse, have less variety in the striding and/or reduce the number of jumps in the combination or drop back to a simple one-stride or a simple triple until calmness and confidence are restored.* (See appendix 1, the section on "Starting to Teach Combinations," Steps 6 and 7.)

If a ground crew is available, it is ideal to build a combination from scratch as the combination is being schooled, starting with the first element, an X or low vertical. Trot in; canter out. However, riders may have an inexperienced person helping, or are often in a group with several young horses. In such cases set up the combinations to be used in this period all at one time. Have a one-stride combination, a triple combination, and a quadruple combination, each with simple cantering distances for the young horse being schooled. These combinations should be in locations that allow an approach from either direction and a straight departure with the choice of turning left or right. Further, if schooling a horse that is a Thoroughbred or energetic type, it may be desirable to have a ring fence or barricade on the landing, but usually not closer than six strides. On the other hand, if it is a half-bred or lazy type of horse, it may be prudent to be sure that there is no barrier near the landing. This last will encourage the horse to jump the combination more energetically as he looks off to an open space.

When the horse does the first two combinations correctly, he is ready to try the quadruple during this or the next period. On the other hand, *it may be that, although a variety of combinations are planned, only the simple ones are actually realized. Change the plan if the horse is not mentally calm or performing well.* Further, make certain that all the jumps are low so that they can be jumped confidently and without causing unsoundness.

Also, in the situation with a limited or no jump crew, first trot the last element very low, then trot the second element at an angle, and then put the triple together. The chances of success the first time through the combination will be better. This is, of course, in place of the preferred method of slowly building the combination up from the X to the second element to the third element to the fourth.

If the horse tends to land on one lead more than the other, be certain to turn in the opposite direction on landing. It is important not to upset the horse in the process. For example, use ground poles on each side to go straight and forward in the combination and on landing, and then turn in the direction that he does not favor. Work in a simple interruption of the leads from the trot (or walk), and then continue through the turn. Alternate this with similar exercises after the combinations such as leg-yielding at the trot before cantering off on the inside lead or making a gradual transition to the walk followed by a turn on the haunches or a walk and a halt. Making a fuss about the lead on landing will jeopardize the jumping lesson at this stage, and the horse will become worried about the landing and the departure from the combination.

Also, when trotting single jumps, practice angling them. Alternate the angle unless the horse favors a side. Then angle them to the corner the horse does not favor, away from the drift or favored lead. Do it without jerking the horse's head in the air for the lead or getting unduly concerned about it. The goal will be achieved in time, assuming the horse is sound and the flat work is progressing. At this point keep the drifting, lead, or other problem from becoming the point of focus when the objective should be to develop the horse's ability to figure correct takeoff and develop athletic jumping. Put combinations together in such a way that they will encourage straightness and good form and discourage poor habits from developing. It is important to continue to try to teach or emphasize one thing at a time.

To repeat, working with combinations, plan to go straight on landing and turn in the direction the horse does not favor with a simple interruption of the lead, making sure that he stays mentally calm. If he is stiff in one direction, do not interpret this as stubbornness or resistance. It is simply physically difficult for him, and it will take some gradual work to improve it. Add in flat schooling with all of the jumping. For example, jump a combination, and then along the long wall, make transitions to the walk, halt, back, and walk. Then proceed again to the combination in the direction with the desired approach. The next time, do a simple interruption of leads three times in a row, provided that it is not too taxing on the horse mentally. The next time after the combination, do a half-circle in reverse and approach the combination from the chosen direction. If the horse is naturally energetic with extra reserve energy, do flat work at slower gaits with fewer transitions. If the horse is lazy, try a little extension at the canter and possibly try an extension at the trot, being careful not to exhaust him for jumping. Speed produces impulse, so after a gallop or lengthening on the lazy horse, return to the trot for the approach to the combination. There should be more reserve energy created for the jumps.

The jumping and flat exercises should be integrated. Riding currently has become so commercialized that inadvertently some things are done for convenience rather than for the good of the horse. For example, lessons are given for a limited or previously fixed time. In other situations, lessons are offered by a traveling coach or teacher who may have a package lesson for the day. One either fits into it or does not. This in itself is not suitable for a young horse on a regular basis. Some horse-show coaches used to doing flat work, schooling jumps, and then going into the jumping competition build their lesson around the competition warm-up. In fact, a few of them offer instruction only at horse shows between divisions or before classes, at the end of the horse show, or early in the morning before the horse show starts. This can be good for teaching the rider in certain situations, but it is often not in the best interest of the young horse's schooling to be fixed by time, location, or lesson plan.

At the beginning and end of any type of jumping session, be sure the horse is stabilized on the approach and departure of the jumps. If not, do not proceed with the lesson until the horse can at least do something simple demonstrating that he can maintain the gait and speed at the approach and departure; i.e., a low vertical or simple one-stride in-and-out trotting in.

On a particular day, at the end of the combination work, do a little light, easy flat work by itself or go for a hack with a mature, well-behaved horse. Integrate the flat work, hacking, and jumping in different ways each time the horse is schooled over jumps. At this stage avoid following the exact order or routine, especially for some horses.

Introducing simple, low courses at the trot should be fairly easy provided schooling has been done in different locations, jumping a variety (color and shape) of individual, low fences and combinations such as one-stride and simple triple combinations. Begin a jumping course by ensuring the horse can trot each fence on the course individually, maintain the gait and speed on the approach, and be calm and stable on the landing. Then put together a line of jumps (at a minimum of seventy-two feet apart, which would be five cantering strides or, trotting into the line, six cantering strides) with a single fence in, a ramped oxer out, and then a second line, and perhaps on another day a third line. Eventually the horse should be able to *trot in and trot out of the lines* going straight and looking for the next jump while maintaining the gait (trot) and speed asked for by the rider. Later, when first going to a strange place, put a very low course together and trot all of it. In the next period, consider trotting in and cantering out of the lines. This should easily follow the combination work that has been done. When the horse finally goes to his first local horse shows in the seventh or later schooling period, trot the courses even though he is doing more at home. Low-level hunter horse shows provide a valuable education for field horses, cross-country horses, and jumpers, as well as hunter show horses.

In summary, be sure that the horse is very confident, calm, and bold trotting courses in a variety of settings. Begin by trotting individual fences and combinations. Then put a course together trotting one line at a time over a period of several schooling sessions that also include flat work.

FIELDWORK WITH JUMPING

In the field, continue the longitudinal exercises over uneven terrain, but begin to expect a good performance at the canter; that is, the horse should begin on his own to shorten the canter down the hill, lengthen or open up the stride going uphill, and return to the ordinary canter on the more level part of the field.

Before emphasizing the canter over uneven terrain, it is important that the horse has learned at the trot to shift his weight on his own going downhill with a minimum check-release reminder from the reins and voice of the rider, and to lengthen the stride going uphill with a minimum effort from the rhythmic squeeze-release leg of the rider. In this way the horse is able to maintain the speed as well as the gait, by shortening downhill and lengthening uphill. When he has nearly perfected this at the trot, he is ready to undertake it at the canter, which is more difficult because it is a three-beat rather than a two-beat gait and it is faster.

A young horse has to learn to coordinate his legs and body under the additional weight of the rider while staying balanced and maintaining the gait and speed going downhill and uphill. Make it as simple for the horse as possible so that he can engage, disengage, or stay connected, moving in one piece, without being inhibited unnecessarily by the rider's weight.

The rider should be certain to keep the horse's back free; that is, get up in the stirrups in two-point or galloping position when going uphill. The horse should feel the weight shift, which will encourage the lengthening. This will take a good strong engagement (the swing of the hind leg under the belly) and disengagement to keep the pace even uphill. Going downhill, the horse shortens the stride. The rider should be certain to keep the horse's back and loin free of weight by keeping most of it in the stirrups. On a steep downhill let the hip angle open to avoid getting the upper body ahead of the horse's motion.

Include single low jumps with stabilization in open fields. Be certain that the jumps are on fairly level ground and located thoughtfully; that is, keep in mind the horse's individual needs while jumping, and be sure to plan ahead so that each time is a successful jumping effort. If this is going well, begin to add a little natural variety in a field, such as brush, to the single verticals. On another day, move the vertical to a slight incline up.

Much later when the horse is ready, jump the vertical down the slight

To develop boldness and experience, jump a variety of low fences in the open as well as in a ring. The horse is starting the landing phase, the front left leg on the ground first. The head and neck are raised for the landing. The hind legs will fold tighter when they reach the top rail of this low jump. *(Frances C. Hooper, rider; Keedie Grones Leonard, photographer)*

incline. Continue to ensure that the footing is suitable. By the end of the fifth period, the horse should be able to jump single jumps over uneven terrain at the trot. Do not consider cantering these fences until the horse is very stable cantering over uneven terrain and can jump very well on the flat from the canter with correct figuring of takeoff through combinations and over single fences.

Individual jumps in the open will allow the horse to integrate jumping with his flat work over uneven terrain and will also develop boldness and confidence jumping in any setting.

Gradually increase the periods of the canter over uneven terrain. This will help develop the young horse's wind and stamina as well as teach him to be stabilized at the canter and the gallop. These long canters in the open should always be under control with the horse mentally stable. If he starts to become upset, stop, return to the trot or walk, and then try again on that or another day. Avoid having long periods of canter in the open on days when the horse is frisky due to weather or lack of sufficient turnout. If the young horse bucks and becomes playful in the open, do not find this amusing, because it will become a lifetime habit. It will not help the horse to be a consistent performer in the open if he associates the field with running off or bucking.

The early introductory lessons at the slower gaits in the previous periods will help make this month's objective to canter in the open for a longer time and at different speeds more attainable.

All longitudinal and lateral agility exercises should be applied in the open with the same rein and leg aids that are used on the flat. Most important, the horse should respond as cooperatively, softly, and precisely in the open as he does on the flat in a ring. This is a point that currently escapes some riders and trainers. Perhaps this is due to overspecialization and focusing on a finished competitive, isolated performance. Some horses today seem to be drilled on the flat, in the ring, or between the dressage boards with intended emphasis on "suppleness" and "obedience," but the same horse in the field is strong and less responsive. Their training for obedience to the hands and legs seems not to exist in the open. Something may be wrong with the training program or the system if the schooling on the flat does not carry over to uneven terrain, the jumps, and different settings.

Often one sees horses getting so upset that they ignore the rider's aids. Horses in "training" seem to take considerable extra hardware, muscle, bracing, and setting to crudely control them in the open. However, all the schooling on the flat is supposed to make them more ridable in different settings, including riding over uneven terrain and riding outside the ring in a field.

It is not unreasonable to expect a correctly schooled sport horse to jump a course of hunter fences in the open or especially for a jumper to cleanly and calmly jump a stadium course in a field.

GROUP WORK

Schooling a horse to perform with manners in an under-saddle class or to be a hunter/hack type that can go to a local horse show on one weekend and later be in a hunter trials or hunter pace or possibly participate in a group trail ride requires a horse that is trained to obey rein and leg aids in the open and in company. Correctly trained, he will be a more pleasant ride and a safer and sounder horse.

At the least, a sensible four-year-old or an older horse being reschooled with the right temperament that is started correctly in the earlier periods should, by the fifth month, be doing hunter exercises at the walk and the trot and passing the group of four or five at the canter.

When schooling a young horse aged three to five with no previous experience, it is more realistic to expect the hunter exercises to be done at the walk and trot and to reserve the canter in this exercise for the next period. There are obvious exceptions; for example, a half-bred or lazy horse may need to develop more stamina outside and will not be troubled by cantering in and around other horses. As a matter of fact, he may enjoy it more and develop some reserve energy through the faster gaits and the conditioning that will help his contact work and flat schooling.

SCHOOLING ON THE FLAT

LONGITUDINAL AGILITY

During this fifth period, the longitudinal agility exercises are more advanced and precise as well as soft.

In the exercise "three speeds of the trot," the strong trot develops some consistent lengthening. The lengthened trot is introduced on a straight line on a flat area in short sessions. Be sure the horse is fit enough and prepared for the exercise. The horse must remain mentally calm, although it will be necessary for him to be alert with reserve energy. Some horses, such as Thoroughbreds, do lengthening more easily than others. If they do it easily in this period, do not practice it often. Work on the ordinary and short trot. If the horse does not do a strong trot with some lengthening easily, do the ordinary–strong–ordinary trot often with appropriate rest periods. Eventually he will learn to have a consistent strong trot and some lengthening.

For the canter, the horse should be doing the ordinary–long–ordinary canter well by the end of this fifth period. All transitions are more prompt provided the horse is coordinated enough.

In this month begin to improve the short canter: ordinary–short–ordinary. This is done by starting with the ordinary canter, sitting down, opening the hip angle, and holding the shoulders back for the weight aid. In rhythm with the balancing gesture, take back a little more, follow forward a little less, and repeat, keeping the rhythm of the canter. With the use of the voice ("slooow") and a supportive lower leg, the horse begins to understand a little shorter canter. It will take three to six weeks before the horse can actually do it softly and consistently. Later in the horse's career when he can canter with a balancing gesture at a shorter-than-ordinary canter to a fence requiring a small arc jumping into a line, the merits of having taken time teaching the short canter will be obvious. If the horse can do it softly and be rated easily with a slight balancing gesture at the short canter, he has been taught successfully.

Unfortunately, the short canter can be forced in a lesson or two. A certain kind of rider can feel that he has made a great accomplishment. However, if the short canter is forced, the horse can learn to be heavy on the hand or pull—exactly what should not happen when the horse is being rated on a course of jumps at the canter.

The modern sport horse should be soft, cooperative, athletic, and fluid at the ordinary and shorter-than-ordinary canter. He should not be heavy, upset, or overflexed with a set head and neck. The goal is an energetic and alert but calm athlete.

Three speeds of the canter is one of the important exercises to be schooled at a high level given the horse's natural athletic ability, quality of movement, and temperament.

Spend a great deal of time on the flat asking the horse to lower his head and accept the soft contact in a connected, athletic, agile balance with precision. Often horses on a serious course of jumps will get their head a little high because they are anxious, not well prepared, or a little upset and ambitious, or because the rider is a little anxious, perhaps using too much spur and/or holding too much with the hand. It does take a special kind of competitor to stay calm and consistently use the controls the horse has been taught. Even an experienced working hunter doing the four-foot to four-foot, six-inch, courses can become aggressive in anticipation of the challenge that he is about to be asked to complete. It is important that the rider remains soft as well as precise in rating the stride. Doing so will yield a more fluid performance, and in show hunter competition, a rough performance will be penalized. However, in the stadium phase of a horse trials or in a jumper competition, especially at the lower levels, the riding can be at the expense of a smooth performance and sometimes without any penalty.

The subjectively judged working hunter rider will try to ride smoothly and in an educated way between jumps, but the jumper rider may become more aggressive and interfere with the softness and at least the aesthetic performance. Further, course designers build for the exceptional few horses in a top jumper class. Over time, as our riders and horses have met the challenge, the courses have become more difficult. Many horses struggle to meet the big and difficult courses. Eventing has the same course design problem, as it too is judged objectively (i.e., faults are scored, not quality performance). However, the top competitors are often pleasing to watch because the horses have been trained to the challenges of the course (turning, ratability, form), and both horse and rider have above-average talent.

The use of the weight aid in developing the longitudinal agility of the horse is important. It can be a valuable preparation or signal to the horse that the hand is about to ask for a transition down. This will also be useful in riding a course of jumps, either in a ring or cross-country. The horse will begin to feel the weight change and shorten or steady himself with the weight if he has been taught in earlier training to pay attention to and obey that natural aid. (See tables 1 and 2 in chapter 2.)

In longitudinal exercises, especially on a young horse, get up in the stirrups when lengthening the canter. It makes it easier for the horse in that it frees his back and allows the engagement and disengagement. Later, at the end of his schooling, the rider may sit to lengthen on the flat if a stronger leg is needed or if that technique works better. Always get up in the stirrups off the back when cantering, trotting, or walking uphill. Uphill, the horse will have to lengthen at each of the gaits in order to keep the pace even.

CHANGE OF LEADS   The change of leads with a simple interruption is a longitudinal agility exercise, but it can be added to lateral exercises, such as half-circles, half-circles in reverse, serpentines, and very large figure-eights. Up to this point, the simple interruption has been at the trot with many steps. To avoid anticipation, do not pick up the canter until the horse is calm and listening. The goal is to reduce the trot to three to five steps during the transition. For example, in doing the half-circle in reverse, on the diagonal line when leaving the rail, trot three steps rather than eight, pick up the inside lead, and continue to loop back to the fence. If the horse should begin to "hurry" the change of lead, simply increase the number of steps at the trot until he is waiting. Combining this exercise with lateral movements is very useful in the training of the horse. Be sure to allow some space for the horse to mentally and physically perform the transition and the turn. If too many of these are added or the horse is pressed too hard, he will begin to stiffen and worry, and the lesson will become counterproductive.

Normally, the young horse is not yet ready for decent, straight, flat, prompt departures through the walk. This requires more connection and reserve energy. Teaching the horse to canter from the walk too early often results in a lifting of the front end and a disconnected first stride. Later this learned poor departure will have to be corrected, and it is difficult to reverse.

LATERAL AGILITY

Lateral agility is simply the ability of the horse to turn athletically. Ideally the horse should be connected and on the line on the turn. The pace should stay even, along with the reserve energy or impulse. It is very useful to have a rail or fence on one side when first teaching or practicing lateral movements. A rail helps the young horse to be straight—for example, when doing a turn on the haunches or a half-circle in reverse along the rail. The rail may also be used so that the half-circles and circles are better planned, an even size, and therefore more productive as well as simpler for the horse.

SERPENTINES   Before cantering a serpentine with simple interruptions in the center, the horse should be able to canter half-circles and half-circles in reverse well.

The serpentine at the canter is a very useful lateral exercise. Adjust the size of the loops to fit the level of schooling of the horse and the purpose of the lesson. For example, if the horse is young or is not well coordinated under the weight of the rider at the canter, the loops should be large and the serpentine first done at the trot. Once the horse is doing ordinary–long–ordinary canter and is shortening at least a little from the ordinary to a shorter canter, he probably is ready to canter the serpentine with a simple interruption at the trot.

When first introducing the serpentine at the canter, it is best to have a very large, flat, enclosed ring. When doing them in a field, mark out corners to have an idea of the boundaries and to make the loops consistent and even. If the horse begins to anticipate the lead change, trot a loop and canter a loop. Canter a loop and trot a loop. In that way both sides are worked evenly at each gait. (See also the section on "Serpentines" at the trot in the fourth period in chapter 10 and the line drawings at the end of chapter 9.)

If the horse is not ready for the serpentine at the canter yet, there is no need to worry. It can be taught in the next period. The only cause for concern is forcing it, stiffening the horse, and setting up a pattern for resistance in this and other movements.

In time the horse should be able to canter the serpentine maintaining the counter-canter. Later in schooling it will be done with the flying change and other variations of lead changes in the center of the loops.

ZIGZAGS   The zigzag at the trot can be improved in this fifth period, provided the horse is first walking them well. Start with the short sitting trot and plan to have long lines of the "zig" and the "zag," as well as fairly sharp turns. This will be a series of quarter turns on the haunches from the slow sitting trot. Do not plan to do zigzags at the canter for at least the next two periods, if appropriate at all. However, the zigzag at the canter may be possible sooner for an older horse being reclaimed. Cantering a zigzag is not an essential exercise for most horses. (See the line drawing at the end of chapter 9.)

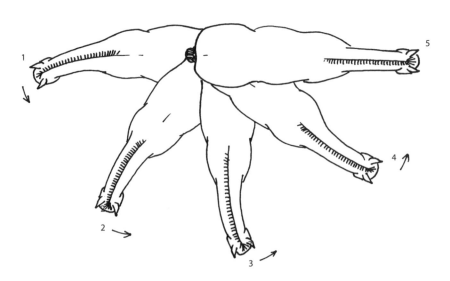

HALF-TURN ON THE HAUNCHES—LEFT
The head and neck are bent slightly left in the direction of the turn. The right foreleg crosses over the left foreleg. The leg aids are the dominant aids. The horse should walk forward promptly after the last step. First teach it from the walk. Later the same aids can be used to teach a short turn at the canter, which is useful on a jumper course.

HALF-TURN ON THE HAUNCHES   A half-turn on the haunches from a walk should be performed fairly well in this period. If the horse can do a fluid short turn at the walk in the fourth period, he should be able to do sharp, fluid turns on the haunches in the fifth period. Start to teach the turn on the haunches, with outside forefoot crossing in front of the other forefoot while the back feet essentially mark time in place. It should easily evolve from the fluid short turn at the walk. It may be necessary to teach it one step at a time. Halt and reward after each step. The horse's head and neck should be extended and the mouth closed through the turn on the haunches, with a soft bend of the head and neck in the direction of the turn. In the finished movement the horse walks into and out of the turn on the haunches. The aids are an inside holding leg, an outside displacing leg (starts the turn at the girth and finishes the turn four inches behind the girth), and two direct reins of opposition. The inside rein can be slightly opening, and the outside rein can be a bearing rein as needed. The corrective rein, inside rein of opposition behind the withers, may be used.

SCHOOLING POINTERS

In general the lateral exercises involve changes of direction and giving the horse the sense that he is going someplace, thereby making it a little more interesting or less boring for him. This will help hold his reserve energy. Avoid repeating the same circle over and over and having some kind of battle about falling in or out. Keep it practical and interesting.

The lateral aids thus far have been reinforced by teaching turns on the forehand and haunches, with a little leg-yielding from the inside to the outside on the half-circles returning to the rail and on the serpentines with the diagonal line. Keep it simple for the young horse. Do the exercises that will give the most return for the time and energy the horse has in training; i.e., turning at the canter and longitudinally rating the canter stride (three speeds of the canter). The canter is the gait used to negotiate a course of jumps. The horse needs to learn to turn easily at the canter as well as to adjust his stride.

Both the experienced trainer and pupils just learning to school should remember that the horse can become not only physically tired but mentally fatigued while doing lateral and longitudinal agility exercises.

Plan all exercises (longitudinal and lateral) so that they make some sense in the daily routine of schooling the horse. Prepare with some kind of warm-up plan that progressively leads the horse from simple movements that he understands to the new lesson of the day. Achieve some success and then move to something easier. Simple interruptions with long periods of the trot should progress to short periods of interruption at the trot between the canter. Canter departures on wide circles lead to canter departures off trotted half-circles and half-circles in reverse. All of these are leading up to several simple changes of lead down the center line, staying connected, straight, and alert but mentally calm. Later the exercise becomes the flying change of leads.

ADVANCED SCHOOLING ON THE FLAT

If exercises have been done correctly using the four natural aids (weight, voice, hand, and leg) with the correct techniques, at first at the elementary level—check-release of the hand off contact—and then with the intermediate/advanced technique of give-and-take back to contact, in coordination with the weight and leg aids (moving from the tap to the squeeze-release technique), the horse is probably ready for flexions. In fact, a well-conformed prospect may have actually developed them naturally through the longitudinal and lateral exercises that have already been done on contact. Therefore not all horses will need this lesson. Remember also that not all riders are able to successfully give the lesson.

Just as other lessons have been introduced in several short periods, such as contact starting in the third period, flexions also should be taught in many short lessons. The schooling to this point and the horse's conformation will determine how quickly he accepts and responds to the lesson. (See the discussion of "Flexions" in chapter 9 before continuing with this section.)

To begin, the muscles of the horse's lower jaw must be relaxed so that, in response to tension stronger than normal contact, there will be a softening or a flexion of the jaw. When shortening the gait, changing the gait, or halting, the chief aids are two direct reins of opposition and the lower leg. The hand technique is a give-and-take action of the rein with the squeeze-release technique of the lower leg in coordination with the horse's efforts. Later the "half-halt" may be used as a hand technique as well.

Because the prospect or young horse has done circles, half-circles, and serpentines on passive contact and now a "soft contact" connected, on the line, and with more reserve energy, the upper third of the length of the neck has become softer and more flexible laterally. Correctly ridden, these lateral patterns will also begin to produce more lateral flexibility in the jaw.

Flexion of the poll should be taught after the flexion of the lower jaw. Lateral flexion teaches the horse to bend his neck slightly and yield promptly while turning and changing direction. The softening and relaxing of the jaw and poll provide softer and more precise control. During this period if the horse requires it, introduce the flexing of the neck at the poll. As a result of increased tension on two direct reins of opposition, the more prompt but soft longitudinal exercises will help develop flexibility at the poll.

SOME CAUTIONS ON ADVANCED SCHOOLING ON THE FLAT

All the longitudinal and lateral exercises, especially in the fifth period, will help the horse develop correct head and neck carriage. Such carriage comes because the horse has learned to carry the weight of the rider in doing these transitions, and the head and neck position gradually changes.

Often today one can see people fake the advanced education of the horse through gadgets, drilling with draw reins and side reins to make the horse carry his head and neck in a manner similar to advanced schooling. They then put an experienced, talented rider in the saddle and present the horse for sale or competition. The horse will indeed look trained to the uneducated eye but will in fact often have a "frozen" head and neck (currently referred to as "the frame") and a resisting attitude and will not really know much about how to carry himself on a turn, in transitions down, or over a course of jumps. Unfortunately, one can observe that, if enough horses have a fake head and neck carriage with a stiff body and poor connection, people begin to see it often, develop an eye for it, and think it is correct. Further, if a judge puts a blue ribbon on such a horse (he is required to give it to one of the competing horses), that ribbon implies that the carriage is correct. Others begin to copy it without realizing that the judge may not have actually approved of it.

In developing the young horse's head and neck carriage, be careful that it comes from transitions and turns progressively developed. The horse then learns to carry himself in one piece under the weight of the rider. The training should bring out the best in the horse's natural athletic ability. Longitudinal and lateral exercises will eventually change the head and neck position as the horse becomes more connected and agile. With a young horse a difference should be noticeable in this fifth period.

Advanced schooling (forward riding) on the flat, if correctly done, can help a horse be more precise and soft in transitions, improve overall performance, and give the horse consistent reserve energy on soft contact. However,

TABLE 4

PROGRAM RIDE

SAMPLE INTERMEDIATE-LEVEL SCHOOLING RIDE FOR HUNTERS AND JUMPERS

This ride is to be ridden on contact unless otherwise specified. Depending upon the horse's progress, the contact can be passive or soft contact with more reserve energy.

Review the purpose of riding on contact and how it is achieved in chapter 2.

The capital letters noted for each movement refer to positions in the diagrams of Schooling Movements in chapter 9.

		Movement
1	A	Enter ordinary trot
	C	Track left
2	H	Slow trot, sitting
	K	Ordinary trot
3	A	Serpentine of four large loops (tracking right at C)
4	C-M	Leave track to approach fence
	MBF	Take trotting fence
	A	Ordinary trot
5	E	Circle, passing through X; returning to E, walk
6	H	Halt; back four steps; walk
7	C	Ordinary trot
	MXK	Change direction
8	A	Circle (same size as previous circle)
9	FBM	Lengthen stride at trot
	M	Ordinary trot
10	H	Canter, left lead
	A	Large circle (approximate width of arena)

if advanced schooling is overdone on the flat, a horse may develop too much reserve energy. That is, the horse's mental calmness may have been disturbed, making the horse too sensitive, energetic, or aggressive for his schooling objectives. This may also reduce the quality of his movement and reduce the horse's usefulness to a large number of riders. It may be desirable, however, for some horses that have poor conformation (which makes good connection, contact, and agility difficult) and for horses that tend to be a little lazy by nature to develop extra reserve energy on soft contact in order to achieve the schooling objectives.

11	FXH	Change direction over fence, changing leads if necessary; simple change through a trot or flying change
12	F	Half-circle; on returning to rail, maintain counter-canter to E, with bend of neck in direction of the leading leg
13	E B	Simple change of leads through walk or a trot Ordinary trot
14	C C-M	Halt; half-turn on forehand; walk Gradually go to loose reins
15	B-F F	Establish contact Ordinary trot
16	A G G-C	Turn down center Walk Gradually go to loose reins and leave arena
17	Stabilization of horse	_____
18	Contact/impulse/quality of performance	_____
19	Position of rider	_____
20	Efficient use of aids	_____

• Large space; minimum of 100 feet x 175 feet.

• Large circles and turns comfortably executed before smaller circles and turns.

• Gradual soft transitions are more important than precise transitions.

• Please see the comments on "Programmed Rides and Evaluation" in chapter 10, Schooling Period 4.

• Individual or several movements may be used in schooling before putting the ride together. Adjust the ride to fit your horse's level of schooling.

Horses that are fully on the bit (classical dressage system) can produce brilliant gaits but can also have a highly alert mental state. This is not conducive to natural athletic jumping; long, low, ground-covering, efficient strides; or manners appropriate for an amateur horse. Do not confuse this system with advanced schooling in forward riding.

If his job is to be a three-foot, six-inch, Amateur Owner hunter, to go in company across country, or to be an equitation horse, it may not be necessary or desirable for him to have some parts or any of the advanced schooling in forward riding on the flat. If, on the other hand, the plan is to develop the prospect into a jumper that has the potential to be a serious competitor, consider doing the forward riding advanced schooling on the flat as part of his program.

In summary, the early schooling periods began off contact with looped reins to teach the horse to respond to the lower leg and to develop a correct three-year-old carriage with stabilization. The third schooling period began passive contact with an extended, low, natural carriage for a young horse. Later, the contact remained passive between the transitions and in coordination with the weight, leg, and hand asked for more quality, prompt, soft transitions. Next a consistent contact with more reserve energy developed as the horse became stronger physically, developed more stamina, carried himself in one piece under the weight of the rider, and accepted soft, precise controls. Some horses will need more work on contact to develop more reserve energy, and some will need less, depending on the objectives. All of the objectives are important. Each requires skill and quality riding. In other words, a quality hunter going cross-country in company is just as important and valued as a jumper that goes cleanly, alertly, and calmly about his work. Each is doing a job well for his rider and with a good performance.

SAMPLE MOUNTED WARM-UP

The fifth period warm-up is done both on and off contact. The more energetic or nervous type of horse should have a longer warm-up off contact, to be sure that he is stable at the ordinary gaits, through transitions, and over low jumps at the trot before moving on to contact. Keep in mind the limitations of the horse's physical strength and mental fatigue.

Walk for ten to fifteen minutes and then trot, canter, and trot low fences off contact, establishing stabilization; that is, maintaining the gait and speed asked for on elementary controls. Work on transitions, changes of speed at the trot and canter, changes of direction on all formal patterns, and backing for one to four steps (always followed by prompt forward movement).

On contact, depending on the horse's needs and temperament, do one or more of the following exercises that he already knows. Do three speeds of the trot. With a younger horse, avoid too much lengthening trot in the warm-up. Do an ordinary–strong–ordinary trot, two speeds of the canter (ordinary–long–ordinary), and the counter-canter in a large area perhaps established on a half-circle or a large full circle. A few of these exercises will not tire the horse either mentally or physically. They should establish the necessary cooperation for the day's work. Select different exercises for another day's warm-up.

Then start the planned lesson—for example, parts of a program ride or repeating one transition, putting together a simple course, teaching better lengthening at the trot, and/or improving the quality of performance in a movement or transition. Be certain to finish the mounted work on a pleasant note.

When that lesson is finished, consider going on a walking hack or at least grazing the horse after he has been ridden and before he goes back to the stall.

When teaching schooling, have a ground discussion with the pupil at this point. For someone who has schooled fewer than ten horses, it is wise to discuss often the horse and his progress with an informed, experienced person and/or to refer frequently to this text.

If you have had a long-range schooling plan laid out on a calendar by days, weeks, and months, consider changing the schedule as you reevaluate your schooling progress. Rewrite the plan and calendar based on the progress of your specific horse.

Developing Quality Movement, Experienced Jumping, and Program Rides

12

Schooling Period 6

As the horse is both mentally and physically able to accept work on contact for longer periods of time, a better quality of performance can be asked for. Continue to practice and improve the exercises and movements introduced in the earlier schooling periods, and throughout the schooling keep a good gauge on the horse's mental and physical stability.

Successfully taught transitions make it much easier to move toward the ideal quality performance of the young horse when building to the end of his schooling. In schooling, precision is not as important as the quality of the movement. For example, in the canter–walk transition, it is more important to have the horse make the transition with his head and neck extended, mouth closed, hind end connected to the front end, and a smooth forward transition into a long, fluid, and forward walk. Making the transition exactly when asked for but with the head in the air, the mouth open, the hind end disconnected from the front end, with the first steps at the walk short, will not lead to consistent quality transitions. Once the horse-and-rider combination begins to feel quality transitions, the precision will be much easier to obtain with preparation and feel.

In order to maintain the best of the horse's natural athletic movement, he should move in a connected forward balance 90 percent of the time. When practicing the short gaits such as the short canter with extra reserve energy and abrupt transitions such as the canter–trot–halt–trot–canter, the trainer must integrate the ordinary and lengthening gaits with the shortened gaits.

Do not confuse advanced flat work for the sport horse, hunter, and jumper with classical dressage tests. The idea is not to progress along the classical dressage steps and simply stop at one point for the hunter and at another point for the jumper. The forward riding system is an entirely different schooling program on the flat that emphasizes the horse's natural athletic forward balance and integrates certain exercises in order that he can better perform his job. In the sixth schooling period, the exercises and schooling "program rides" (large area) have more challenging movements than the lower-level dressage tests (small area). This is as it should be, because the horses are being asked to jump in the open, over uneven terrain, and on courses with different striding and to turn often at speed with agility. Flat work is directed toward jumping in a large flat space and in a field. The position and controls used to teach the horse flat movements in this system are the same for jumping and field riding. It is clearer to the horse, and the rider is able to perform at a higher level using one position and one system of controls in all settings.

KEY CONCEPTS AND EXERCISES FOR
THE SIXTH SCHOOLING PERIOD

In flat work, use program rides to teach the horse to calmly obey a series of different gaits, speeds, and transitions requiring lateral and longitudinal agility.

Lateral agility exercises in this schooling period include short turns at the gallop developed from short turns at the walk, turns on the haunches, and leg-yielding.

Longitudinal agility exercises include three speeds of the canter with soft precision, transitions with ordinary–long–ordinary–short–ordinary to encourage more cooperation with the aids, abrupt transitions to be done smoothly and calmly (trot–halt–trot), and canter–halt–back–canter transitions to develop coming back and impulse forward. They also include practicing ordinary canter–short periods of fast gallop–ordinary canter transitions to stabilize at the gallop and to develop wind and stamina, jumping simple low courses in the field at the trot with cantering between the jumps, and jumping on the flat progressively more difficult courses from the trot and the canter.

For fieldwork, use hunter exercises to teach the young horse to work calmly in company and over progressively more difficult terrain at the trot and canter in different locations. Practice all flat work exercises in the open; and for a field hunter, a hunter trials horse, a cross-country horse, and a competitive jumper, introduce more jumping in the open.

SCHOOLING ON THE FLAT

The program ride exercise and evaluation are a series of schooling exercises on the flat to demonstrate cooperation with the rider's aids and to improve the

Lengthened trot on soft contact in a field. It can be part of a longitudinal agility exercise; i.e., short trot–long trot–short trot. The horse demonstrates a long, low, ground-covering stride. The rider demonstrates a soft contact with impulse and a position based on the stirrup used riding on the flat and jumping. *(Liz Callar, photographer)*

quality of the horse's transitions and movement. The program ride is done in a large area in forward or hunter balance. The ride encourages long, low, ground-covering, connected, efficient strides. The head and neck are extended, and the horse performs calmly on soft contact. The horse should now do movements worked on up to this sixth period with more quality. The transitions are soft, and more precision is required.

The rider must prepare for each transition using the weight aid in advance of the give-and-take hand. The horse cannot perform an accurate transition without preparation and planning from the rider. Consider a situation of cantering and then making the transition to a walk at the letter B or at a marker in the middle of a long wall. The rider feels the degree of energy and contact at the canter and applies a bit more or less leg, using the weight aid to shorten the stride and also give-and-take of the hand in rhythm with the balancing gesture. In order to be precise with the walk at a specific point or letter, the rider either needs to start early with the horse that has reserve energy or start closer to the place where the transition should happen with a horse that does not have much natural energy. The rider needs to prepare the specific horse for the transition to the walk at least several strides before the point where the walk is intended.

It is fairly difficult to ride a program ride that has a number of different transitions in succession while keeping the horse calm and the transitions soft and precise. It takes practice and skill on the part of the rider to help the horse do it.

These skills can be carried over to riding a course of jumps because the balance and movement of the horse and the position and controls of the rider are the same for the program ride in this hunter flat-schooling exercise as they are on a course of jumps. It is not one balance, movement, position, and set of controls for the flat and then a different position, balance, and movement for the jumping course. Therefore do not confuse the program ride in this schooling system with the classical dressage tests.

Be sure that the size of the arena or ring in which the schooling takes place is large, such as one hundred feet wide and two hundred feet long. If restricted by space, limit the number of movements and plan the ride so that there is sufficient time and space between transitions. Better still, move the exercise to an open field and mark four corners for the working area.

Choose a program ride suitable for the horse in this sixth period and make adjustments based on the horse and the working area. Put together two or three movements at a time over at least several schooling days. Sample program rides are discussed at the end of this chapter and chapters 10, 11, and 13.

Practice the specific movements repetitively, and occasionally do them at the same place each time in order to develop in the rider a feel of the timing and distance needed to get the horse to perform at a specific marker. When the horse understands what the transition is, he will be more responsive, and by the third or fourth one the timing will be better. Normally avoid letting the horse memorize the order and location of the movements on the ride.

Performing the entire program ride well is a good indicator of progress. Each transition should be preceded and followed by a different movement. If the horse can remain stable and cooperative doing all the different transitions to a satisfactory level of performance, the rider can be confident that the previous work has gone well. If, however, the horse becomes upset, begins to have poor head carriage, or shows other signs of resistance when being asked to do a series of different transitions, reevaluate the ride. Perhaps the transitions are too close together, the ring is too small, or the horse is being asked for transitions that are beyond him both physically and mentally at this point.

In short, the program ride may be used to evaluate the horse's progress. In some cases it may indicate that he is being asked for too much too soon by the trainer. Therefore, tailor the work on the flat in this period with the information gained from evaluating the program ride.

As on a course of jumps, if the rider is agile, coordinated, and practiced, the program ride will be much easier for the horse. For trainers teaching schooling or for those riders with limited experience, first practicing the program ride on a made horse will help avoid unnecessary complications in the schooling program.

LATERAL AGILITY EXERCISES

Repeat and practice earlier lateral movements such as large circles, half-circles in reverse, serpentines, and zigzags intelligently integrated during warm-up or the day's lesson. The horse should be on *consistent soft contact and connected, with quality reserve energy.* The pace should stay even on the turn. Further, the horse's head and neck should be extended, with the mouth closed. There should be lateral softness in the jaw and a bend in the upper part of the neck in the direction he is going. The horse should turn easily in either direction. If any lateral movement is difficult, consider enlarging the size of the turn and reducing the gait and speed.

The short turn at the gallop can be introduced if the short turns at the walk and turns on the haunches are soft and accurate in both directions, other leg-yielding movements are responsively completed, and the canter is stable (the horse can do ordinary–long–ordinary canter and ordinary–short–ordinary well). The short turn at the gallop or the short turn at the canter can be used by a sport horse such as the show hunter in a handy hunter or equitation class, by the jumper in competition, and on some cross-country courses.

The aids to perform the short turn at the canter or gallop are essentially the same as the lateral aids for the short turn at the walk and the turn on the haunches. Canter down one side of the rail. Open the hip angle—but not behind the vertical—and apply the weight aid to signal the horse that he is about to shorten the canter. Use give-and-take in rhythm with the balancing gestures of the head and neck, or a half-halt, to establish the short canter. Then apply an inside direct rein that becomes a slightly opening rein, combined with an outside neck or bearing rein and an outside active leg at the girth. As

"On-the-line" cantering (second beat) through a turn in forward balance. The head and neck are positioned slightly to the inside on this wide turn. The rider's aids are inside holding leg, outside displacing leg; the inside direct rein has become an inside bearing/neck rein and a slightly opening outside rein. The rider is in two-point position based on the stirrup, and the pony is connected with reserve energy, calm, and stabilized. *(Sari Deslaurieres, rider; Liz Callar, photographer)*

the turn begins, use an outside displacing leg at the girth. The inside indirect rein behind the withers (corrective rein) is a traditional rein aid and may be useful in some cases, but on a course of jumps the former is often more efficient. The goal with a sport horse is not to do classical pirouettes but rather an agile, athletic turn with an extended head and neck, because he may need to jump a fence or to lengthen the stride immediately out of the turn.

When the horse is fairly confident at the short turn at the canter on the flat and is cooperating calmly with the aids, practice doing a short turn by jumping a single fence, performing the short turn on landing to the left or right, and jumping back over the same fence. In preparation for this exercise, set up two standards without any rails. Canter between the standards, do a short turn, and canter back between the standards. When the horse is doing this well, add the jump. In many cases the fence will help the turn and keep the horse interested and understanding what is expected of him. (See the photograph of a short turn at the canter in the color gallery.)

If the horse is performing turns on the haunches from the walk and zig-zags at the trot and three speeds of the canter, and is stable cantering to single fences, he should be ready for this exercise. If, on the other hand, the horse begins to be stressed, stop the exercise and work on the individual parts: lateral turns, three speeds of the canter, stabilizing to single fences, and practicing judging correct takeoff at the canter through combinations. Then come back gradually to teach short turns at the canter.

LONGITUDINAL AGILITY EXERCISES

In the warm-up and in the lesson, integrate previously learned longitudinal exercises such as three speeds of the trot and three speeds of the canter with varied transitions, at first gradual; i.e., canter–trot–walk–halt–back–walk–trot–canter.

Gradually begin to shorten the transitions, making them more prompt, and being certain that the horse is connected and moving in one piece, accepting the contact with head and neck extended and mouth closed. During this schooling period, provided the appropriate large space is available, teach canter–gallop–canter to stabilize the horse at the gallop and to teach cooperation with the rider at faster speeds. Doing so will also develop wind and stamina in the young horse. At first restrict the period of the lengthening to eight to twelve strides.

The horse's temperament and progress to this point will determine how to approach this exercise. If the groundwork and schooling have gone well and the horse is mentally and physically stable at the canter and the easy gallop in the open, this exercise should go quite smoothly. If, on the other hand, it upsets the horse, go back and break up the parts that prepared the horse for the exercise and concentrate on them. Be sure that the horse is getting regular work and turnout before doing any of these exercises, especially the fast gallop.

Provided the person schooling the horse is an advanced rider in this system, jumpers and some hunters will benefit from abrupt transitions and shortened gaits with more impulse. Three speeds of the canter done softly and precisely will set the rider and horse up to be a very ratable and ridable team over a course of jumps. In this period, begin to ask for the ordinary canter–lengthened canter–short canter–ordinary canter with the goal of being able to do the long canter to the short canter with soft, precise controls. The preparation for this should be ordinary–long–ordinary, then ordinary–short–ordinary, and then to drop the ordinary in between. It may be done over a period of time, but if the horse has learned his lessons well through this period, start teaching it and getting some results within one to four lessons. When the horse can be rated promptly and softly from the long to the short canter, it will become extremely useful on jumper, equitation, and some hunter courses.

Riding over progressively more uneven terrain at the canter will enhance the three-speeds-of-the-canter exercises on the flat. This setting also helps maintain the horse's pleasant attitude toward his work.

Backing from a halt after a canter should be preceded by gradual transitions such as canter–trot–walk–halt–back–walk–trot–canter. This can be shortened by dropping the trot and halting through the walk and walking before cantering after backing. This method of teaching transitions should be used to prepare the horse for the eventual canter–halt–back–canter transitions. The exercise will develop the horse's ability to respond to the weight and hand aids softly and lightly. It requires some flexion of the lower jaw and poll. There must be preparation for the transition and coordination of the weight, hand, and leg aids. This exercise also promotes responsiveness to the lower leg and impulse forward. To prevent unsoundnesses, it should be taught gradually, done accurately, and performed in moderation.

It is not necessary for most show hunters to do the short, semicollected gaits. In some cases, it would be undesirable because it could upset them mentally or be harmful to the quality of their movement, especially if these exercises are overpracticed.

Never do the canter–halt–back–canter exercise in anger or as a punishment even though one sometimes sees such behavior in the warm-up area at competitions. Unfortunately for the horse, it is an expedient exercise for riders who have to hop on a poorly trained horse that has no mouth. The rider inflicts a little pain and makes the mouth sensitive. When the horse enters the ring minutes later, that sensitivity might last the length of the course when the rider touches the horse's mouth. Although a prize might be won on that day, the future riders of that horse will have to pay for this quick fix in schooling.

A horse that is pressed with abrupt and crude transitions will develop a very hard mouth and often will become mentally upset after a period of painful techniques. In time the performance over jumps often deteriorates, rails are pulled, the jump becomes flat, and the approach and landing are quick. However, correctly done backing from a halt after a canter can be a sophisticated exercise that advances the horse's longitudinal agility and makes him more cooperative, responsive, and useful for his job.

JUMPING

During the sixth schooling period, continue to keep most of the jumps low, between two and three feet. Continue to add color and variety to certain fences and to jump simple combinations in preparation for the day's jumping lesson. Combinations help teach correct takeoff and jumping form. If the horse remains calm and is able to handle it physically, every one or two weeks introduce a challenging combination. This might include a one-stride to a three-stride to a two-stride. Once the horse masters this and jumps it confidently, change it and build something different. Remember to work up to each new combination by regularly doing individual fences, one-stride, and simple triple combinations that are set for developing confidence, form, and correct figuring of the takeoff. Begin to add some height and width at the end of these simple combinations; i.e., two feet; two feet, six inches; and three feet. Then progress from there: two feet, six inches; two feet, nine inches; three feet, three inches; and so on. Use the combination to teach confidence with height and width. Add the height and width to the course after the horse is comfortable jumping that height and width in combinations.

If the young horse is progressively introduced to increasingly higher jumps in combinations and jumps them in good form at the correct takeoff, he will be more likely to handle that height comfortably and accurately on a course.

To summarize, combinations up to this point have taught the habit of a stable approach and departure, to determine correct takeoff, and to develop an individual horse's jumping form under the weight of the rider. By the sixth period, the individual horse's jumping potential should be fairly clear to the rider. Still, remember that when practicing combinations even on an experienced horse, the reins should be looped and the rider passive. An override through the combination defeats the purpose of the combinations in this schooling program. (See appendix 1, the section on "Starting to Teach Combinations," Step 8.)

JUMPING PROBLEMS

Even with the most careful schooling, for a variety of reasons, jumping problems can arise, and corrective jumping may be necessary in the sixth schooling period, especially for those horses being reclaimed. As the height, width, and variety of single fences increase, be alert to spotting a potential problem. Stop and thoughtfully correct it as soon as it becomes apparent. Review earlier chapters on jumping, and see appendix 1.

Combinations are among the most useful tools for correcting jumping faults provided the horse is physically comfortable and mentally stable doing them. The combinations must be correctly set and on good footing. Reclaimed horses should have been given the chance to relearn jumping, including practicing the approach and departure to single fences, developing straightness and a slow and careful approach, taking many low jumps, and going through combinations to help them develop confidence in determining the correct takeoff. However, they may bring with them to the schooling program certain habitual jumping faults such as drifting, landing on one lead more than the other, or twisting behind. Even a young horse that has been jumping simple courses and individual fences outside can develop some jumping faults as the height is increased if he has physical limitations or a previously unidentified injury.

Be sure that the horse is sound before proceeding. Perform a soundness check from the ground: do joint flexion tests, move on small circles, have a professional watch the horse, and, if necessary, consult a qualified equine veterinarian.

If the horse seems to be worried about the jump and is not mentally stable, reduce the height and retreat to the simplest types of jumping, including rails on the ground, Xs, and low verticals. Proceed from there only when it is clear that the horse has a foundation of stabilization.

It may be, though, that the horse being schooled has height and width limitations to his ability. Actually, most horses do; some simply turn up earlier than others. If this is the case, he may be a nice three-foot horse but tends to struggle and get worried when the jump gets to three feet, three inches. Readjust the schooling goals for this horse. In this case it will be helpful to have done some hacking and work in company along with uneven terrain, flat work, and combinations. The young horse will be more versatile and can begin to specialize in an area that does not require the height of jumps over three feet. On the other hand, if he appears to be an able horse with some jumping problems, stop and fix them now at lower heights.

With accurate observation of how a combination is influencing the jumping problem and with a little imagination, using the basic information in appendix 1, the rider can make insightful adjustments to the distances or the angles that will help correct the problem. Be sure that in fixing one problem another is not developed. Keep an eye out for any resistances that indicate the horse is worried about an exercise. If any are seen, stop and go back to something simpler and try again with another approach.

Most jumping problems or faults are caused or influenced by one or more of the following: the rider's position and/or controls, the history of the horse's flat and jump training, or physical or mental limitations of the horse. One or two unfortunate mishaps along the way in schooling can leave a lasting impression, especially on horses of certain temperaments. Nearly all corrective jumping should start with reinforcing stabilization on the flat off contact and stabilization to low single fences and low, simple combinations. In the majority of cases, corrective jumping plans can be implemented only if the horse is approaching the jumps and departing the low fences calmly maintaining the gait and speed.

Jumping faults that a reclaimed horse may have or a young horse may have developed include any of the following, not necessarily in order of importance or severity: refusing strange jumps, folding late in front, rushing the jump, scooting on landing, drifting to the right or left in the air, consistently landing on one lead more than the other, twisting the forelegs over the top of the jump, twisting the hind legs to one side or the other over the top of the jump, jumping flat in the flight phase and not using the head and neck well, having difficulty standing off and giving a long arc, having difficulty jumping from a close takeoff and a small arc, running out at a jump, unfolding early, not folding well (front legs below the horizontal), showing poor folding behind, or having problems with straightness on the approach and/or departure. If he has a jumping problem, it is best to evaluate it and solve it before proceeding with simple courses.

SIMPLE COURSES

Beginning to teach the horse to negotiate simple courses should go fairly easily provided he is stable at the trot and canter on the flat, is bold and stable to various low fences, has had many experiences over simple combinations teaching correct figuring of the takeoff, and has demonstrated that he is sound and physically able to do the height of the courses. Early courses should be at two feet and two feet, six inches. Increasing height should be introduced first in combinations. When he is jumping well, add that height to the course.

For the remainder of the schooling over courses, first trot the courses on most horses. Then trot into the lines and canter out. When the horse is ready, canter the entire course. This will help ensure that the horse continues to jump boldly and straight. It is important to be this conservative when the horse is inexperienced; the goal is to have all his jumping be successful. This will build a very confident horse with good form over courses. When trotting into and cantering out, be sure to add a stride. The gait of the approach is the trot, but the distances are normally set for the cantering stride in as well as out of the line.

A useful exercise for teaching riders their first experience on courses might be successful with the young horse as well. Jump a jumpless course; that is, a course of single poles instead of normal jumps. These jumpless courses may consist of eight poles: a side (six strides), diagonal (seven strides), side (six strides), and diagonal (seven strides). This will help give the horse the idea and may help the rider be a little better organized as well when the jumps are added. This is very effective for a trainer schooling his first five projects. Trot the "pole" course first, and if it suits the horse pick up the canter on a preparatory track for the long approach to the first pole set between the standards. Canter down the lines, and do simple interruptions from the trot for the lead changes.

When introducing simple courses, keep in mind that the green horse has not read the course diagram. He does not know where he is going, and the young horse has no experience jumping a course. Part of the goal for most horses, in teaching simple courses, is to get the horse to calmly but alertly anticipate by looking for the next jump on the course and figuring correct takeoff. As in all flat riding and schooling, connect the horse from leg to hand and ride ahead with your eye by setting advance points—in this case, the lines, turns, and approaches on the jumping course.

At this time stay with the simple interruption for a lead change on the courses. Avoid the temptation to press for a flying change. The horse is learning a great deal by jumping a series of jumps; do not add a second lesson at the same time. Many trainers in a hurry to get to the show ring or to a sale rush the lead changes. The young horse may become mentally upset during the lead change on the corner and rush or quicken to the jump after the lead change.

If the lateral and longitudinal work on the flat is done correctly, including simple interruptions, and if the horse is sound, there will be no difficulty with gradually teaching the flying change. Teach jumping simple courses first and then add the flying lead change.

In this sixth schooling period, it is important, as with hacking out and fieldwork, to bring the horse to different settings to work on the flat, practice part of a program ride, and possibly put one together. Jump simple combinations, individual jumps, and eventually simple courses in a different setting as well. In short, get him used to going to a strange place and doing his job well.

To get started, jump each of the fences on the new course individually at the trot. Once the horse is straight and stabilized over one fence, then go on to the next. Jump it several times if necessary. If a particular fence offers problems, either do not proceed with schooling the course or remove that particular fence from your planned course. Select the fences that are the simplest and most natural for the horse to jump. However, for a few horses it is better not to school individual fences in the order of the simple course because they over-anticipate. This may be the case when reclaiming more experienced horses as well.

Once the horse is stable and confident at the trot, trot into the lines and canter out, and then canter all of it.

At first the young horse will be surprised to see the fourth fence, and then the fifth and sixth. If the jumps are low and the course has been first trotted, he should be fairly confident by the time the canter is added into the lines as well as out.

It may be that in one schooling session the time taken to jump the fences individually has been enough for the horse. The original plan may have been to jump a simple course, but it will be much faster in the long run to spread this process out over several sessions and avoid overworking the horse. When the horse has performed simple courses well in one place, go to another and repeat the same slow process. It might take all month and into the next before he can go to a new place in one session, jump the individual fences, and put a simple course together at the trot and canter without being spent physically or mentally.

When going to a competition, use these steps in introducing the competition course to the horse. First of all, go to a competition that allows schooling. Jump the fences individually. Practice trotting in and cantering out and then canter the whole course. Some horses will eventually be predictable to the rider; i.e., once they do a line or two of trotting in and cantering out, it is possible to just canter the rest of the course. Variations like that should be anticipated so that the horse can be saved for the actual competition.

While jumping simple courses, if the horse begins to stop, rush, or be frantic, recognize that something has been done too soon or incorrectly. Retreat promptly to a less complex task until the horse is stable—trot a low vertical and return to simple flat work and combinations. Avoid blaming it on the horse's breeding or personality. It is the trainer's job to deal with these characteristics, taking into account any peculiarities of the young horse's temperament that might require different preparation and more time than another horse. Face up to the problems promptly or risk developing a permanent jumping fault. In jumping simple courses, resistance or jumping form limitations will not correct themselves in most cases. Reevaluate the schooling plan. Review the foundation of schooling in this system. Take a step back and start again more carefully and thoughtfully. Don't allow a problem to become a habit.

See appendix 1 for sample distances and schooling exercises, and particularly the section "Moving toward Your Horse's Jumping Specialty."

FIELDWORK

Gradually, three speeds of the canter over uneven terrain should become fairly easy for the show horse, jumper, and field hunter. On a more level part of a field, use the ordinary canter. The downhill slope calls for a short canter, and the uphill requires a lengthened canter to keep the pace even. Riding over uneven terrain can help develop the horse's condition, mental stability, and longitudinal agility. The horse should perform outside on soft contact, connected, and moving in one piece with the head and neck extended and the mouth closed. All transitions should be softly and precisely executed. Look for the same quality performance over uneven terrain as seen with three speeds of the canter on the flat. This exercise will become very useful on hunter courses, jumper courses, and outside hunter trial courses.

Building on work outside at slower gaits by his sixth period, the young horse should be able to successfully do short periods of the fast gallop. This should be done in a large, fairly flat area or field before going to uneven terrain. It is also useful for conditioning the horse and developing stamina.

The "hand gallop" should be taught to the horse over uneven terrain so that he becomes mentally stable at that gait and speed in the open. Never let the horse become out of control at the gallop. The rider should be able to stop or change the gait in a few strides at any time during the gallop exercise. The horse should stay mentally stable at the gallop just as he does at the lengthened trot or a canter.

This exercise is a longitudinal agility exercise in that the horse canters, gallops at speed, and then returns to the canter. The horse has to learn to lengthen without getting mentally upset and then cooperatively shorten. If the

The canter (three beats). The hind left supports the horse, and the balancing gesture of the head and neck is at the highest point. As the dynamic balance shifts forward, the balancing gesture will become the most extended, as the right leading leg supports the horse. Shortening and lengthening the stride and also riding over uneven terrain develop longitudinal agility. *(Pam W. Renfrow, rider; Reinhold Tigges, photographer)*

only time the horse gallops is when he is on a course with a line that requires lengthening or when he competes on an outside course, he will tend to get strong and upset when he lengthens. Therefore, teach the horse to gallop and stay mentally under control regardless of the situation.

HUNTER/GROUP EXERCISES

Up to this point the individual performer should have benefited from hunter exercises at slow gaits.

Hacking teaches boldness. Hacking is an essential exercise for a field hunter or hunter trial horse if it is done correctly and has advantages for show hunters and jumpers as well.

Group exercises that build on hacking in small, slow groups should be integrated into the rest of the schooling program. If the horse is to be a jumper or an individual performer, it is not necessary to spend more time or develop more skill and experience with these group exercises, especially those at speed. However, if the horse is to go on to be a field hunter, hunter trial horse, or a hunt team horse at horse shows, then proceed with more difficult exercises at speed.

Hunters under saddle will need to practice group exercises up to a point. They would not be required to work at faster gaits. If, however, the horse has a nice temperament, no harm will be done by proceeding cautiously with the hunter exercises at faster gaits. Indeed, it will make this type of horse more versatile should he have to change his career goals at a later date.

A sample group exercise involves the whole line trotting while the horse at the rear gallops to the front and takes up the trot at the front of the line. Hunter exercises with jumps may also be added. For example, the first horse trots up to the jump and circles to the rear of the line, the second horse jumps the jump, the third horse circles to the rear, and so on. Have a course of three or four jumps and involve four to six horses. This exercise is fun to do, but it also requires that the horse be listening, obeying, and cooperating with the rider on the flat and approaching jumps, and not just following the herd.

Hacking out with an experienced horse in strange country is a good exercise for nearly all horses. The future field specialist should "lark," if possible, at the trot over some hunting panels, possibly taking a lead from an experienced horse.

When in a group of three or four, try the following exercise. Walk and trot between the jumps in pairs or doing slow hunter exercises. Line up parallel to the wing (or fence line) of the jump. One at a time, coming out of the lineup, without a lead, jump the fence at the trot or canter. Green horses should trot and take a lead, if necessary. Upon landing and walking, that horse should start a new parallel line exactly opposite and as close as possible to the horses lined up abreast on the approach side. Stay clear of the approach and departure line, because that will tend to make the next horse quicken. This is a nice, relaxing, useful exercise for individual performers, as well as for the specialist horses going across country under control in company. It teaches calmness in company and boldness and introduces new types of panels. Later, if schooling experienced field hunters, use this exercise to restore obedience and stability after a particularly exciting day in competition or with hounds.

It is disheartening to see people take their young inexperienced horses to a novice-level cross-country course where schooling is not allowed and then try to go cold over the jumps. Especially in the United States, where horse

A field hunter participating in a horse show as part of his schooling program to ride with hounds and jump in safe form. The rider demonstrates crest release and a correct design of position based on the stirrup for jumping at a horse show or riding in an uneven field. *(Mary S. Robertson, MFH, rider; Al Cook Photography)*

Horse standing quietly with hounds. The field hunter should be educated with the same riding and schooling principles and exercises as a show hunter. At the end of the schooling period, emphasize field riding and jumping in company. *(Mary S. Robertson, MFH, rider; W. A. Robertson, photographer)*

Connected walk from the leg to soft contact. The rider's position allows the leg to be used at the girth, while the stirrup is short enough to ride over uneven terrain and jump in unity with the horse. The rider demonstrates "driving rein" technique to follow the balancing gestures and maintain consistent contact. This technique is useful when riding certain young horses and in teaching contact and following arms on the flat and jumping. *(Liz Callar, photographer)*

trials might be just two feet, six inches, to two feet, nine inches, a strong rider with a whip and spurs can get a young, kind horse to the other side, but the quality of the performance and the habits the horse develops can be negative. It would be better to school slowly across country in company, and when ready do a hunter trial course. Many jumping problems that might develop can be avoided with this approach.

For the first field competition experience, select one that allows the jumps to be individually trotted in advance. Assuming they are natural-looking, inviting fences, there should be no problem to put them together as a course. The goal should be to avoid resistance and develop confidence. Bring an older horse for support, especially during the early experiences.

TABLE 5
PROGRAM RIDE
SAMPLE INTERMEDIATE-LEVEL RIDE FOR HUNTERS AND JUMPERS
This ride is to be ridden on a soft contact with more reserve energy unless otherwise specified. A higher level of performance on contact is required in order to do these movements both softly and precisely.

The capital letters noted for each movement refer to positions in the diagrams of Schooling Movements in chapter 9.

		Movement
1	A	Enter ordinary trot
	C	Track right
2	M	Slow trot, sitting
	B	Half-circle in reverse
3	B	Halt five seconds, proceed ordinary trot
4	C	Serpentine of four loops, track right at A
5	KXM	Lengthen stride at the trot
	M	Ordinary trot
6	C	Leave track early to approach trotting fence
	HEK	Take trotting fence
7	A	Walk
	F	Lengthen stride at the walk
	B	Ordinary walk
8	M	Canter on left lead
	C	Large circle at canter (approximately thirty meters)
9	HXF	Change direction over single jump, change leads if necessary; simple change through the trot or flying change

Do not show the horse a strange jump, let him sniff it, and then make another approach to the jump. It is better to jump it on the first approach or to take a lead where the horse sees it for the first time and follows another horse over it.

Working over courses or outside fences should continue to develop the confidence in jumping that has been started with the young horse. To reinforce jumping form and correct takeoff, return to the foundation of careful and progressive training through combinations. Continue hacking out with an older horse through the woods and over low jumps, and eventually, the confident young horse should be able to jump a hunter trial or lower-level

10	H	Walk
11	C	Half-turn on the haunch
12	H	Right lead counter-canter maintaining bend in direction of leading leg
13	B	Left lead canter (preceded by simple change of lead through trot or walk)
14	CEA	Gallop
	A	Ordinary canter
15	B	Ordinary trot
	B-M	Gradually go to loose reins
	C-H	Establish contact
16	E	Halt, back four steps, proceed at walk
17	K	Ordinary trot
	A	Turn down center line
	G	Walk, leave arena on loose reins
18	Stabilization of horse	_____
19	Contact/impulse	_____
20	Quality of performance	_____
21	Position of rider	_____
22	Efficient use of aids	_____

• Large space; minimum of 100 feet x 175 feet.

• Gradual, soft transitions are more important than precise transitions.

• Please review "Schooling on the Flat" sections in chapters 10 to 12, Schooling Periods 4 to 6.

• Adjust the Program Ride to suit your horse's schooling level.

cross-country course without advanced schooling and in good form with a calm, cooperative attitude.

SAMPLE MOUNTED WARM-UP

Walk for ten to fifteen minutes on a hack. Work in halts using short turns at the walk, neck bends, and lengthening at the walk. This should be done primarily off contact.

In the working area or in an open field, trot and canter off contact to be sure the horse is stabilized. Move to contact at the trot depending upon the

100-Mile Trail Ride competitor at the trot, on contact, with the head and neck extended and the mouth closed. The horse demonstrates a connected, ground-covering stride with good horizontal engagement of the right hind leg. *(Sally Young, rider; Ira Haas, photographer)*

Working hunter. This horse demonstrates excellent jumping form in the flight phase of the jump. The balancing gesture of the head and neck is extended and round, and the front legs folding over the top of the fence are even and tight with his knees above the horizontal. *(Louise W. Serio, rider; Teresa Ramsay, photographer)*

horse's needs. Work in low, single fences. Include some spreads and color. Start with the simple and what he knows and does well. Then move to the more difficult lateral/longitudinal agility exercises in the warm-up or go on to the day's lesson.

If the day's lesson is something special, a short warm-up geared specifically to that session is in order. Preliminary exercises in the particular setting will be necessary for some or all of the following lessons: (1) uneven terrain work at the gallop: stabilize at the slower gaits and the canter first, (2) program ride exercise: practice certain movements before doing the ride, and (3) a course of jumps: work up gradually to the height that the course will require. First trot, then canter out of the line with simple interruptions for the lead before putting it all together at the canter.

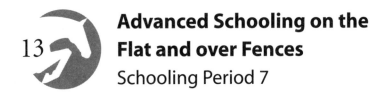

Advanced Schooling on the Flat and over Fences

Schooling Period 7

The seventh period primarily covers four to five weeks of developing exercises previously introduced. It begins during the seventh to tenth month of schooling. There is some emphasis on the schooling or career objectives for the horse being educated.

Begin to work on improving all the flat work that has been introduced and emphasized in this schooling program that is directly related to the objectives for the horse. For example, the horse being trained to be a jumper on a higher level will need to do the advanced-level flat work well. Some of these exercises are discussed in this chapter. A horse that is a better-than-average mover, has good form over jumps, and is geared to be a show hunter will need to be able to do well three speeds of the canter, connected straight laterally agile turns (on the line), and the flying change, and to hack nicely at the walk, trot, and canter in company. The field hunter will need to work stabilized in company over uneven terrain and jump safely and obediently in company.

All flat-work exercises should be geared toward improving the horse's quality of movement and working toward soft, precise transitions. The educated movement and quality transitions need to be carried over to work in company for horses in under-saddle classes and group riding. The advanced schooling level flat work may be harmful to certain sensitive temperaments in that it may make them less useful to the average amateur rider and may not be necessary for well-conformed show hunters to be successful at their job. Some exercises and movements will be necessary for some horses and will not be necessary in schooling other horses toward their specific objectives.

Upon entering the seventh schooling period decide whether the plan is to keep the young horse. If the schooling project has turned out well and it looks as though he is progressing toward the objectives set out for him—for example, he has demonstrated that he has enough scope and jumping ability to continue with the jumper schooling, or that he has the mental stability to be a field horse, or that he moves and jumps well enough to be a show hunter in the preferred division—that is fortunate. However, if the horse is falling short of expectations, it may be time to change his career goals and consider finishing off the schooling so that he will be a nice horse for someone else and thereby have a good life because he is performing his job well.

If the plan is to sell the horse, integrate different riders into the horse's schooling schedule. He may be going beautifully with one person who has been schooling him through these six or seven periods, but he needs to get used to different weights of riders, different feels, different leg pressures, and different hands. Under supervision, begin to let someone do a little more with the horse as a regular part of his training and preparation for moving on to another rider. When a new rider tries him, the horse should not be worried if he has had slow, easy introductions to different riders. The kindest young horses with the best trainers often need this exercise, not to mention those young horses with more difficult temperaments.

KEY CONCEPTS AND EXERCISES FOR THE SEVENTH SCHOOLING PERIOD

Practice jumping combinations to reinforce correct judgment of the takeoff: a variety of low jumps for boldness and confidence, simple courses at the canter in different settings, and corrective jumping if required.

Perform a flat-work review of longitudinal and lateral agility exercises undertaken in this schooling program. Flat work should always be integrated with the jumping sessions.

Emphasize exercises on the flat that the horse will need to do in his chosen job—turns at speed, flying changes, leg-yielding, and other lateral movements as well as longitudinal agility exercises such as the three speeds of the canter.

Emphasize exercises that the individual horse needs as a result of his conformation or a potential schooling problem.

Use fieldwork to teach balance and agility and to develop calmness in company. Slow work in company can also benefit the individual competitor; for example, jumpers and show hunters. Practice exercises with faster gaits and speeds in company and exercises jumping in company, which are essential for the prospects that are being directed toward fieldwork, hunter trials, and hunter pace events. At this point in schooling, field horses should do most of the flat work in an open area or field and some over uneven terrain.

To prepare for a competition or new activity, practice schooling on the flat in situations and settings similar to competitions, introducing a small sampling of the courses or activity that the horse will eventually be expected to do.

Interval learning and turnout breaks are important factors when schooling a horse. For example, when horses are put "out" on Friday for a two-day break, they quite often will come back on Monday and perform a movement or exercise well that they were introduced to the previous week. The same is true for a longer break. If they take their break at the end of a successful schooling period, when riding resumes they will remember their lessons remarkably well. Unfortunately, this can also include negative experiences. Plan ahead with pleasant work sessions before the break and avoid introducing a new exercise or risking ending the work period with a problem before a break.

JUMPING

In the seventh period, jumping exercises are primarily a review. In warm-up, trot a vertical rather than an X to encourage the horse to fold more evenly. Horses having a problem with straightness will need to use ground rails. Keep the one-stride and simple triple in-and-outs, but begin to increase the spreads (three feet to four feet, six inches) and heights. Introducing different spacing of the combinations in triples, quadruples, and quintuples builds the horse's agility and confidence for figuring correct takeoff at the canter. Continue to trot courses, trot in and canter out of lines, and canter lines. The courses should become progressively more difficult in terms of variety of jumps and in the distances—require waiting on one line and moving forward on the next, and have more spreads, which will help develop the horse's scope and flight phase at the jump. To be certain, there should be no traps. Everything should be introduced progressively, as earlier discussed, and then the course put together. The experiences should always be positive and successful. What is done on the days before schooling over jumps is at least as important as how warm-ups are conducted for jumping courses. In teaching schooling, do not expect pupils to fully appreciate this point. However, planning ahead and preparing properly means the trainer will be much more likely to ask the horse for something he can easily do. (See the diagram of sample schooling exercises at the end of appendix 1.)

Corrective jumping for specific problems, if the horse has them, should figure into all flat schooling and jumping. For example, if the horse tends to drift, combinations should always be set up with placing rails to keep the horse straight on the approach and landing and with adjusted distances. If the fault becomes worse with height, then wait until it can be corrected over lower jumps. Continue to be alert to the fact that jumping faults can occur if the height and width that the horse is able to do, either for his experience and confidence level or ability, have been exceeded.

If the horse takes off from the correct place ten out of ten times and jumps properly—that is, straight and folding well—then he is learning correct takeoff and good form. However if five or six times out of ten the horse drifts right, favors a lead, or twists, then he is learning those jumping faults rather than correct takeoff and form. Jumping faults may be caused by the rider—even experienced riders—by "ducking," uneven leg pressure, limited release on one side or too-short a release, "tilting" or uneven depth in the heel in the flight phase, and so on. During periodic evaluations, try to catch these potential problems early. Practice on a made horse, and have an educated rider with a good position school the young horse.

It is important in this seventh schooling period to take the horse to a neighboring farm or farms and school over different jumps, occasionally putting a simple course together. This last assumes that everything is going well at home. If the horse has been hacking out consistently with an experienced horse, he has developed a certain level of boldness that will carry over to different settings.

SCHOOLING ON THE FLAT

The program rides vary in level and may be used in a variety of ways. For example, after a vacation, take a few of the movements from the elementary ride or foundation ride off contact and make them the flat lesson for a day or so until the horse maintains the gait and speed asked or becomes restabilized. A sensitive or spirited horse may take a little longer to return to his prior level of work. Notice that the elementary program ride has gradual transitions that are far apart and circles that are large and suitable for starting a horse up after a holiday. In this seventh to tenth month after warm-up, consider performing the foundation ride all on contact (rather than loose rein and contact) for the day's flat lesson. On another day, this program ride might be used for warming the horse up for a trotting and cantering course.

The other program rides are progressively more difficult and can be used in part to prepare for uneven terrain work, jumping combinations, and courses. These higher-level program rides include movements that should be taught. Repeat selected movements several times until they are done on a satisfactory level, and periodically put a group of them together, creating your own program ride tailored to your horse.

The chief goal for a show hunter or jumper at this point is .o have the horse on a consistent soft contact with impulse that produces soft, precise transitions and improves the quality of his movement. Fine-tune all the transitions and gaits so that the horse is performing them to the best of his physical, mental, and athletic abilities for his age, stage of schooling, and his schooling goal.

Keep in mind that in modern advanced hunter/jumper schooling a third of the work should be on looped reins, most of the contact will be on a soft contact with reserve energy, and, depending on the schooling objectives for the individual horse, a smaller portion of the flat riding may be on a soft contact with a higher degree of impulse.

In this seventh period it should be easy to identify any lateral stiffness or resistance in longitudinal movements. Plan flat work to help eliminate these weaknesses in the schooling program. At the same time, if the horse has a jumping fault, he may have a related flat work problem. Therefore, it will be necessary to work every day on gradually improving the horse in the direction or in the transition with which he is having difficulty. This does not mean to force any lesson. On the contrary, if the horse is stiff turning, work both sides, but when going to the stiff side start on larger circles and turns. When he is soft and laterally agile turning on wide circles, the turns can gradually be made smaller. Also, it is most probable that more work will be done on the stiff side, albeit with larger turns, than on the softer side.

THE FLYING CHANGE

In preparation for the flying change over the last six schooling periods (six, seven, or more months), the work has been on canter departures primarily from the trot. In the last period there were some canter departures from the walk. These should be going very well before attempting to teach the flying change. The canter departures from the walk and trot should be straight, soft, and precise with a prompt response from the horse to the lower leg. After the departure the first canter stride should be flat, with the head and neck extended and the mouth closed with no resistance such as head-flipping or rolling under or behind the bit.

The progressive movements with the lead changes have been canter departures from the trot and then the walk on circles in both directions, off a half-circle, a simple interruption on the diagonal through the trot or walk, and down the center line with simple interruptions. Further, in preparation for the flying change, the horse should be able to counter-canter in both directions and easily pick up the counter-canter from both the trot and the walk. This is a useful outline for teaching the rider on a made horse as well.

Other exercises exist to help the rider learn to use the leg and hand aids accurately for the flying change. The rider needs to be able to feel the movement and at the right moment apply the (outside) displacing leg, the direct rein on the side of the desired lead (diagonal aids for the lead), and the holding/urging leg. For example, practice switching leads with simple interruptions to develop the rider's leg aid coordination and to teach the horse to respond calmly to the lead-change leg aids. Establish a very large circle in a flat field or an unusually wide ring, avoiding corners. Canter from the walk or trot on the inside lead for twelve to fifteen strides, then walk or trot and canter on the outside lead for twelve to fifteen strides and repeat. Do not proceed to teach flying change to the horse or rider until this and similar exercises are consistently being completed successfully.

On courses of jumps, simple interruptions through the trot have been done, preferably on the straightaway after landing from a line of jumps or a combination. Be sure that these simple lead changes on the courses have the same qualities as canter departures in the schooling on the flat. This relates to the rider being in the same position and using the same controls and the horse being in the same balance on the flat and over a course of jumps.

Do not ask for the flying change at the end of a line of jumps if the horse is not stable at the jumps or is not doing simple lead changes well. Transitions from the canter to the trot or walk to the inside lead should always have been soft, precise, straight, and flat, with the horse's head and neck extended and his mouth closed. The horse should do the transitions easily and cooperatively without getting upset.

The turn on the forehand is a good tune-up to remind the horse about the displacing leg before doing the flying change. Use a reinforcing stick or spur if the lazy horse does not respond positively to the cue of the outside squeeze-release technique of the displacing leg for the turn on the forehand.

Be sure that the rider consistently uses correct aids for the lead change. Aids not applied in coordination with the movement and gait and not consistently accurate will "worry" and quicken horses. It is wise for the rider or trainer to practice the aids for the flying change on a made horse if at this point he has been schooling mainly younger horses.

The basic aids for the flying change are an inside holding leg (straight horse), an active outside displacing leg, and an inside direct rein. From the start of schooling, these are the same aids used to teach the horse to take the correct lead from the trot and the walk. There are several other methods to teach a horse to take the desired lead, but in moving up to teach the flying change from simple interruptions the consistently used diagonal aids are the most efficient.

FLYING CHANGE FROM A COUNTER-CANTER ON A LARGE CIRCLE

Pick up the outside lead and move onto a large circle. When the horse is connected, straight, and consistent in the counter-canter, stay on the pattern of the circle (do not inadvertently steer to the center and a smaller circle), and ask for the lead change by using an active outside displacing leg with squeeze-release technique, and keep the horse straight with an inside holding leg. Position the head and neck slightly in the direction of the lead.

TIMING AND THE FLYING CHANGE

The rider's coordination and feel for the horse's movement are important to "timing," or asking for the change at the right moment. The following may be useful to some riders having difficulty with timing and perhaps to some teachers. First, ensure that the rider and horse consistently produce straight, flat departures in forward balance from the trot and from the walk. The rider sits evenly over the stirrups (especially not leaning to one side or ahead of or behind the motion), keeps the horse straight with an inside holding leg, and then cues the horse for the lead change with an outside active displacing leg. The inside direct rein positions the head and neck slightly in the direction of the new lead. In this schooling program, the aids used for the flying change are the same as those used when asking for simple straight, flat departures. Next, the rider should practice flying changes of leads in forward balance on a made horse until the rider's aids are precise and the timing is consistently accurate.

In preparing to ask for the flying change of lead, the rider should mentally rehearse the planned pattern, the feel and timing, and the application of the aids, and then do flying changes on an experienced horse. For example, while at the counter-canter on a circle, the rider's inside leg is the active leg in the displacing position, and the outside leg is at the girth. The horse's head and neck are bent slightly toward the outside lead. Essentially the rider's leg positions will be quietly switched. It is at this moment that the rider could unintentionally miscue the horse. As the horse is about to take the third beat on the counter-canter lead, take the inside displacing leg off and quietly move the outside leg from the girth back to the displacing leg position. Ask for the swap from behind with an active outside displacing leg. For straightness and to urge as necessary, put the inside holding leg in place at the girth and ensure that the head and neck are positioned slightly in the direction of the new lead. The hand should continue to follow the balancing gestures. Be careful not to set the hand against the balancing gestures at the time of the change.

If the horse does not respond to the rider's active outside displacing leg and does not change to the inside lead on the circle, calmly trot a step or two and pick up the inside lead, staying out on the large circle. Make one to three attempts to do the flying change. If applicable, make these first attempts changing toward the side or lead he prefers. Stroke him and reward with voice when he takes the lead. If necessary, reinforce the leg with a spur or stick or "cluck" accurately and thoughtfully, without quickening the horse. Finish by doing something he knows and likes, but include departures with simple interruptions. Then let the lesson go until the next day or so.

When the horse does change cleanly from the counter-canter to the inside lead on the circle, promptly tell him "good" with the voice, keep him connected and straight, stroke him on the neck, and stay cantering on the circle on the exact pattern that has been established. He has just made an extra effort with his hind end to make the change. If he quickens through the change, try not to grab him on the outside rein. Rating the stride in rhythm with the balancing gestures, stay cantering on exactly the same large circle until he is calm. Repeat this lesson almost immediately if things have gone well. If the horse changes in front but not behind promptly (within one step), trot, pick up the lead, and stabilize the canter.

Anticipation from the horse may help him learn, but it may also cause the inexperienced trainer to set the hand against the reserve energy necessary before, during, and after a change.

At the start, asking for the change in the same spot on the circle may help some horses better understand the lesson. However, if the horse begins to anticipate too much, regularly change the spot where you ask for the flying change.

FLYING CHANGE FROM THE COUNTER-CANTER AT THE END OF A SHORT DIAGONAL

Take up the canter and, when it is straight, connected, alert, and stabilized, canter across the short diagonal of a large ring. At the last quarter of the diagonal line, nearly at the ring fence or other barrier, ask for the lead change using outside displacing squeeze-release leg, inside holding leg, and inside direct rein on the side of the new lead. If there is no response, use the spur also in rhythm with the mechanics of the gait. When the horse swaps, follow the balancing gestures, rate the stride in rhythm with the canter, reward, and continue. Avoid using the long diagonal, as many horses can anticipate and quicken. If the horse's pace becomes a little too alert after the change, establish a large circle, keeping the horse straight, until the canter is soft and the horse is mentally stable. Be certain to say "good" and stroke.

FLYING CHANGE OFF A HALF-CIRCLE

Another method for teaching the flying change is to work on half-circles with a simple interruption at the trot. This method relies on the horse calmly anticipating the change. If the horse has found it easier to take the right lead from the beginning, then do a half-circle to the left on the left lead with a simple interruption of three to five steps of the trot and then pick up the right lead on the diagonal line before getting back to the rail. Repeat the half-circle to the left several times to get the number of steps of the trot reduced to one step and then zero. The horse may begin to anticipate the lead change, which could help, but if he quickens after the lead change, rate the canter in rhythm with the balancing gestures, canter a large circle at the end of the ring, and stay on it until he is calm.

Avoid setting the hand against the mouth and the balancing gestures. Rate the stride in rhythm with the balancing gestures, using the voice to help shorten and calm. Repeat the lesson several times with the simple interruptions. If one flying change is obtained, reward and consider stopping or attempt only one more, depending upon your horse.

Never let your horse or pupil inadvertently practice the cross-canter or disunited canter. If there is a change in front and no change behind, or cross-canter, try promptly to walk or within one stride to trot or skip behind, pick up the inside lead, and, with voice and soft hands, rate the stride. Be certain the horse does not run from the change or become frightened by the rider's aids. At no time should the rider get frustrated with the horse and jerk him up.

Leave this exercise doing a half-circle in both directions with a long period of interruption through the walk or trot, ensuring the horse has not been rattled, and try again another day.

Do not drill on the flying change exercise. Short periods once or twice a week may be sufficient. This will be determined by the mental stability of the horse, the stage of the horse's education, and the success of the method and techniques used.

Teaching flying changes to horses and riders is often more successful with the counter-canter, because it is simpler for most horses. Gradually reducing the number of simple interruption steps (from five down to zero) from the half-circle makes a good exercise for teaching the rider on a made horse. However, off the half-circle a young horse can anticipate too much, causing quickening and the rider to set against him.

Conservatively speaking, do not ask for the flying change on a course of jumps until the horse is comfortable with it on the flat. Often when the horse quickens or worries about the lead change, it will lead to a poor jump following it. The horse might learn to associate the troublesome flying change with the courses and the jumps. Should this happen there will be two problems instead of one.

If appropriate on a course of jumps, intersperse soft, gradual trot and walk transitions to the halt on a straight line. Then walk and change to the inside lead, continuing to the corners and to the jump. Straightness from the hind end, which is possible through accurate and effective leg aids, must be emphasized throughout all transitions and movements.

Horses are often pressed for a short-term objective such as to be sold, go to a competition, or have a chance at a good ribbon by doing the flying changes on the course. However, if the teaching of the flying change to the horse is hurried, he may learn to do the changes automatically on slight turns before the rider's aids ask for the change. This may be desirable in the short run for lower-level riders, but it will not make for a useful equitation horse. Also, horses can learn to be quick and hurried at the lead change, and many then can become fairly useless in the equitation and hunter divisions, although they move and jump well. Some "automatic lead change" horses can develop a habit of changing leads on a straight line between jumps to balance themselves, a very undesirable habit, especially for a show horse. Teach the horse to hold the counter-canter or desired lead and change only when the rider asks or cues him for the change.

If both sides of the horse have been worked with a focus on the weaknesses or a stiff side, moving into the seventh period should not present any problems with the flying change.

If all the right steps have been taken without success, consider a second opinion by employing a qualified professional rider who rides softly and rhythmically. Prepare the horse well in advance by repeating schooling basics on the flat. Ask the professional to work the horse up through the simple interruptions or through the counter-canter, whichever system is preferred. The professional may have another approach, but emphasize that the goal is to do this without frightening the horse and to have the horse be able to change when signaled (diagonal aids) with an average rider in the saddle. When the professional rider has finished the session, the rider might ride the horse for a cooling-out walk or something simple such as working in some halts and/or a turn on the haunch. It may well take several quiet, slow, short sessions. Through observation and discussion, the rider should be able to figure out the problem and develop a plan to solve it.

It is not unusual for a professional rider who shows many horses to get a flying change on a green horse while schooling the horse over a course of jumps. The horse is cantering forward, the rider's timing is accurate, and the rider does not set against any temporary quickening. The horse will anticipate and change. However, this does not always mean that the horse is being educated in the flying change for average amateur riders.

There are professional and amateur riders with a natural feel who can get a flying change on almost any horse in this setting. However, there are others who can inadvertently do considerable harm to the horse's understanding of the lead change and the job expected of him on the course of jumps.

Finally, it is most important that the horse jumps straight and in good form with an even pace in a connected, efficient stride and canters through the turns on the line with consistent contact. The flying change can be over-emphasized in training. If the green horse is constructed so that he is awkward and the lead change will take some time, keep working on his jumping and course experiences and use simple interruptions, with three or two steps of the trot, preferably before the first part of the turn, or the counter-canter in some cases throughout the course. Emphasize straightness and always think hind end first, using the leg aids. As long as he continues to stay calm and obedient, he is consistently receiving a foundation for correct flying changes.

If the horse is to be a jumper, training for the flying change need not be rushed. Start going to different courses and trot the lead changes before the turns in competition. In the green and low hunter divisions, maintaining the counter-canter through the turn is a correct training exercise for a young horse. It is, however, not appreciated by most contemporary judges. Do not ever allow the cross-canter on a turn. Either hold the counter-canter or do a simple interruption on a straight line before the corner. Avoid waiting for the corner, where the straightness can be lost.

It is possible to purchase a horse that has been frightened by the flying change or cannot do it consistently. First be sure that the horse is sound. Consider having a chiropractor who is well known for work with horses check him out. Then start from the very beginning with lead changes from simple interruptions on circles. Do not ask for any flying changes for some time. When they finally are indicated, ask for the flying lead change in a setting that the "worried" horse is not used to and when such a change is not anticipated; for example, in a field. This is not to say, though, that one cannot move right along in developing other aspects of the horse's education and experience with the variety, width, and height of jumps; uneven terrain; and schooling on the flat. In short, adjust the schooling program to the individual horse.

Whether teaching flying change or another movement, most disobedience occurs because the rider unintentionally has incorrectly cued the horse or because the rider is pressing the horse too hard. A system of riding that promotes consistent clear communication is important.

The conformation of the horse and his natural agility and balance, as well as his progress in this schooling program, will determine to a large degree how easily he does flying changes. If the horse mentally and physically accepts and cooperates with the rider's accurate aids and he is conformed in an athletic way, the lead changes are usually very easy. On the other hand, a horse with a similar temperament and education but poor conformation, such as long in the back and loin or not naturally united, will find it difficult to make a clean flying change. The latter will take more schooling on the flat to prepare him for these first lessons.

TURNS AT SPEED

There is no way to teach the horse to gallop turns at speed with agility other than to gallop them. Be certain to practice turning, first at the trot, then at the canter, and then at the gallop. During this seventh schooling period the horse should be very stable at the canter and gallop in the open and in the ring. He should be able to stay mentally calm while lengthening on a line of jumps, lengthening on a straightaway, or galloping through a turn. Practice turns at speed so that the horse is maintaining his stability and coordination through the turn.

LEG-YIELDING

Leg-yielding has been taught almost from the beginning of this schooling program (see especially the discussion in chapter 10). To summarize, the term *leg-yielding* has been used to mean any reaction to a leg aid that asks the horse to move away from the pressure created by the leg. The purpose of these exercises is to improve lateral agility and responsiveness to the lateral aids. The horse moves away from the leg in a cooperative manner, while still maintaining forward movement. Basic leg-yielding exercises should also encourage the horse to accept contact.

Preparation for successful leg-yielding is important. The horse should be able to move forward at all three gaits, with good energy, and on consistent soft contact. In addition, the horse should be able to do the following in both directions: correct turns on the forehand yielding to the displacing leg, turns on the haunches from the walk, and half-circles with a few steps of leg-yielding at the trot off the rider's inside leg on the straightaway returning to the rail.

During this schooling period the horse can be asked to trot first on the quarter or center line, moving laterally toward the outside rail. Coming off a circle or turn to the quarter line, the horse's head and neck are positioned to the inside (position left/right), which will be away from the direction of the leg-yielding movement.

The horse yields to the rider's inside leg with both sideways and forward movement from the quarter line toward the outside wall. Moving on four tracks, the inside legs cross over the outside legs toward the outside wall. It may be sufficient in teaching leg-yielding for some hunters to be satisfied with just the inside hind leg crossing over the outside hind leg. The rider's inside displacing leg is the active leg. The outside leg at the girth holds and urges. Two direct reins of opposition are the main rein aids and, with the legs, maintain the slight inside bend of the head and neck away from the direction of the movement. The outside direct rein can be slightly opening for a few steps to help guide the movement. The outside direct rein can also become a bearing or neck rein for a few steps if necessary to prevent the shoulder from falling out. The exercise should finish by going forward with energy and connection on a straight line. Maintain consistent contact throughout the exercise. Later, if appropriate, leg-yielding can be done on a circle and off a diagonal line. (Again, see the discussion of "Leg-Yielding" in chapter 10.)

Having the horse yield to the leg and move over is not the only objective.

He should also move forward remaining alert and mentally calm, with the head and neck extended and the mouth closed. If the horse becomes cranky or gets behind or above the bit, it is possible that either the rider is using incorrect hand or leg aids or the horse is not ready for the exercise. If this occurs the rider should practice on a made horse and/or go back to doing short turns at the walk, turns on the forehand, turns on the haunches from the walk, walking and trotting a zigzag, position left/right on the long wall, and simple exercises turning the horse using correct lateral aids.

SHOULDER-FORWARD   This exercise, shoulder-forward, correctly ridden at the walk, trot, and canter, should be an important objective for the high-intermediate and advanced hunter or jumper being schooled in forward balance. It can enhance straightness as well as responsiveness to the lateral aids. It will improve the "ratability" of the horse on a course and specifically help establish the straightness necessary for a clean, calm, timely lead change on course. It also helps both intermediate and advanced riders develop coordination and feel.

If position left/right (see chapter 10) has been introduced earlier when teaching half-circles, turns, and serpentines, shoulder-forward should easily evolve at this time.

To summarize:

1.   Shoulder-forward is basically similar to a shoulder-in but requires less angle (15 percent). It can also be referred to as "shoulder-fore." Technically the horse's shoulders are slightly farther away from the long wall than the hindquarters or, because of the position to the inside, the outside shoulder is ahead of the inside shoulder.

2.   On a large circle before the long wall, position the head and neck to the inside. Proceed out of the corner on a straight line. Maintain position left/right just as when turning on a circle, but continue to move on a straight line. With the head and neck softly positioned to the inside, the shoulder is displaced to the inside about 15 degrees. The horse moves on four tracks. If viewed from the front, the track of the outside foreleg is between the track of the two hind legs.

3.   Aids
     • Inside urging/holding leg at the girth (to keep the horse on track). The main aids are the inside leg and the outside direct rein.

- Outside displacing leg behind the girth only as needed to keep the quarters straight.
- Inside direct rein. Position left/right should be achieved before attempting the aids for shoulder-forward. In teaching, be alert to correct riders who might pull the head to the inside or use an inside indirect rein in front of the withers in place of an inside holding/urging leg.
- Outside direct rein. The outside direct rein encourages the shoulder to move in.

4. The rider must follow the gestures of the head and neck at the walk and canter.

5. This can be a valuable exercise for hunters and jumpers that should be easily integrated into the schooling program. When practiced at the canter it helps improve the horse's performance on a jumping course. It can promote straightness without interfering with good "hunter movement" or the mental stability of the horse.

The following three lateral movements could be useful for teachers, professional riders, and some advanced amateurs in the process of their riding education. They should be able to perform them at least mechanically or be technically accurate. However we must concede that it is a fact that historically many successful show hunters, jumpers, cross-country horses, trail horses, and other quality horses have either never been taught these three exercises or have never accurately performed them. They were successful without them.

Regardless, some riders may like to continue by teaching shoulder-in, haunches-in, and two-tracks. These are exercises that aid in teaching the rider coordination of lateral aids and, if done correctly, help teach the horse to yield to the leg and improve straightness and lateral agility. These should be done only if the horse and rider are ready.

These lateral movements are a gymnastic to develop efficient movement, better engagement, and agility. They can be a means to an end for the field horse, hunter, or jumper. Avoid aiming for perfection or complete precision in the execution of schooling movements with a hunter or jumper. However, the horse that will specialize in upper-level dressage should aim to perfect these exercises in order to move toward collection and central balance.

SHOULDER-IN This exercise, if it is suitable for the horse-and-rider team, should be taught to a horse in training by an experienced rider. Riders should first practice on a made horse with an instructor before teaching it to a less-experienced horse. Before starting, all previously discussed leg-yielding exercises and steps should be executed at least in a technically accurate manner by both the horse and rider.

Shoulder-in is a lateral movement and a schooling exercise used to help a horse become straight and, if appropriate, to help teach a rider aid coordination and feel. For some in advanced dressage the objective is to perfect this movement, because it is the first exercise in collection. There are three tracks in a shoulder-in: (1) the outside hind, (2) the inside hind with the outside foreleg, and (3) the inside foreleg. The horse moves actively forward with the head, neck, and shoulder slightly positioned to the inside. (See the illustrations.)

To summarize:

1. Shoulder-in can be executed on three tracks at three gaits, although it is difficult at the canter and not necessary or recommended for most schooling objectives. Trial runs can be practiced at the walk, but the trot might be a better gait for an experienced rider.

2. When first starting, put the horse on a circle at the end of a long wall. Close the inside leg at the girth to urge/hold the horse on the track and use the outside leg behind the girth only as needed to keep the quarters from falling out. First position the head and neck slightly to the inside (see position left/right) and then move the shoulder to the inside (30 degrees).

3. Continue out of the circle, pushing the horse onto the straight line with the inside leg urging at the girth and the outside displacing leg four inches behind the girth if needed to keep the haunch straight. The reins rate the energy and softly direct. The main aids in a successful shoulder-in are an inside leg at the girth (to keep the horse on track) and an outside direct rein.

4. Hold the shoulder to the inside at first for one or two steps. Weeks later maintain the shoulder-in until the end of the long wall, or when the quality of the steps is lost. Then promptly put the horse back onto the rail with the inside leg, emphasizing forward, straight, connected movement. This exercise should be done only for short periods. Shoulder-forward is a more appropriate and useful exercise for most riders and horses.

In the beginning of the twenty-first century, this exercise is being introduced in some clinics to horses and pupils who are either not ready for the exercise or are not able to do it without supervision after the clinic lesson. The results are often set aids and cranky horses. Keep in mind that this exercise was introduced by the Duke of Newcastle, who taught classical dressage in the mid-seventeenth century. But some of the seventeenth-, eighteenth-, nineteenth-, and twentieth-century explanations, such as bending the horse's spine or ribs around an inside leg, are not literally possible. The interested horseman should read Littauer's *How the Horse Jumps* to learn more about the rigid back and how the aids influence the skeleton and muscles of the horse.

HAUNCHES-IN   Haunches-in should be discussed at this point to ensure the reader knows why and how a rider or trainer may want to use it as a schooling exercise. It is perhaps an easier exercise than shoulder-in, because it is more natural for some horses to do. Keep in mind that flat work is done in order to improve the sport horse's performance. It is not necessary nor in many cases desirable to perfect the exercise unless your goal is to specialize in dressage. Again all previous lateral exercises should first be done responsively and well (e.g., the turn on forehand, turn on haunches, leg-yielding, and shoulder-forward as described earlier).

Haunches-in will help the rider's coordination and feel. If it is done correctly and in the right amount it will improve straightness. It can also improve some horses' ability to turn sharply on jumper courses.

Start from a circle in the corner and move to the long wall. Both forelegs should travel straight, with the head and neck positioned slightly to the inside. There are three tracks: (1) the inside hind, (2) the outside hind with the inside foreleg, and (3) the outside foreleg. For the leg aids, use the inside leg at the girth and an outside displacing leg. If the haunch is only slightly inside, there will be four tracks. The hands (direct reins) are used to lightly control speed and direction, with even contact on both sides. The head and neck have a slight position to the inside. Avoid use of an indirect rein in front of the withers, because the horse could become overflexed and heavy-headed. The rider needs to emphasize the leg. (See the illustrations.)

To summarize:

1. Horse's legs:
    • Three tracks at the walk, trot, canter. (It may be desirable to ask for four tracks; the haunch is only slightly inside.)

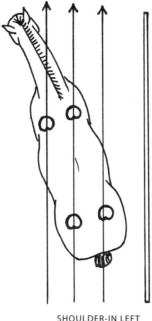

SHOULDER-IN LEFT

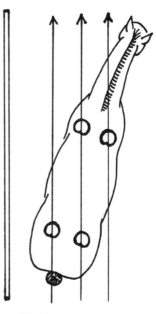

SHOULDER-IN RIGHT

There are three parallel tracks: outside hind, inside hind and outside foreleg, and inside foreleg.

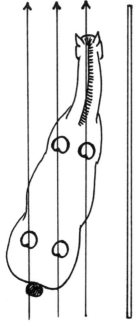

HAUNCHES-IN LEFT

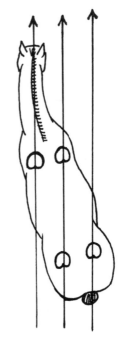

HAUNCHES-IN RIGHT

There are three parallel tracks: inside hind, outside hind and inside foreleg, and outside foreleg.

• The forehand moves straight forward on the planned track (the front legs do not cross over each other).
• The outside hind leg steps over and in front of the inside hind leg (the hindquarters are toward the inside).
• The outside hind leg and the inside foreleg are on the same track.
2. Aids:
• Legs: outside leg behind the girth (displacing leg) moves the haunch in; inside leg at the girth (urging/holding).
• Hands: direct reins with even contact on each side. Neck rein for a few steps may be necessary. The horse is positioned left/right or to the inside.
3. Reminder: If appropriate at all, most sport horses should practice haunches-in only for short periods and not often.

TWO-TRACKS   Two-tracks is a lateral schooling movement in which the horse moves forward and sideways at the same time, with his front and back feet making two sets of tracks. It can be performed at the walk and canter, but the trot should be the easiest gait to teach, because it has no balancing gestures and it is a two-beat gait with forward impulse. The head and neck should be slightly positioned in the direction of the movement. The forehand leads the hindquarters through the exercise. This exercise can develop the engagement of the hindquarters and the extension of the shoulders.

Practice two-tracking off diagonal lines, or it may be easier for some off the center line. It can also be done out hacking on a lane or wide track. It should be easier to teach two-tracks after shoulder-in and haunches-in. However, I have had success teaching the hunter or jumper rider two-tracks on a trained horse after basic leg-yielding and shoulder-forward.

To summarize:

1. First teach the horse basic leg-yielding, shoulder-forward, shoulder-in, and haunches-in.
2. On a diagonal line, the horse's outside legs cross over the inside legs, with the head and neck positioned in the direction of movement.
3. Aids:
• The inside leg at the girth (urging/holding) moves the horse forward on a line.
• The outside leg behind the girth (displacing) moves the horse over or sideways.

• The inside direct and, when needed, slightly opening rein.

• The outside direct rein with the neck rein or bearing rein for a few steps as needed to give direction.

4. Head, neck, shoulder:

• While the horse gains ground both to the side and to the front, the head and neck are positioned in the direction of movement.

• The forehand should always lead the hindquarters with even energy and consistent contact.

5. Reminders:

• The rider needs to plan ahead and look for the diagonal line of the two-tracks.

• Should the hind end begin to lead the forehand or should the shoulder fall in, promptly correct it by moving forward on a straight line.

• Start with a few steps at a time and work up to more over a period of weeks. To do two-tracks with even a degree of success is difficult.

• For their objectives most hunters and jumpers that have achieved consistent connected forward balance do not need to perfect this exercise.

FOCUS ON SCHOOLING OBJECTIVES/ USE MOUNTED TIME EFFICIENTLY

One caution for the sport horse rider: During the seventh period, emphasize schooling on the flat that will help the horse negotiate courses in the arena or in the field. A modern understanding of how a horse moves, including his agility and coordination, indicates that practicing turns at speed, schooling on uneven terrain, and practicing the longitudinal and lateral movements discussed earlier in this text are efficient and practical exercises for reaching most sport horse objectives.

PRECOMPETITION OR PREACTIVITY SCHOOLING

In situations and settings similar to the competition or activity, introduce a small sampling of the courses or activity. Throughout this program suggestions for developing boldness and mental stability have included changing the setting where the horse jumps, where he goes hacking, the field in which he works, and the ring in which flat schooling is done. This approach will certainly help the horse adjust to the settings where competitions or activities are held. Eventually he should become comfortable settling quickly into a new environment.

At home, consider an evaluation day that includes a flat hunter ride or a program ride, a course of jumps, and then a jumpless course over uneven terrain. Prepare for this the evening before by memorizing the flat movements (use a caller as well if needed), by setting up the course with the distances and the type of fences and spreads desired, and by planning the route of the jumpless course (ground poles).

The next morning or afternoon when the simulated competition is scheduled, warm up for the program ride and perform it. Have a qualified friend watch and evaluate it. Dismount, loosen the girth, and discuss the flat ride. Then think over the jumping course, mount, and school the horse one fence and line at a time, trotting and then cantering. Leave the schooling, go out of the ring, and reenter. Take up the canter on the preparatory track and jump around according to your plan. Dismount, discuss how things went on the course, and then move to the jumpless course over uneven terrain, also to be followed by an evaluation. Having it all videotaped should help as well.

Those riders who compete on many horses at each competition have developed considerable skill, timing, and rhythm for fixing and riding different horses over a course of jumps. However, these kinds of precompetition exercises will help the rider with fewer opportunities prepare for the horse show as well as the trainer and rider to evaluate the horse and prepare him to do the course by entering the ring and getting the job done. Take this exercise to another farm once the horse is doing it well at home.

The field hunter trainer should organize to hack across country with some slow-paced horses, larking primarily at the trot over low chicken coops or natural panels in new territory, or should ride at the rear of a group, having an acting field master who is willing to walk and trot and keep looking back. If correct spacing and distance out hacking have been insisted on from the beginning, it will be a simple matter to reinforce it in this exercise. When the field master begins to make a transition down to a trot, walk, or halt, start making a transition immediately, without waiting for the horse in front to make the transition. The aids are the same as those used for making any transition on the flat. The position and the controls are the same ones that the horse has been schooled with since the beginning of the program. This is one advantage of an efficient modern system of riding and schooling.

The precompetition or preactivity schooling is less expensive and may be more useful for some than going to a horse show or an actual field activity. It is possible to control the experience to suit the horse. If something starts to go wrong, stop and fix it, reevaluate, and proceed—or stop and replace the existing exercise with something less challenging at the moment.

Next give the horse actual competitive and activity experiences. These will be much easier to introduce to the prospect if the suggestions in this schooling program have been consistently followed. Update the three-month projections and schooling calendar to include schooling, competitions, and vacations.

FIELDWORK

Fieldwork is done to teach calmness in company, balance, agility, and boldness. For the individual competitor, such as the show hunter, work in company should be done at slow gaits. Faster work, including jumping in company, is done with a horse that is going to be a field hunter. Field riding gives most horses a relaxed attitude about work. The uneven terrain helps develop strength and stamina, as well as longitudinal agility for all horses, regardless of their final objectives. Show hunters and jumpers often have to do a course on a sloped ground and often have to warm up in an uneven area with a large number of horses. Jumpers will need experience over natural obstacles such as water and banks. If the prospect has been brought along in the program with consistent work in the open and over uneven terrain, he will be ready. A field hunter should be going to horse shows and green classes in hunter trials, which will help prepare him. Fieldwork on the appropriate level should develop boldness and confidence for a range of schooling objectives.

It is difficult to explain to some cross-country competitors that they need to go for an even, smooth, cooperative, slow-gaited, quality performance for at least the first year of competition. It does not take much skill to go fast on an outside course of jumps, but it will take a great deal of skill to undo the mental and physical damage if it is done too soon. To teach the horse to go under control at speed over uneven terrain and jump with agility takes considerable planning and technique. Ideally, the horse on an outside or cross-country course should be as obedient to the hand and leg as he is when schooling on the flat.

Similarly, there is a risk of ruining the horse by going out on an active trail ride or with hounds in the faster front group too early. If the prospect is a three-year-old coming four, delay going out with hounds until he is four or five years old. Ensure your prospect is doing well at the hunter exercises discussed in earlier schooling before going out in a larger group. Spend the first season exercising hounds or at the back of the field walking and trotting, and canter only when necessary. The horse first needs a foundation of obedience and stabilization in company at the rear. In preparation it is wise to continue to go out with a calm older horse as a babysitter. It allows leaving and rejoining the group as the horse needs.

Finally, for all objectives, all of the prospects should be able to perform their flat-schooling exercises and jump well in an open field, maintain the gait and speed asked for, be alert but mentally calm, stay on contact consistently, and be connected and moving efficiently in a ground-covering stride.

POINTERS FOR HACKING OUT IN A GROUP

It might be appropriate here to note some points to keep in mind when hacking out across country or trail-riding in a group. There are several things to consider before starting:

1. What is expected to be accomplished: have a plan for the ride.
2. The weather conditions and footing.
3. The time of day and how much time is available for the ride.
4. The horses' condition and when they were trail-ridden last. A slow warm-up is very important. It is also better to first get a "hidden" buck due to highness or cold weather out of the mount by a short lunge or an individual ride in a flat area. It is assumed that the horse has been turned out.
5. The experience of the riders and horses. The ride must be conducted for the least-experienced rider or the greenest horse on the hack.

When training horses in a group, one person should be in charge if the schooling session is going to be efficient and successful. Three to four horses are an ideal number to teach stabilization in company and on the trails. The person leading the session, whether the group is small or large, should consider the following:

1. Give preliminary instructions concerning the ride:
    a. A communication system for passing commands forward and back in line. Riding in double-file where possible will make communication easier and often horses more settled.

    b. Distance to keep; i.e., two to three horse-lengths.

    c. Order of going depending upon manners and experiences.

    d. A short explanation of how to keep up, how to keep horses from running up, how to keep horses walking up and down hills.

2. While conducting the ride:

    a. Look back often to check riders, distance, and horses. Readjust positions if necessary.

    b. Announce any increase or decrease of gaits. Make trots slow enough in front so that a horse at the end of the line will be able to trot comfortably. All transitions should be gradual. Keep in mind the "whip" effect at the end of a long line and that the objective is to train horses to go calmly in company.

    c. Think ahead and try to anticipate any trouble that may occur. Be aware of possible problems in large fields and "spooky" areas; i.e., when entering an open field from the woods.

3. Be certain all riders are wearing well-fitting hard hats and safe, comfortable riding attire.

4. The first ten to fifteen minutes should be walking. Check girths after the walking period.

HUMANE TREATMENT

As your horse should be at least nearly ready to start his job—show hunter, competitive jumper, field horse, etc.—it is appropriate to discuss the humane treatment of horses in schooling, in competition, and in work.

First, I recommend using a consistent system of riding and schooling to prevent and solve schooling problems.

It is important to say here that horses are not motorcycles. Some uninformed parents, spouses, or owners who write a check for a very nice prospect or for a trained young horse expect the horse to start going to the horse shows and win from January to December. Horses subjected to these schedules can and do break down mentally and/or physically. Even with good riding and schooling, on a tough schedule they will slowly become sour and stiff. These people need to be educated to consider the horse's well-being. The days off and the breaks must be regularly scheduled throughout the work year. The time period before and after breaks should have light "let down" and "leg up" work.

A few trainers and professional riders also need to be educated or remind-ed to consider the horse's well-being. The horse's spinal column is fragile, and serious damage can be done by just one rough, painful halt from the canter, or smashing into an arena wall, or a similar action. Also, there is always the temptation to fix a schooling problem quickly with gadgets or tricks. Forcing a horse to turn tight circles on his stiff side either through riding or lunging in gadgets is but one example. These can do irreparable damage physically and destroy a good attitude.

It is important that the competitive jumper, show horse, trail horse, cross-country horse, or field hunter has a reasonable workload. Many people pay considerable money for a horse and then expect too much. Following the A-level horse show circuit or going to all the meets on the card or chasing points on the local circuit without considering the health or well-being of the horse is not humane treatment.

Longevity for the horse seems to no longer be a concern for some profes-sionals and their customers. If not interested in the horse's well-being after a competitive season, at least consider the economic aspects for the owner. Buying another horse and starting training again requires a cash investment sooner than it should be needed. Sadly, a few professionals, however, feel it is better business to replace these horses because they will receive a commission or sell another horse sooner rather than later.

Young horses need to be turned out daily, and on those days when the weather prohibits it they should be lightly lunged in a large circle and/or ridden on elementary controls until they stretch down, loosen up, and relax both mentally and physically. If poor weather lasts several days in a row, try lunging and giving an elementary-level ride off contact and then, after a rest, ride a second time that day asking the horse to work on contact, assuming he is ready for that lesson. Lunging may not be an option, because some horses may have been scared by poor lunging or may find it physically uncomfortable. It is important to turn the horse out every day or give him some equivalent mentally relaxing physical exercise.

In addition, horses need one or two days off each week on a regular basis. They also need longer breaks at least twice during the year. Plan, in laying out a schooling and activity calendar over a twelve-month period, weekly days off and two vacation periods of fifteen to thirty days of turnout for the horse. Ideally the breaks should come at convenient times such as in the winter dur-ing cold weather and during the more humid parts of the summer. Improvise if facilities are limited. If turnout is not for a long enough period each day, include a combination of turnout and light, short lunging or long periods of hand walking and grazing. If mounted exercise must be done during the horse's break, avoid having the horse develop any habits of shying or bucking because he is feeling frisky. Normally some looped-rein riding, head and neck stretching, interesting walks, and trots in an open field or in the woods will be relaxing for the horse. Long daily turnout is, by far, preferable for most horses.

Do not confuse the suggestion of days off and two long breaks with the schooling methods of some trainers. The horses are mentally upset, stiff, and strong in their competition, so they are given four or five days off. Then the day before a competition, the trainers work the horses very hard, hoping they have unfit, tired, but calm-appearing horses for the competition. In fact, the horses are tired and muscle-sore, not educated and obedient. This is really inhumane treatment, and it will eventually lead in most cases to a mentally upset and unsound horse with too much hardware in his mouth.

A number of very talented, expensive, and successful horses have been ruined through overwork, schooling methods, and poor conditioning. They made it through the circuit for a few years this way before they gave out. It is troubling that several generations of juniors have come up through the ranks in the midst of this process.

These are some concerns in dealing with the equine athlete. It is difficult to understand why perfectly reasonable and well-informed people allow their horses to be treated in this manner. Fortunately most professionals and amateurs treat their horses very well.

Each trainer, owner, or pupil must have his own personal standards and ethics in schooling, competition, and planning the horse's schedule. There will be pressure to do too much or to short-circuit the schooling plan. The professional rider sometimes feels pressure from the owner or owner's family, who may want to do more and win more than the horse can reasonably be asked to do. If the owner is unhappy he finds another trainer. The pressure on amateurs and owners can come from coaches, professional riders, and horse organizations to be a profitable customer and to chase points for year-end awards.

Unfortunately, it is necessary to comment on drugs, gadgets, and other temporary shortcuts.

Persons who use drugs to mask a sore horse so that he can continue to work, to achieve calmness without schooling, to establish stabilization, or to press a young horse for a flying change without progressive schooling are primarily unethical in their treatment of the horse. These people may also be deceiving an owner, rider, or prospective purchaser, who is unaware of the unethical use of drugs in association with an individual horse's soundness and/or training. Because some people do it and may be rewarded does not make it okay. Have your own standards that have the ethical treatment of the horse as a central principle.

At the end of the last century and the start of the twenty-first century, draw reins have become nearly standard equipment at many riding levels and on a range of horses whether they benefit or not.

It can be argued that draw reins can be a useful training tool if used correctly by an expert rider in a particular schooling situation, but used incorrectly they can be a disaster, especially for the horse. Remember, if an artificial aid improves a certain problem but causes several others, then it is not a constructive tool. Further, if when the gadget is removed the problem still exists, what is the point?

The improper use of draw reins can cause restriction of the back, breaking the neck too far back, a dull mouth, and the horse to go behind the bit.

Other gadgets such as the Chambon-degogue cannot substitute for horsemanship. Evaluate your horse's schooling and soundness and set a plan for a progressive education or reschooling to achieve a lasting goal.

Despite the popularity of some gadgets, many professionals and advanced amateurs have observed that horses have been ruined by incorrectly used draw reins and/or a Chambon-degogue. In the end with most horses an educated riding and schooling system will help achieve a made cooperative horse in a shorter period of time. Gadgets are not an educated horseman's answer to training the horse.

Just because a catalog sells it or a top rider may use a gadget on a particular horse does not mean it will be useful to you, your equine pupil and partner, and your human pupils. In fact a good horse may well be successful in spite of it, not because of it. Develop your system of riding and schooling to the point that the majority of horses respond and progress without special effects.

PASSING ON YOUR HORSE TO A NEW RIDER/TRAINER

Do remember that when selling a young horse every effort should be made to try to find a suitable owner.

The schooling project will be better off with a new owner who sits well, has good controls, and has an understanding of training or will be riding under someone who has an understanding for schooling a horse. The horse will last longer for the new owner and will have a better life for himself. To accomplish these goals it may be necessary to require the purchaser to work with the horse's rider or trainer for one to two weeks and ride under supervision. That will put things on a good footing for the new owner, and the horse's schooling during these six to seven schooling periods will be more highly valued.

If the seller is willing to give the time, it is worth the effort for the horse's sake. However, some professionals want or need to sell the horse, cash the check, and get the horse off the property as soon as possible. Some alternative could be worked out. Ride it one or two days per week for the new owner at its new stable, or the sold horse could go to a professional trainer who would supervise the new owner daily. This will work provided the professional trainer understands how the horse has been schooled. Situations involving a more difficult equine temperament or a less-educated and less-confident professional in schooling young horses or an amateur or junior rider with no experience require extra time if the transition to the new rider is to be successful.

SAMPLE WARM-UP

At the end of each schooling period we have suggested a warm-up procedure to prepare the horse for the day's lesson. It is offered as a reminder and summary pertinent to the schooling level. The rider or trainer needs to adjust the warm-up to fit the individual horse's current work and its schooling progress.

Adjust the routine to the location, horse's level, and temperament. Begin off contact, on a loose rein. Move from the simple to the more complex depending on the horse's level and his condition—large circles and turns before smaller ones, gradual transitions before abrupt ones. It will not be necessary, especially with an experienced horse, to do some of these exercises at both the trot and canter each time.

The rider's personal condition and physical comfort will influence the riding and schooling. Before mounting, the rider should spend at least three minutes doing stretching exercises to prepare for riding.

The girth should be tightened gradually in three steps: (1) loosely when first saddled, (2) tightened walking to the mounting block, and (3) tightened

TABLE 6

PROGRAM RIDE

SAMPLE HIGH-INTERMEDIATE-LEVEL SCHOOLING RIDE FOR HUNTERS AND JUMPERS
This ride is to be ridden on soft contact unless otherwise specified. More impulse and reserve energy will be required in order to perform these movements softly, fluidly, and with precision.

The capital letters noted for each movement refer to positions in the diagrams of Schooling Movements in chapter 9.

		Movement
1	A	Enter ordinary trot
	C	Track right
2	B	Slow trot, sitting
		Circle, passing through X
3	F	Ordinary trot
	KXM	Lengthen the trot
	M	Ordinary trot
4	C	Zigzag of six turns, tracking right at A
5	K	Canter, right lead
6	E	Half-circle in reverse with a flying change of lead on diagonal line
7	F	Ordinary trot
	B	Turn left
8	X	Halt five seconds, back four steps; ordinary trot
	E	Track right
9	C-M	Leave track to approach fence
	MBF	Take trotting fence
		Ordinary trot to A
10	A	Canter, right lead
	K	Gallop
	F	Canter

after five to ten minutes of walking.

Mount softly and walk for ten to fifteen minutes. After standing in the stirrups for the first steps of the walk, sit softly in the saddle. The walk can be a hack in the woods or in the work area for that day. Try to avoid always walking in a ring, especially indoors in the winter, in order to give the horse some variety and mental relaxation.

In cold temperatures or if there is an unusual change in weather, use extra

11	A	Turn down center
	X	Simple change of lead
	C	Track left
12	E	Slow canter; circle, passing through X
	K	Ordinary canter
13	FXH	Change direction over two jumps
14	M	Ordinary trot
	M-B	Gradually go to loose reins
	F	Establish contact
15	A	Walk
	K	Lengthen the walk
16	H	Half-turn on haunches; walk to E
17	E	Canter, left lead
	A	Turn down center
18	G	Halt through the walk, halt five seconds
	G-C	Walk. Gradually go to loose reins. Leave arena
19	Stabilization of horse		_____
20	Contact/impulse/quality of performance		_____
21	Position of rider		_____
22	Efficient use of aids		_____

• Large space; minimum of 100 feet x 175 feet.

• Review "Points and Distinctions of Contact in the American Hunter System" in chapter 2, and the "Schooling on the Flat" sections of chapters 11 to 13, Schooling Periods 5 to 7.

• The quality of movement is more important than accuracy.

• Use these movements to help plan your schooling calendar.

• When both previous Program Rides and portions of this ride are being performed well, consider putting this ride together.

walking throughout the ride to avoid stiff muscles and possibly tying up, as well as to relax him mentally.

While walking for ten to fifteen minutes do (1) mounted rider exercises: half-seat or two-point, rotating arms, shoulders, neck, ankles, (2) half-circles in reverse and serpentines, (3) walk–halt–walk transitions using the voice, (4) turns on the forehand, (5) ordinary walk–lengthen the walk–ordinary walk, and (6) turns on the haunches from the walk in both directions.

TABLE 7

PROGRAM RIDE

SAMPLE ADVANCED-LEVEL SCHOOLING RIDE FOR HUNTERS AND JUMPERS

This ride is to be ridden on soft contact unless otherwise specified. Review "Points and Distinctions of Contact in the American Hunter System" in chapter 2, and the "Schooling on the Flat" sections of chapters 11 to 13, Schooling Periods 5 to 7. Not all horses are capable of performing upper-level rides well. This ride is recommended for schooling jumpers, 3 feet, 6 inches/4 foot hunters, and human pupils wanting to compete and train on these levels. To achieve soft, precise transitions and connected quality movement, the ride requires a soft contact with varying degrees of increased reserve energy/impulse.

The capital letters noted for each movement refer to positions in the diagrams of Schooling Movements in chapter 9.

		Movement
1	A-X	Enter ordinary trot
	X	Halt five seconds
	X-C	Proceed ordinary trot; track right
2	B	Circle, passing through X
		Ordinary trot to K
3	KXM	Lengthen the trot
	M-H	Ordinary trot
4	H	Half-circle in reverse
	E-H	Slow trot, sitting
	H	Ordinary trot
5	HCM	Trot over low fence off track
6	B	Halt; walk forward on loose reins
	F-A	Establish contact
	A-K	Canter, right lead

Trot first on a large circle on loose reins. Be certain to give the horse a walking break between some of the exercises at the trot. Use these exercises: (1) gallop position or two-point exercises for a position tune-up, (2) neck bends at the walk and trot, (3) trot–walk–halt gradual transitions using weight aid and voice, (4) wide serpentines, large half-circles in reverse, and large half-circles on contact, (5) stabilize over single poles and low verticals, (6) position left and right, and (7) three speeds of the trot on a soft contact with reserve energy.

For canter work, start cantering off contact on a large circle until sta-

7	E	Circle, passing through X
8	C-A	Serpentine of four loops (between first and second loops, simple change of leads; between second and third loops, simple change of leads; between third and fourth loops, flying change of leads)
	A	Track left
9	FXH	Change direction over two jumps
10	F	Short turn at the canter
		Canter to M
11	M	Halt; back four steps; proceed canter, left lead
12	E	Circle, slow canter, passing through X
	K	Ordinary canter
13	F	Gallop
	E	Ordinary canter
14	A	Turn down center
	X	Halt five seconds
		Leave ring on loose reins
15	Stabilization of horse	_____
16	Contact/impulse/quality of performance	_____
17	Position of rider	_____
18	Efficient use of aids	_____

• Large space; minimum of 100 feet x 175 feet.

• Soft, precise transitions are the goal. However in schooling the quality of the movement is more important than accuracy.

• When previous rides and portions of this ride are being performed well, consider putting this Program Ride together. If needed, adjustments to suit the horse and/or rider are encouraged.

bilized. Then begin the following on a soft contact with impulse: (1) transitions, gradual to a halt (canter–trot–walk–halt–walk–trot–canter), (2) large serpentines, half-circles, and half-circles in reverse with simple interruptions on the straight line, (3) ordinary canter–strong canter–ordinary canter, with emphasis on the weight aid when shortening and responsiveness to the lower leg to maintain a connected canter, (4) simple departures through the trot and walk on the center line, (5) following the balancing gestures when cantering and walking, (6) flying changes from the counter-canter in both directions (end of the seventh period or later when ready), (7) backing a specific number of steps and promptly walking forward (toward the end of trot/canter warm-up) combined with halts from a walk or trot, and (8) integrating low jumping from a trot and canter. Review anything that is needed for the day's work, and then begin the day's lesson.

GOOD RIDING AND GOOD LUCK TO YOU

This ends the seven periods of schooling using modern twenty-first-century schooling and riding principles, skills, and techniques of the American forward riding system. Please let me hear from you if you have any questions, suggestions, or comments. Ask yourself often what your horse might think of you. Best wishes for many enjoyable and successful hours with your horse. We are all very fortunate.

Appendix I
Setting Combinations and Jumps
for Different Levels of Schooling

Read the riding and schooling theory, progressive schooling program, and related levels of controls and techniques contained in the text. This appendix complements the main text and is offered as a sample of possibilities.

Like the sample Program Rides, the size of the working area must be large. All turns, especially for young horses, should be large or wide, transitions gradual, and individual parts practiced separately before putting a combination or a series of jumps and combinations together.

Both the equine and human pupils should remain calm, alert, and confident. The rider needs to coordinate the four natural aids with the horse's efforts and use techniques suitable to the horse's schooling level. If the horse or rider shows any sign of stress, stop the exercise, move to a simpler exercise, and reevaluate the schooling plan.

The horse must be allowed to carry himself under the weight of a passive rider in a combination. The horse learns to correctly judge takeoff and to use himself athletically throughout the phases of the jump. This basic, modern American training through combinations is directly rooted in Caprilli and Littauer early in American hunter/jumper riding.

The trainer sets the correct distances and jumps and then allows the horse to jump freely through the gymnastics. The horse uses his instinctive ability to figure correct takeoff while developing his natural athletic ability.

The rider's job is to approach the combination keeping the horse straight, centered, and maintaining the gait (trot or canter) and speed necessary (stabilized) for the jump or the specific distance in a combination.

Gymnastics can be done on straight lines, broken lines, or circular lines.

Gymnastics ensure that the horse jumps consistently from the correct takeoff and in good athletic form throughout the stages of the jump.

Combinations and gymnastics develop longitudinal agility. They require an athletic jumping effort, correct takeoff, and rhythm with consistent energy.

In general, verticals require horses to jump up, and spreads ask them to jump up and out (scope).

BASIC PRINCIPLES AND GUIDELINES FOR
SETTING COMBINATIONS OR COURSES

1. All distances should be set comfortably for the horse's or pony's stride and ability. Do not try to make the horse do something he is either mentally or physically unable to do. Even if the distances/combination/course is set before mounting, it is helpful to have a person on the ground to adjust the poles/jumps.

2. The average horse has a twelve-foot canter stride. A person's walking step is three feet, so four human steps equal one stride of a horse.

3. Most lines and combinations are set on a twelve-foot canter stride when the jumps are set at approximately three feet in height.

4. The distances for courses and combinations are set by the gait and speed of the approach and the height of the jump.

5. The location and footing (i.e., indoors, field, away or toward the gate or barn, deep or hard footing, nice cushion) will affect distance.

6. Approximate distances between poles on the ground for cavalletti:

   a. Walking: 3 feet to 3 feet 6 inches

   b. Trotting: 4 feet 6 inches average but can range from 4 feet to 4 feet 6 inches depending on the horse and the objective of the exercise

   c. Trotting, last pole before a jump: 7 feet to 12 feet; adjusted for specific problems

   d. Cavalletti may be used on a circle or in a straight line trotting.

   e. Cavalletti may be used to teach a horse to trot to a single fence.

   f. Cavalletti may be cantered if set at 12 feet.

   g. Cavalletti and combinations with low jumps can be useful in training horses without requiring higher jumps that could risk unsoundness or injury.

7. Constructing courses and combinations:

   a. When building a course, set poles on the ground where you think a jump should be placed before actually building the jump.

   b. Jumps should be set in an inviting way that promotes good jumping form.

   c. Usually avoid airy jumps that have no ground lines.

   d. Gates should have poles on top of them.

   e. Ascending oxers also promote good form and should be used whenever possible, particularly at the outs of lines.

   f. In general, try to make jumps appear top-heavy; i.e., with two poles or more at the top of the first element instead of one, to encourage good form.

   g. Generally, build lines with the first jump lower than the second.

   h. Basic measurements for setting jumps and distances:

   1) In-and-out with trotting approach: 18 feet

   2) In-and-out with cantering approach: 24 feet to 25 feet depending on height of the jumps, location, etc.

   3) One-stride to two-stride oxer with trotting approach: 18 feet to 30 feet or 33 feet

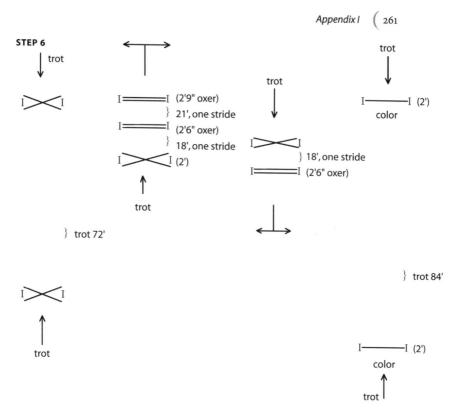

STEP 6

Approximately twelve to sixteen weeks into this schooling period, you may continue your flat and jumping schooling with these steps. The Foundation Level Program Ride should be part of the schooling program at this time. Adjust the cantering fence in the program ride to a trot fence or to a trot-in one-stride in-and-out. The Program Ride exercises are an important part of schooling to jump. (See chapter 10, Schooling Period 4.)

Step 5. Periodically change the location of the schooling poles and fences once your horse is stabilized over ground poles, single low fences, and a trotting in-and-out. Use a large space, preferably enclosed. Keep turns wide and transitions gradual. Continue to repeat earlier steps at the trot and begin to add color. Alternate turning on landing. Integrate elementary control exercises such as half-circles, short turns at the walk, two speeds of the trot, and canter departures. Because the horse is stablilized to the fence, you do not need to set ground poles to stabilize the approach. (See chapters 10 and 11, Schooling Periods 4 and 5.)

Step 6. Although the flat schooling is increasingly done on contact, continue to warm up on the elementary level and to teach jumping on the elementary level at this step. Trot low lines, add a triple in-and-out, develop progressive program rides, and integrate flat work or program ride movements with jump schooling. Be flexible and consistent, repeating movements and combinations. Do not move on unless the horse is completely stabilized and confident doing the flat and jumping exercises to this point. (See chapter 11, Schooling Period 5.)

Step 7. Practice combinations individually and in a series integrated with schooling exercises. Repeat earlier steps warming up. Remember to make wide turns in both directions. These distances should be adjusted to fit the individual horse. It is better to start with a low height, adjusting the distances as the fences are raised, and to start with one or two jumps, building up to multiple combinations similar to those presented here. The rider and/or ground person must know the horse's capabilities and the horse's experience and athletic ability. Apply that knowledge to schooling combinations and courses. The predominant fence is a low, ramped oxer. (See chapters 11 and 12, Schooling Periods 5 and 6.)

Step 8. Schooling on the flat in forward balance is an integral part of this jump schooling program. In schooling, the horse should be able to put together a series of flat movements with some low jumps and remain stable while under soft controls at both the elementary and intermediate level. Practice the three program rides in whole or in part recommended in the fourth, fifth, and sixth schooling periods. Because these are practiced in a large area (100 feet x 175 feet to 125 feet x 250 feet), they directly relate to schooling over a course of jumps. Repeat any earlier steps necessary as part of a warm-up to this exercise. Adjust to your horse's needs. As the horse becomes stable and confident, change the schooling

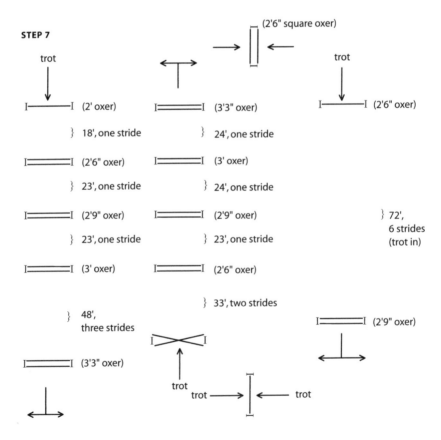

STEP 8

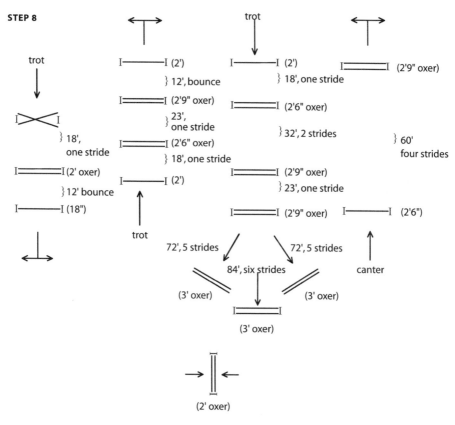

location. In a new location, ensure he is stable on the flat on elementary controls before jumping.

Adjust the height and distances to the horse's schooling progress. When in doubt, less is better. Gradually build up the number of fences in the gymnastic or combination. Remember that disobediences usually occur because the horse has been asked to do something he does not understand or does not feel confident doing. It is better to err on the low and slow side until you are encouraged to move forward by your horse's confidence, calm attitude, and developing ability.

Keep in mind that horses are not all created with equal abilities. Some may find their comfort level at 2 feet 6 inches or 2 feet 9 inches or 3 feet. Some may be confident and have athletic jumping form at 3 feet 3 inches but not higher, etc. Recognize your horse's limits promptly and adjust the combination accordingly. Occasionally, if the horse is physically ready, introduce a bounce from a trot to help develop agility. Set two low jumps, with ten feet between them if approaching at the trot, and later twelve feet if cantering. If the horse quickens in the bounce, return to a comfortable combination for him. The most able jumpers will also benefit greatly from learning to jump with a gradual progression over low fences with easy distances. (See chapter 12, Schooling Period 6.)

MOVING TOWARD YOUR HORSE'S JUMPING SPECIALTY

The following are comments and suggestions that should be useful as the horse progresses through Schooling Period 7 and beyond. (See chapter 13, Schooling Period 7.)

1. Move the single low fences and combinations suggested in the first eight steps to an open area or a fairly level field while continuing to practice combinations and courses in a large, flat area.

2. Prepare to jump a course by trotting in and out of lines and then trotting in and cantering out of lines. Adjust the lines to make it comfortable for the individual horse. Keep the fences low—2 feet 6 inches to 2 feet 9 inches. Also do simple interruptions for the lead changes before the corners as well as flying changes if the horse is ready. Occasionally circle out to the corners at the end of the line.

3. Continue to adjust the distances and heights in combinations and lines to the individual horse's characteristics and schooling level. Again, start with two fences and gradually build the multiple combination.

4. At this time, if the horse is ready, build more combinations and lines to be approached at the canter. The canter is the gait used in recognized hunter and jumper competitions.

Practice in forward balance on the flat, lengthening and shortening the canter in a correct forward position. Then add this exercise to simple course lines in both directions. This will develop the horse's feel and eye for coming forward out of a turn to canter down a line, his response to the rider's rating the stride with a soft following arm and hand, and his response to the rider's lower leg on landing to move up promptly and softly. A following arm (advanced-level jumping) through the arc of the jump as well as at the canter will make this easier to accomplish softly and efficiently.

Jumping parts of courses and at lower heights keeps your horse sound and fresh for the competitions. Further, if you regulate the number and level of competitions you undertake, you will have a confident partner for a longer time.

5. Practicing courses to prepare for a specific competition:

• If the rider needs to practice, do not use your schooling project. Practice on a more experienced horse. If that is not possible, use a "jumpless course" (single poles set at cantering distances). This can be helpful to a rider without pressing a young horse.

• If the rider is less experienced on courses, trot into combinations and also trot into lines and canter out when schooling courses. This will help the horse find consistently correct takeoff distances.

• When schooling the horse for a competition, it is better to school parts of a course and include circles, especially to the outside, to reestablish rhythm and pace, and include soft transitions between some lines.

• Later when the horse is jumping more serious courses (3 foot 6 inches hunter courses and then low jumper courses), continue to school mainly low heights at home in order to keep him more attentive at the competition as well as sound and comfortable.

6. If you have a competitive jumper prospect following the principles and schooling outlined in this text, plan a schooling competitive program. In general, start with the low hunter and then the green working hunter division (up to 3 feet 6 inches), and not before age five or six gradually progress to low jumpers, medium jumpers, and high jumpers.

At age seven or eight, if the horse exhibits comfortable confidence with consistent ability, enter the 1.30-meter and later the 1.35-meter divisions. Again, when schooling at home do not jump maximum height or width. Even for those competing on the top levels, four feet should be sufficient. This will keep your horse cheerful, attentive, sound, and confident.

7. Preset distances for combinations and courses to establish a place to initially put the jumps. The rider and ground person need to intuitively adjust the distances and height for the individual horse. From competitions you attend, plan to get ideas for combinations and parts of courses that will suit your horse. Also use the annotated bibliography (appendix 2) for further ideas of combinations and courses that might improve your schooling plan and that you can adjust to your horse's talent and experience.

Remember, when ready to start competing, go to different locations to experience colorful jumps, and go to competitions with nice courses to school, not to compete—circle back into a corner or trot a fence during your judged round. Always aim to finish a schooling session or competition with a sound, calm, confident horse.

The following is an easily set sample schooling exercise.

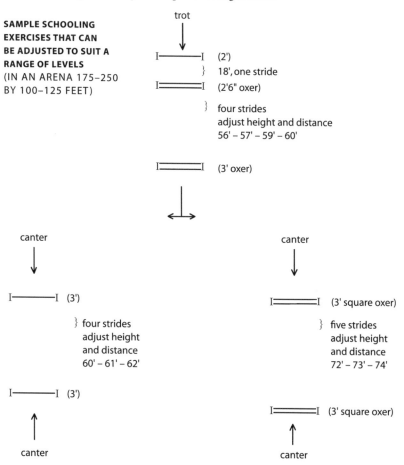

SAMPLE SCHOOLING EXERCISES THAT CAN BE ADJUSTED TO SUIT A RANGE OF LEVELS (IN AN ARENA 175–250 BY 100–125 FEET)

trot

I————I (2')
} 18', one stride
I========I (2'6" oxer)
} four strides
adjust height and distance
56' – 57' – 59' – 60'

I========I (3' oxer)

canter

I————I (3')
} four strides
adjust height
and distance
60' – 61' – 62'

I————I (3')

canter

canter

I========I (3' square oxer)
} five strides
adjust height
and distance
72' – 73' – 74'

I========I (3' square oxer)

canter

Appendix II
References for Forward Riding, the Sport Horse System, and American Hunter Riding

The following books and references may be of interest to professional teachers/riders and serious amateurs.

Caprilli, Capt. Federico. *The Caprilli Papers.* Translated/edited by Maj. Piero Santini. London: J. A. Allen & Co., Ltd., 1967. Santini had previously translated and edited five articles titled "The Caprilli Papers" by Federico Caprilli (1868–1907) in the Australian magazine *Hoofs and Horns* from September 1953 to January 1954.

Lectures and articles written by Caprilli in 1901. A simple and clear presentation of the new system (Caprilli) in the history of educated riding. It presents a method of schooling, controls, and position that became the foundation of modern forward riding and the American riding system. It is brief, to the point, and brilliant, considering it was all new to print. Many European horsemen were either unwilling to change lifetime methods or were not informed enough to realize that this system was more than a position over jumps; it was a completely revolutionary system of controls and flat schooling as well. The text is reinforced by some fascinating historical photographs.

In 1904, Caprilli, after significant controversy, was allowed by the conservative classical dressage–oriented Italian military school to teach his revolutionary method of riding and schooling horses.

America was an ideal laboratory for the new system because the U.S. military was not immersed in more than three hundred years of the classical dressage system. In addition, the democratic and economic conditions in America allowed a wide range of amateur riders interested in jumping and speed to participate in equestrian sports. There was also an abundance of open spaces for breeding horses, riding to hounds, racing, cross-country riding, and jumping competitions.

Chamberlin, Harry D. *Training Hunters, Jumpers and Hacks.* New York: Derrydale Press, 1937.

Chamberlin significantly developed the basic principles of Caprilli, especially in the area of training the horse. Chamberlin was sent by the United States Army to study in both France (Saumur) and Italy (tor di Quinto), where he learned Caprilli's revolutionary Italian system. When he returned, Chamberlin laid down the Fort Riley training methods based on the forward riding system he had learned. He influenced generations of American sport riders who either trained at Fort Riley or were taught by Fort Riley–trained instructors. The list of the progeny from this school is impressive, carrying well into at least the 1960s and 1970s in the American hunter and jumper fields. This deserves further research. However, at the same time, it is interesting that the U.S. Pony Clubs for children were modeled not only on the effective organizational structure of the British Pony Club but also on the British Horse Society (BHS)/British Pony Club (BPC) riding methods. Both were based on the German/Austrian Classical Dressage system brought to England especially after the World War II occupation of Germany. This occurred even though England had the innate tradition of forward riding cross-country and of breeding good horses for riding cross-country. The BHS and the BPC essentially ignored the Caprilli revolution in riding. The U.S. Pony Club, following the BHS/BPC system, also did not embrace the American hunter/jumper riding system (Fort Riley/civilian riders), which was both successful and admired in the United States and Europe, especially in the 1960s, 1970s, and 1980s.

Chamberlin's chapter 3, "Head Carriage and Objectives of Training," is recommended. Chamberlin suggests the idea of levels of contact later developed in the current modern system. He clearly presented the importance of allowing the young horse its natural head and neck carriage. These horses were started on a passive (driving rein) contact rather than the looped rein currently used. Through gradual stages of schooling, the horse begins to carry the rider and himself with confidence and natural athletic ability. The second stage of head carriage represents the direction of the American hunter equitation. In the third stage, Chamberlin describes some exercises and some of the types of horses he dealt with. He understood collection as a classical dressage school concept. What he proposed was a change from the traditional wisdom for schooling the hunter and jumper.

Chamberlin places importance on some key modern forward riding control concepts, such as riding at the horse's level regardless of how advanced the rider might be [this author's words]; allowing the low, extended natural carriage of the head and neck until the horse has learned to frankly accept the bit; the "oscillations" of the head and neck; the dangers of collection for the sport horse; and the relationship of calmness to head carriage.

Although it is nearly seventy years old, this is still a theoretically sound book on the forward riding and schooling system and is still referred to by many leading American trainers and riders.

Dillon, Jane. *School for Young Riders*. New York: ARCO Publishing Co., 1960.

This book is a good introduction, especially for children, to the theory and practice of forward riding. It is especially good for position. Mrs. Dillon very successfully taught hundreds of Washington, D.C., Virginia, and Maryland juniors in the 1950s, 1960s, and 1970s, including at least two who went on to the international level: Kathy Kusner (several U.S. Olympic teams) and Joe Fargis (Gold Medalist, 1984). Mrs. Dillon was a student of V. S. Littauer, and he gave regular clinics to her pupils. She also produced a useful and entertaining book called *Form over Fences,* New York: ARCO Publishing Co., 1961. For decades she was influential in writing the VHSA Equitation guidelines that were forward riding–oriented. These, in turn, contributed to the USEF (AHSA) hunter seat rules from the 1950s to the 1970s. The USEF (AHSA) rules are interesting to review, as they changed throughout the latter part of the century. For example, the "driving rein" and "foot at home" were dropped only relatively recently, the latter probably reflecting the young female dominance of the equitation division. Teachers like Jane Dillon fed the National Circuit trainers and team coaches with the best-quality educated riders, many of whom went on to successful national teams.

Littauer, Vladimir S. *Common Sense Horsemanship.* New York: Van Nostrand, 1951, 1st edition; 1963, 2nd edition.

Now in its second edition and seventeenth printing in English, it has been translated into Spanish and German as well. It includes many advances today in America such as the leg position used on the flat and jumping, control techniques on three levels, advanced schooling, riding the young sport horse on soft contact rather than on the bit, connection rather than collection, the three levels of controls for jumping, and so on. If Chamberlin was based on the American military, Littauer represents the vanguard of educated riding for the American amateur sportsman. Littauer, more than any other, was not only a creative horseman but a scholar, researcher, and historian of educated riding. The principles and techniques he contributed deserve special research. He developed many amateur riders, professional riders, and teachers who are active and successful in U.S. equestrian sports.

SUMMARY OF LITTAUER'S CONTRIBUTIONS TO MODERN RIDING

Littauer was devoted to developing the modern forward riding system for American amateur sportsmen and sportswomen and for their professional teachers. His focus on forward riding for the American amateur is an important distinction in comparing these texts and in understanding the social and economic influences of the periods in which the authors of the texts rode, taught, and wrote.

The following outlines V. S. Littauer's contributions to educated riding:

1. He recognized controls as a component of a system. Controls are integrated with position theory and schooling.

2. He defined in detail the three levels of controls for teaching the rider and schooling the horse and further developed reasonable goals for amateurs. He developed the idea that advanced controls are not necessary or desirable for everyone. Riders can ride at a high elementary level or intermediate level with pride and satisfaction.

3. He stressed the voice as an aid for the elementary level in a teaching program. At the elementary level, the voice is used very much in forward riding. When learning to ride, the pupil should be on a horse that has been well schooled on this level. There are many instances in the United States, especially in the era of the modern efficient riding school in the 1960s, 1970s, and early 1980s, where people gave excellent lessons with five to seven horses in the group, all going on looped reins on voice commands from the rider and sometimes even from the teacher. This is in contrast to the British Horse Society (BHS) method that I observed in England in the 1970s. The BHSAI (Assistant Instructor) functioned as a groom as well as an individual horse leader from the ground, often with

one assistant for each beginner. When off the lead line they often went nose-to-tail in a closed line in a small space (1800s *manège*/military style), which helps keep the horses under control. Riders used the reins and mouth to balance their bodies while learning to post. It is not an efficient method from many points of view: the horses are abused in this routine, riders will need to relearn the use of the reins, it is costly labor to have runners or leaders on foot (although it is a must with handicapped riders), and the horse burns out or becomes less useful fairly soon.

Littauer moved from the military-oriented drill-group teaching approach to a modern and efficient method of teaching children and amateurs in groups (stabilization and elementary controls). If each pupil learns from the start to ride nonabusively, the horse will last longer, be more versatile, respond on the flat and jump better, be ring-sour less often, and be a better investment as a school horse. Many of the horses used in Littauer's system were what are called three-quarter- and half-bred types that, with training, were cooperative and kind. They were trained to have the foundation of stabilization. It was this foundation that made the school horse on this level more useful. In the forward riding system, the same foundation is given to quality prospects for the higher levels. (This is discussed in more detail in the text in part 3.)

4. He advocated sophisticated use of the voice, especially at the elementary control level and in schooling the young horse.

5. He developed the loose-rein method and technique in detail for beginner school horses, young horses, reclaiming horses, and warming up advanced horses.

6. He defined the concept of stabilization, which is the foundation for schooling a modern sport horse.

7. He was one of the first to place in print the three levels of controls for jumping.

8. He further developed the concept of connection rather than collection.

9. In *Common Sense Horsemanship,* his chapter entitled "Imagine You Are the Horse" predates the philosophy of the twenty-first-century horse whisperers by more than fifty years. It was a consistent part of his schooling system.

10. He did original research and was the first riding teacher to present a complete and accurate analysis of the gaits and the mechanics of the jump.

Other references of interest to teachers and serious riders include the following:

Abby, Harlan D., ed. *Showing Your Horse.* New York: A. S. Barnes, 1970.

A series of articles with photographs by some of the top U.S. coaches and riders of hunters and jumpers in the 1960s to 1980s. It describes the individual approaches of riding and schooling in this period. The basic principles of modern forward riding or the American riding system are very interestingly presented in a number of different approaches by outstanding horsemen, including Rodney Jenkins, George Morris, Daniel Lenehan, and David Kelly. Although it is not a formal riding text, it does document the application of the principles of the American riding system that developed through the show hunter competition and, to some degree, the influence of field riding so available in the U.S. open countryside such as hunter trials, hunter paces, and even riding to hounds.

Allen, Linda L. *101 Jumping Exercises for Horse and Rider.* North Adams, Mass.: Storey Publishing, 2002.

This is a presentation of ground poles, cavalletti, combinations, and courses with advice on how to set and use them. Select what suits your horse and modify these exercises to fit your schooling program.

The concern is that the ambitious reader, rider, and/or trainer will make the exercises and courses too complicated for their horse's schooling level. Throughout this text, *Schooling and Riding the Sport Horse,* the well-being of the horse is the first concern. When in doubt, slow and low is best. Always consider the horse's physical and mental stability.

A centered, sound athlete in connected forward balance is the goal. To get the most out of Allen's book, use good judgment to select a few exercises and tailor them for your horse. Always keep in mind the forward riding principles and system.

Chenevix-Trench, Charles. *A History of Horsemanship.* Garden City, N.Y.: Doubleday, 1970.

This book is a serious contribution to accurately analyzing the development of educated riding. It was favorably reviewed in the *New York Times* Sunday book section as a scholarly work. Trench, on American riding and specifically on Littauer and Chamberlin, wrote that "Chamberlin ... rewrote the American Manual of Horsemanship and Horsemastership and had an influence on American riding second only to that of Vladimir Littauer, who set up the 'Boots and Saddles Riding School' in New York in the 1920's. The fruit of their teaching was the success of America in international competition between the wars" (257). The plates are especially good, and the text has a comprehensive approach to the subject. The book begins with an account of riding in the Ancient World, the Dark Ages, and the Middle Ages before following the events and people that led to modern-day horsemanship.

Budiansky, Stephen. *The Nature of Horses: Exploring Equine Evolution, Intelligence, and Behavior.* New York: Free Press, 1997.

This is an objective, documented account of the evolution, physiology, and psychology of the horse. It is a source book for students and a useful text for serious horse people.

Felton, Sydney W. *Masters of Equitation.* London: J. A. Allen & Co., Ltd., 1962.

This is an excellent review of the development of riding theory through a researched presentation. It was reprinted for use by the U.S. Pony Club. It presents enlightening facts on the development of the American riding system.

Hedge, Juliet, DVM, ed. *Conformation and Anatomy.* Tyler, Tex.: Equine Research, Inc., 1999.

This is a well-written and -presented pictorial approach to equine structure and function. Other equally good works on the subject are available.

Kulesza, Severyn R. *Modern Riding.* South Brunswick, N.Y.: A. S. Barnes, 1966.

A teacher in his later years in both Canada and the United States, Kulesza was formerly an officer in the Polish cavalry. He makes excellent use of his European background and his progress to the new system. This is a well-presented book on riding the sport horse in a modern system.

Kursinski, Anne. *Riding and Jumping Clinic.* New York: Doubleday, 1995.

The author is a very successful competitor in the American Hunter and Jumper Divisions. She stresses the objective of teaching the horse to go in "natural" self-carriage. The horse becomes mentally responsive to suggestive rather than forcible aids and is physically able to rebalance himself without depending on the rider to hold him up. The "clinic" approach, common from the end of the twentieth century into the twenty-first century, is the format used to present the material. Basic American Hunter Equitation is reviewed and developed into an advanced system of controls for riding and schooling jumpers.

Littauer, V. S. *The Development of Modern Riding.* New York: Macmillan, 1991; foreword by William C. Steinkraus.

This is a carefully researched work on the history of horsemanship. The development of educated riding, primarily in Western Europe, is divided into three periods. The aristocratic period (1550–1820) was the golden era of the high school, which ended with the French Revolution. The military period (1850–1900) marked the emergence of the second system and the beginning of two schools of thought for educating the horse. The democratic period (1920–present) fostered the amateur sporting era with emphasis on speed, jumping, recreational riding, and competitions.

This is a well-written, entertaining, and excellent scholarly presentation of the masters in the history of equitation, the importance of social and economic influences in the progress of horsemanship, and the development of educated riding. It is highly recommended.

Morris, George. *Hunter Seat Equitation.* Garden City, N.Y.: Doubleday, 1971.

Where Gordon Wright left off in the competitive arena, his most famous teaching pupil, George Morris, picked up the torch for American competitive hunter riding. Through his own riding, his pupils' national success in equitation finals, his writings, and his traveling to conduct clinics, Morris helped solidify the popular acceptance in America of the hunter seat for hunters and jumpers based on the stirrup as opposed to the dressage position based on the seat for the *manège.* He adapted Littauer's three levels of controls for jumping for the show ring and wrote one chapter considered for decades to be the "bible" for etiquette and rules in hunter seat horsemanship classes.

Perhaps the intermediate control "crest release" for the national Medal/Maclay level has been taken too far by some trainers and has handicapped the progress of the advanced level of controls in hunter equitation as presented by Morris. It is interesting to compare photographs from equitation competitions—the quality of advanced controls over jumps in the 1960s and 1970s to the intermediate control "crest release" in the late twentieth century. Commercial pressures in the late twentieth century were directly related to changes in riding techniques considered advanced as many parents began to buy children expensive, sensitive, quality athletes in the 1980s. Crest release, an important level of intermediate controls, became necessary in advanced competition so that the horse was not upset or abused by unsteady hands and position. Juniors and amateurs could then ride better-quality horses without upsetting them.

As any teacher knows, too much crest release without a ground teacher can lead to ducking, leaning on the neck for support, and/or pinching with the thigh and knee. The quality of position slipped as the intermediate control level dominated hunter seat equitation competition. As taught by Morris, advanced controls (automatic release/following arms) demand a correct forward seat based on the stirrup and consistent, soft, precise contact. The horse will resist if it is not done well.

Morris has written numerous interesting articles as well as other books promoting American hunter seat equitation and educating hunter and jumper riders throughout the United States.

Muybridge, Eadweard. *Horses and Other Animals in Motion.* New York: Dover Publications, Inc., 1985.

Muybridge was an early pioneer (late nineteenth century) in the research on how animals move. His theories still hold up very well. This publication is useful and informative.

It is interesting to reflect on the fact that equestrian authors and riding masters had Muybridge's information available to them for more than ninety years. However, they either chose to ignore it and remain loyal to traditional wisdom, or they were unwilling to drift too far from their usual circle of information.

Wright, Gordon. *Learning to Ride, Hunt and Show.* Garden City, N.Y.: Doubleday, 1966.

Published primarily for the show hunter rider, this book is a straightforward simple "period" presentation of modern hunter seat equitation position and controls. Wright must be considered one of the most influential coaches and trainers in the competitive arena (from 1950 to the 1960s). As with other pupils under the Fort Riley influence, his position and controls had the stamp of a modern method of riding sport horses. His initial influence in the Northeast spread to all sections of the country through his clinics and competitive successes. He also edited the *Fort Riley Cavalry Manual* for publication. His pupils included William Steinkraus and George Morris. He and other Fort Riley–connected teachers helped develop the quality forward seat that nearly every rider who moved on to the U.S. jumping team had before joining it in the 1960s to 1980s.

The combination of good horses and experience in European competition, combined with the riders' solid American hunter basics, produced quality U.S. Olympic riders not seen before.

Related rulebooks and indirectly related texts include the following:

Intercollegiate Horse Show Association Rules and Regulations. Executive Director, 569 Fairfield Beach Road, P.O. Box 108, Fairfield, Conn. 06430.

The IHSA competition is based on USEF Hunter Equitation Rules and Objectives. It uses USEF hunter judges. Collegiate riders draw for horses of the host college. They compete in group flat equitation classes on the beginning through open levels. The jumping classes are judged on the rider's position and controls over a hunter course in a ring on the novice through open levels. All riders are on the team, which makes it an excellent learning and recreational competition.

The flat classes in company on strange horses cannot allow for advanced flat work, and there is no uneven terrain or outside test. However, this competition is designed to eliminate the cost of shipping horses for each team, and it allows large numbers to compete in a short time period. It is a successful collegiate competition in the United States based on the modern American hunter equitation system. Each year it involves hundreds of collegiate riders.

Loehr, James E., EdD. *The New Toughness Training for Sports.* New York: Plume. Published by the Penguin Group, 1995.

"Mental toughness has nothing to do with a killer instinct or ruthless play." A flexible, responsive, strong, and resilient equestrian competitor will be suited to successful riding competition with a horse for a partner. Loehr provides a modern emotional, mental, and physical training program for both the professional and amateur. Videotapes and a special series for equestrian competitors are available.

Madden, Frank, and William Cooney. *Fit to Show: The Guide to Grooming Your Horse.* New York: ARCO Publishing Co., 1985.

This is a stable management text that reflects the growth and standards of the hunter, jumper, and equitation competition. It details an individual stable's approach to horse care for the A-level show hunter competition. It is basic, simple, and traditional American management. The foreword by George Morris gives an excellent historical update on hunter stable management in the United States.

Affiliated National Riding Commission, *Riding Standards* and *Intercollegiate Riding Championships Rules and Regulations.* Reston, Va.: American Alliance for Health, Physical Education, Recreation, and Dance, 2000.

The Affiliated National Riding Commission (ANRC) was founded in 1936 to educate riders and instructors in the American forward riding system through clinics, seminars, and a series of clearly defined riding levels that provide riders and instructors a systematic progression for learning and evaluation. Rider ratings are given at special rating centers.

The ANRC is a committee under the American Alliance of Physical Education, Recreation, and Dance (AAPHERD). It is also an affiliate of the U.S. Equestrian Federation Inc. The ANRC is in the process of developing a series of educational videos that outline each riding level for their ratings.

For more than twenty years the ANRC has sponsored a National Intercollegiate Riding Championship. The collegiate team riders are required to provide their own horses for each of the three phases, which are judged on American hunter equitation standards. This allows riders to school and prepare themselves with a horse before the competition. Some of the colleges that have participated with teams include the University of Virginia, University of Oregon, Mount Holyoke College, Goucher College, University of Maryland, Sweet Briar College, Stanford University, West Point Military Academy, St. Andrews College, Miami of Ohio, Davidson College, University of Kentucky, and Saint Lawrence University. The competition is open only to four-year colleges.

The flat phase, "Dressage Sportif," is a program ride in hunter balance or forward balance. It is a modern flat-schooling ride for the hunter. It consists of a series of movements in a large arena, approximately 100 feet x 175 feet. The horse is to be in a connected forward balance/hunter balance on soft contact.

The second phase is an inviting hunter trial course, or "outside course," in the open over natural, uneven terrain and is judged on the rider's equitation. The third phase is a medal course modeled on the USEF hunter equitation classes.

The number that can participate is limited because of the individual performances and the three settings, but this limitation also leads to higher-quality education and performance. These championships represent some pioneering in American riding and the influence of the American forward riding/hunter equitation system. This educationally oriented format should be used by other riding organizations.

Stoneridge, M. A., ed. *Practical Horseman's Book of Horsekeeping*. New York: Doubleday, 1983.

This book comprises an excellent compilation of horse-care articles on a range of subjects, including choosing a horse, feeding, grooming, tack, stable management, loading, and special horse-care problems, written by American horsemen of different backgrounds. It is very useful for the amateur rider who cares for his own animals. It includes practical and up-to-date American standards.

U.S. Equestrian Federation Rule Book. Lexington, Ky., 2004.

Hunter and equitation committees define performance objectives, which are based on the American riding tradition. Especially the hunter divisions and the hunter seat equitation divisions are clearly based on the principles of Caprilli's, Chamberlin's, and Littauer's forward riding system. Note the descriptions of the rider's hands, the position in motion, the criteria for judging hunter jumping classes (i.e., horse's jumping form, manners, pace), and under-saddle classes in company (light contact, movement, manners). It is interesting to research these rules (USEF and the old AHSA rulebooks), especially the descriptions of position as well as the changes in horse performance expectations by judges; i.e., flying change for young horses, how and when the descriptions/judging changed, and which of these changes were influenced by sound riding theory and which by social and economic factors having little to do with horsemanship.

Index

trot (*continued*)

period six, 201–2, 206–7, 210–12, 219, 221; in schooling period seven, 224, 227, 230–31, 240, 252–53; two-point position in, 30–31, *133*, 155, 252. Transitions: canter-trot-halt-trot-canter, 200; canter-trot-walk, 47, 121; canter-trot-walk-halt-back-walk-trot-canter, 206–7; canter-trot-walk-halt-walk-trot-canter, 14, 253; canter-trot-walk-trot-canter-trot-walk, 148; posting trot–slow trot sitting-trot, 31; trot–canter, 132, 227; trot-canter-trot, 144; trot–halt, 122–23, 181; trot-halt-back-trot, 180; trot-halt-trot, 201; trot-halt-walk, 231; trot-short trot-trot, 119; trot–slow trot sitting-trot, 121, 134, 149, 175; trot–strong trot-trot, 155, 188, 199; trot-walk, 16, 30, 33, 40, 50, 55, 73, 129, 131, 134, 147, 155, 175; trot-walk-halt, 252; trot-walk-halt-walk, 176; trot-walk-halt-walk-trot, 119, 142; walk-halt-walk-trot-walk-trot-walk-halt, 132; walk-trot, 52; walk-trot-canter, 144; walk-trot-walk, 49, 119, 121. *See also* piaffe; posting trot; short trot; slow trot sitting; strong trot

turning out, 115, 128, 134–35, 143, 206, 224, 246–47

turns, 14; at the forehand, 103, 158, 164–66, 193, 227, 234, 252; on haunches, 144, 158, 164, 180, *192–93*, 201, 204–5, 234, 252; lateral agility exercises and, 64–65, 142, 150, 177, 192–93, 204–6, **cg8**; leg aids in, 52; rein aids in, *54*, 56–57, 142, 150; in schooling period two, 129–30, 132; in schooling period three, 142, 144, 148, 150; in schooling period four, 158, 164–66, 177; in schooling period five, 192–93; in schooling period six, 201, 204–6; in schooling period seven, 223, 227, 234, 238, 252; short, at canter, 204–6, **cg12**; short, at gallop, 201, 204,

233; short, at walk, 142, 144, 150, 155, 158, 164, 177, 193, 201, 204, 219

two direct reins of opposition, *54*, 132, 148, 194–95

two-point position, *27*, 29–31, 67, *133*, 185

two-tracks, 240–41

uneven terrain, riding over: longitudinal agility and, 14, 161, *163*; position and, 23, 29–30, 185

United States Equestrian Federation (USEF), 8, 39

United States Hunter/Jumper Association, 8

urging leg, 16, 27, 40, 52–*53*, *59*, 61, 227, 235, 240–41

vertical jumps, 151, 171, 209, 224, 253

veterinarians, 85, 98–99, 209

vibrations, 15

voice aids/techniques, 16–17, 47–*48*, 50–52, 55; in canter transitions, 160; in competitions, 50; discipline and, 19, 47, 60, 119–20; in lunging, 51, 105, 113, 118–20, 123; as rewards, 119, 123; in schooling period one, 113, 118–20, 123, 128; in schooling period two, 130; in schooling period three, 147; in schooling period four, 160; in schooling period seven, 229–30; stabilization and, 11, 81, 113; in trot-walk transitions, 16, 33, 40, 50, 55

walk, *217*; leading at, 103, 123–24; lengthening of, 129; longitudinal/lateral exercises and, 131; lunging at, 105, 113, 119, 128; mechanics of, *18*, 60–61, 87, **cg7** (bottom); neck/head carriage in, 79, *130*; over poles, 123–24, *133*, 155, 259; position in, *26*, 29, *130*, 139–40, 190; reserve energy in, 145; in schooling period one, 113, 119, 121–24; in schooling period two, 139–40; in schooling period three, 142, 145, 150; in schooling

period four, 169, 171, 175; in schooling period five, 188, 190, 198; in schooling period six, 201, 204, 206–7, 219; in schooling period seven, 231, 250–52; short turns at, 142, 144, 150, 155, 158, 164, 177, 193, 201, 204, 219; two–point position in, 30, 139. Transitions: canter–trot–walk, 47, 121; canter–trot–walk–halt–back–walk–trot–canter, 206–7; canter–trot–walk–halt–walk–trot–canter, 14, 253; canter–trot–walk–trot–canter–trot–walk, 148; canter–walk, 30, 47, 200, 202–3; trot–walk, 16, 30, 33, 40, 50, 55, 73, 129, 131, 134, 147, 155, 175; trot–walk–halt, 252; trot–walk–halt–walk, 176; trot–walk–halt–walk–trot, 119, 142; walk–halt, 122–23, 155; walk–halt–back–walk, 161; walk–halt–walk, 121–22, 134, 231, 252; walk–halt–walk–trot–walk–trot–walk–halt, 132; walk–trot, 52; walk–trot–canter, 144; walk–trot–walk, 49, 119, 121
warm-ups, *54;* in schooling period one, 128; in schooling period two, 131, 139–40; in schooling period three, 143, 150, 155; in schooling period four, 175–78; in schooling period five, 194, 198–99;

in schooling period six, 219, 221; in schooling period seven, 224, 249–54
weight aids/techniques, 16–17, 40, 47–50, 55; in canter transitions, 160; longitudinal agility and, 190; position and, 24, 26, 28–31; in schooling period two, 130; in schooling period four, 160; in schooling period five, 190; in schooling period six, 202, 204, 207; stabilization and, 11; in trot–walk transitions, 55
western riding neck rein, 56
whips, use of, 105, 118–19, 122, 217

X fences, 134, 150–51, 171, 209, 224

young horses: ages for mounting/schooling of, 106, 113; attention span in, 105; controls and, 16, 40; crossties with, 103; hunter exercises and, 20, 188, 201; lateral agility and, 14; leg aids and, 51; neck/head carriage in, 79, 114–15, *130, 137;* on-the-ground training of, 51, 102–6, 113–14; rewards for, 102, 105; stabilization of, 11, 82, 116, 131, 141

zigzags, *157,* 169, 171, 180, 192, 204